"Be quiet, or I'll kill you."

The man spoke softly. Mary Katherine didn't move a muscle. She pretended to sleep, watching through half-closed lids as the man ordered Elizabeth out of bed. His voice was almost pleasant. He was tall, but not very tall, about the size of her brother, Charles. She couldn't see his face very well.

The man nudged Elizabeth toward the closet. He told her to get a pair of shoes. "Ouch!" Elizabeth cried out, stubbing her toe. That was when he ordered her to stay silent.

"Why are you doing this?" Elizabeth asked. She slid her feet into her bright white sneakers. He steered her out of the room, into the dark hallway.

HELD CAPTIVE

The Kidnapping and Rescue of
ELIZABETH SMART

**MAGGIE HABERMAN
JEANE MacINTOSH**

AVON BOOKS
An Imprint of HarperCollinsPublishers

HELD CAPTIVE is a journalistic account of the 2002–2003 kidnapping investigation of Elizabeth Smart in Salt Lake City, Utah. The events recounted in this book are true. The personalities, events, actions, and conversations portrayed in this book have been constructed using interviews, police reports, personal papers, research, and press accounts. Quoted material has been taken verbatim from interviews.

AVON BOOKS
An Imprint of HarperCollins*Publishers*
10 East 53rd Street
New York, New York 10022-5299

First Avon Books paperback printing: July 2003

Avon Trademark Reg. U.S. Pat. Off. and in Other Countries, Marca Registrada, Hecho en U.S.A.
HarperCollins® is a registered trademark of HarperCollins Publishers Inc.

Printed in the U.S.A.

10 9 8 7 6 5 4 3 2 1

ACKNOWLEDGMENTS

Unraveling the complicated story of the crime committed against Elizabeth Smart was difficult, for two reasons: the horrific nature of the crime, and the roadblocks we ran into along the way. Several doors were closed as we researched this case, in Salt Lake City and beyond. However, many more graciously gave of their time in an effort to try to ensure a true account. We thank them, and are deeply grateful. Many of those people are named in this book; others, at their request, are not.

The information in this book was culled from interviews with people closely involved in this case, as well as court documents, transcripts, and news accounts of the most publicized abduction in years.

All information attributed to the Smart family is based on interviews we conducted with Tom, David, Angela, and Dorotha Smart in the days immediately following Elizabeth's return, as reporters covering the case for our respective newspapers, or from transcripts of press conferences that are part of the public record. Ed and Lois Smart declined to be interviewed. We did not interview Mary Katherine Smart. All attributions to them, as well as to other Smart family members, are based on transcripts and statements the family made publicly, on television, and at press conferences.

The abduction of Elizabeth Smart also directly affected two other families. Members of the Mitchell and Barzee families were instrumental in documenting the history of Brian David Mitchell and Wanda Barzee. We are appreciative of their honesty and their openness. As painful as some of their recollections were for them, they were always open and forthcoming.

A special thanks to Sarah Durand, Chris Goff and Beth Silfin, who patiently took all of our calls, answered all of our questions, and saw this project through to the end.

We especially thank Ed Kosner, editor-in-chief of the New York *Daily News,* and Col Allan, editor-in-chief of the *New York Post,* for letting us write this book. Thanks also to *Post* metro editor Jesse Angelo and *Daily News* editors Michael Goodwin Richard Belsky, Dean Chang, Mark Mooney, Linda Hervieux, and John Oswald.

Maria Fernandez, Bruce Furman, Adam Benson, Juan Arellano, Paul Armstrong, Brigitte Stelzer, and William Bastone pointed us in the right direction for research, and we couldn't have finished this project without them.

Several people sustained us with support, friendship, food, water, and vast reserves of patience. They are Martin Pollner at Loeb & Loeb; Natalie Collins, author of *SisterWife;* Robert Hardt Jr., Tom Topousis, Kerri Lyon, Sean Gannon, Paula

Froelich, Lisa Colangelo, Michael Saul, Brigette Harrison, Lisa Marsh, Ian Spiegelman, Greg Gittrich, Richard Wilner, and Maureen O'Brien.

We are also grateful for the help and direction we received from those who know too well the pain of having a child abducted. Gay and Bob Smither at the Laura Recovery Center and Patty Wetterling at Team Hope were most generous with their time and insight into this national epidemic. For more information, please visit Laura Recovery Center at *www.LRCF.org* and Team Hope at *www.teamhope.org*. There is also the National Center for Missing and Exploited Children at *www.missingkids.com*.

—Maggie Haberman and Jeane MacIntosh
May 2003

Jeane gives thanks to Maggie Haberman, who's a first-rate reporter and even better friend, who did the heavy lifting and whose focus made this project happen. To my parents, siblings and extended family, who pitched in with babysitting and gave me the time I needed to do this, supported my choices, and have given freely of their love, laughter, and encouragement. To my husband, Tom, a man who knew what he was getting into and jumped in anyway. Thank you for keeping the hall light on. And, finally, to Kate, who makes me realize how lucky I am.

Maggie gives thanks to Jeane MacIntosh, a wonderful friend and idol whose perseverance, doggedness, and ability have always amazed me. To my three parents and my brother and sister, who have always supported me in whatever I chose, and who have always put up with whatever I've done. A special thanks goes to my mom, whose insights—and there were many—kept us on course every step of the way. Finally to Dareh, who knows exactly what he did.

HELD
CAPTIVE

PROLOGUE

Angela Dumke rushed to the Kinko's copy store in Salt Lake City, her heart leaden. She was on her way to pick up a batch of "kidnapped" fliers. Her niece, Elizabeth Smart, had been stolen from her bedroom by an intruder hours earlier.

Outside the copy shop, a robed man approached her. He asked for money. He said he was a preacher of the Lord's word and needed help.

Angela was struck by the man's appearance, both Christ-like and unnerving. There was something off about him, she later said. She made no move to give him anything.

"What do you need money for?" Dumke asked him. He wouldn't answer. He broke eye contact and shied away. Angela turned to go into the Kinko's. She picked up the posters. When she came out, the man was gone.

But something about the man rattled Angela. The image of his face stayed with her. She described the odd encounter to her brothers later that day.

Angela later came to believe the man she'd seen was Brian David Mitchell, a homeless drifter who had been paid $5 by Elizabeth Smart's mother to help fix a skylight on their home in November 2001.

During his encounter with Angela, the robed man knew exactly where Elizabeth was, investigators would later say. She was hidden in the mountains behind her family home, tethered to a tree, and terrified.

The meeting outside Kinko's was just one in a series of bizarre twists and missed opportunities in the Elizabeth Smart case, a knifepoint abduction in the dead of a June night that ended nine months later, 20 miles away from where it had begun. Elizabeth was discovered by two alert couples as she walked with Mitchell and his wife, Wanda Barzee, on a main street in a Salt Lake City suburb on March 12, 2003.

She was taken, investigators said, as a "plural wife" for Mitchell, fulfilling one of the prophecies of a rambling religious manifesto he'd spent six years writing. The abduction was every parent's nightmare. A thief in the night stole the Smarts' little girl, and the kidnapper's trail disappeared just yards from their house. But for two months of her ordeal, Elizabeth was held captive just four miles away, in the thick brush of the mountains around Salt Lake City. Later, she was hiding in plain sight.

Two dramatically different worlds collided the morning Elizabeth was taken.

Mitchell's was a life marked by neglect, broken dreams, failed marriages, accusations of abuse, delusions, and a "revelation" that instructed him to live among the homeless of Salt Lake City. His 14-year-old captive led a life warmed by harp recitals and school medal ceremonies, doting parents and services at the Church of Jesus Christ of Latter-Day Saints.

Mitchell and Barzee were from middle-class families who struggled to make ends meet. Elizabeth Smart was from an affluent, socially and politically connected family of doctors, lawyers, journalists, and businessmen that could trace its roots back to the days of Salt Lake's early pioneer settlers. Her grandfather, Charles Smart, was one of Utah's most respected oncologists; one of her aunts is married to the son of a former Congressman, and another married into a major philanthropic family in Salt Lake City.

Set in the valley of the gently sloping Wasatch Mountains, Salt Lake County is laid with clean, wide boulevards and low-sitting buildings—it is a skyline unmarked by the skyscrapers that crowd other major cities. Some Salt Lake neighborhoods seem trapped in time, unchanged for decades, their neatly manicured lawns the picture of perfection. The nine unincorporated towns of Salt Lake are lined with strip malls and parking lots; the less-affluent areas are populated with tract-housing and trailer-home parks. The city's large homeless population tends to gather in the south end of town, near the shelters and soup kitchens, and in warmer weather fans out to makeshift camps they set up in the mountains behind town.

Salt Lake City itself is cosmopolitan. There is the

expected smattering of malls, and Starbuckses dot
the corners. In the middle of town is Temple
Square, a ten-acre plot of land that marks the
headquarters of the LDS, or Mormon, church. The
centerpiece of the square is the six-spired granite
Salt Lake Temple, which faces the famous domed
Tabernacle.

Salt Lake City addresses begin at the gates of
Temple Square. The streets are laid out in a grid
pattern in square blocks, and addresses indicate the
distance from the four main streets—North, South,
East and West Temple—bordering the square.

The LDS church has 11 million members and is
among the fastest growing religions in the world. It
does not disclose its finances, but its holdings have
been estimated at about $25 billion. Most of that
money, church leaders have said, comes from
tithing—members are required to contribute at
least 10 percent of their annual income to the
church. The church's vast holdings include financial, telecommunications, and agricultural businesses. In Salt Lake, one of the church's holding
companies owns the state's second-largest newspaper, the *Deseret News,* and KSL television station.

Church officials say that Utah is about 73 percent Mormon, and in some towns nearly the entire
population belongs to the LDS church. But Salt
Lake City is an anomaly—Mormons make up just
half the community. Salt Lake officials have
boasted of the religious melting pot in their city as
a sign Salt Lake has grown with the times. Jews,
Catholics, Presbyterians, and other religions are

all represented. And, though the state is 91 percent white, Salt Lake boasts more ethnic diversity. It is also a college town, with an active counter-culture of artists, musicians, and writers. Still, there is a palpable divide between Mormons and "non-Mormons," evidence of cultural boundaries that were set more than a century ago. The church also dominates cultural and community activities. Despite renewed efforts to integrate its various cultures and religions, the heavy church stronghold in Salt Lake continues to spark political and social debates between Mormons and the non-LDS community.

Utah is called "The Beehive State," and the state food is JELL-O. The state motto is industry, and Mormons follow that edict closely. Mormons believe strongly in charity and in helping those in need. The church's missionaries are known as friendly and community-oriented. LDS church members who aren't deeply religious generally consider themselves "non-practicing."

Mormons are led by a "living prophet," who is also the president of the church. God speaks to President Gordon B. Hinckley, and the membership follows. Mormons refer to themselves as Saints and believe they will lead the rest of society to salvation. The church is led by men; women are not allowed leadership positions. Instead, men have the "Priesthood Authority"—or the literal power of God and the authority to act in his name—and the women "enjoy" the priesthood authority through their husbands, Hinckley has said.

For Mormons, the key to eternal life lies in proving oneself worthy. As a result, they are extremely industrious and, in addition to holding secular jobs, are urged to devote hours of free time to community service and church-related activities.

The Mormon church was once widely regarded as "strange" and cultish, mostly because it's a relatively young faith as far as the way the Western world views religions. In recent years, the LDS church launched a campaign to change its image. Its membership has soared, although some practices of the church remain an issue among other Christians. For instance, some Christians find the concept of a "living" prophet blasphemous. Others have taken issue with the church's temple rituals, which members aren't supposed to discuss. They are not secret, members say, they are sacred, and therefore they should be kept quiet.

One of the most controversial LDS practices—polygamy—remains a sore point for the church. The practice was instituted as doctrine in the late 1840s after the church's first prophet, founder Joseph Smith, received a revelation. It was abolished in 1890 by a subsequent prophet as a condition of Utah's being granted statehood. The LDS now considers plural marriage an excommunicable offense, but pockets of polygamy still thrive in the state, and the practice remains a contentious one. The early advocacy of plural marriage remains part of current LDS doctrine, and according to Mormon doctrines, polygamy is a hallmark of the afterlife.

In the LDS faith, fathers are expected to preside over the family with love and "righteousness," and to provide for their families. Mothers are primarily to be responsible for raising their children, according to Hinckley. The family, not the individual, is the basis of LDS salvation. The center of a Mormon family's religious universe is the neighborhood "ward," similar to a local congregation. Each ward belongs to a bigger district called a "stake."

On June 5, 2002, the Federal Heights Ward where the Smart family made its home was shaken to its core. The families of Mitchell and Barzee were equally horrified at the events that would tragically link them to the Smarts.

Before the details of her nine-month ordeal emerged, Elizabeth's homecoming was an uplifting moment for a nation steeped in bad news. The country was still reeling from the memory of the terrorist attacks on September 11, 2001. The United States was preparing for a controversial war in Iraq, and the nation's economy was limping through a protracted recession marked by lost jobs and struggling families.

Elizabeth being found alive seemed nothing short of a miracle, one that was nourished by her media-savvy family, who pressed to keep the national press focused on the case. It was also a hard-won miracle, and there were unpleasant days following the national euphoria that marked Elizabeth's initial homecoming.

There were recriminations that police had made

mistakes and had been less than diligent in the search for Elizabeth. There were disturbing details of the torment Elizabeth had suffered at the hands of her captors that trickled out in news accounts within hours of her return.

Her captors' motives, and their splinter religion, put the Mormon church on the defensive again over a controversial piece of its history—polygamy. The homeless community of Salt Lake City, many of whom searched for Elizabeth after she went missing, faced a backlash simply because Mitchell had lived among them.

Elizabeth Smart had become the most famous abducted child in decades. Within hours of her disappearance, her tight-knit Mormon community sprang to action. LDS President Hinckley sent out a nationwide bulletin, urging his followers to help find the girl. Within days, Elizabeth's kidnapping was an international news story.

Salt Lake police spent $1.5 million on the search for the teen, investing 53,000 man hours on the investigation.

Her case generated a media interest rivaled in the last 30 years only by the abduction of publishing heiress Patty Hearst in 1973. In the age of 24-hour cable news channels and the Internet, the picture of the missing, angelic blonde had people around the world mesmerized and praying for her return.

Few missing children cases generate the kind of interest Elizabeth's did, and most don't end the way hers did. For every Elizabeth Smart, there are roughly 100 children abducted by strangers each year. The chances of one of those children returning alive after more than 30 days missing are fewer than 2 percent.

Elizabeth Smart survived nine times that long.

June 5, 2002,
By Rich Vosepka,
Associated Press Writer

SALT LAKE CITY (AP) - Police have issued a statewide alert to find a 14-year-old girl apparently kidnapped at gunpoint from her home in an affluent neighborhood early Wednesday.

Elizabeth Smart was taken about 2 a.m. when a man broke through a window in her Federal Heights home, police said. Her parents were asleep in their bedroom at the time.

The neighborhood abuts the University of Utah.

Police say the man threatened Smart's 9-year-old sister and said he would harm Elizabeth if her sister said anything. The two girls share a bedroom.

The man let the girl take a pair of shoes with her, police said.

The sister waited several hours before alerting her parents because of the threat, said Dwayne Baird, a Salt Lake City Police Department spokesman.

Searchers were scouring the area east of downtown Wednesday morning, looking for clues. Neighbors began the search in the pre-dawn darkness. Police were called at about 4 a.m.

The man is described as white, with dark hair and wearing a tan denim-type jacket, a white baseball cap. He is about 5 feet 8 inches tall and was very soft-spoken, the sister told police.

He gained access to the house by forcing open a window, Baird said.

Police also were searching nearby foothills Wednesday morning. Tracking dogs also are being used, Baird said.

Police say there is no indication that the man knew the girl.

The girl has blonde hair and was wearing red pajamas.

The suspect didn't call the victim by name, nor did he appear to know his way around the house, the sister told police. He had a small black handgun.

"A two-hour window gives anyone the opportunity to be away from this area," Baird said. "That does pose a problem."

ONE

He called himself the "true prophet," but his was a religion of two.

Brian David Mitchell was a fixture in downtown Salt Lake City, standing on street corners draped in purple robes. He held a wooden staff in his hand and loudly preached what he called the word of God to anyone who walked by. His wife, Wanda Eileen Barzee, stood silently by his side.

"He was commonly called the Jesus guy among our homeless friends," Pamela Atkinson recalled. "He talked about his work as God's messenger."

Atkinson spent more time around Brian David Mitchell than most members of his family in the three years before he crossed Elizabeth Smart's path.

Atkinson, a British transplant with silver hair and a soft, clipped voice, is a homeless advocate in Salt Lake City, who often offered Mitchell and Barzee hot showers and meals and supplies like socks and toiletries when she ran into him on the streets.

She also tried to bring him into the larger homeless community, urging him to seek shelter and mental help. It was an uphill battle.

"He wasn't well-liked," Atkinson said. "He was

always preaching—nobody could ever get a word in edgewise with him."

Brian David Mitchell seemed to fancy himself the voice of God, and he was struggling with a religious fever.

Fastidious and attentive to neatness, he seemed to want to attract people with a clean-cut appearance. Yet he almost instantly repelled them once he started talking.

"It got to the point where our homeless friends would cross to the other side of the street to avoid him," Atkinson recalled.

"If he came into the Salvation Army for a meal, people would get up from the table and move to another. He tended to irritate everyone with his incessant preaching. Many of our homeless friends don't want to be preached at. And Brian would only talk about his faith—the others felt like he was invading their private space."

Mental health experts and homeless advocates say he is the victim of a troubled mind. Elizabeth Smart's family sees a darker motive.

"He is not just sick. He is evil," Elizabeth's uncle, David Smart, said. "He is a wolf in sheep's clothing."

Whatever it was that drove Brian, he was a study in contrasts, and always had been.

"This whole pattern dovetails together," said Shirl Mitchell, Brian's father.

Shirl sat about 20 miles from the enclave where his kids were raised, in his ramshackle home with surprisingly distinctive architectural detail.

From the front hall to the kitchen, the floor is covered with dusty exercise equipment, boxes of papers, broken furniture, and old family photos, including several with a smiling, clean-cut Brian David Mitchell.

Shirl Mitchell, once a broad-shouldered, handsome man with a clean shave and a head of white hair cropped short, is now stoop-shouldered and tired. He wears a scraggly beard and folds his gnarled hands in his lap as he talks about his children in his thin, high-pitched voice.

Like his son, Shirl Mitchell is a complicated tangle of intelligence, charm and a host of painful memories from years past. Unlike his son, Shirl openly admits to having interests that many would consider unusual.

Shirl seemed surprisingly eager to talk about his son's decline. He ticked off a list of fragmented memories from Brian's childhood that he thought could explain what went wrong, even as he acknowledged that the two were never very close. And some of Shirl's recollections differ from those of others in the Mitchell clan.

Shirl and his tumultuous marriage to Brian's mother had a much greater influence on his son than he realized at the time, he admits now. Shirl had his own brand of rambling theology and a dysfunctional union with Irene Sidwell Mitchell, a woman for whom he can barely mask his anger, even twenty years later.

"I'm responsible for it, my ex is responsible for it. She has her limitations, and I have mine," Shirl

said as he picked apart Brian's psyche, moment by
defining moment. "He has been plunging reflex-
ively and reactively all his life."

Shirl said Brian seems to have "two personalities," one docile, the other angry and attention-
seeking. He's careened from one to the other all his
life. On paper, however, Brian David Mitchell
should have had a relatively normal, if bumpy,
childhood.

He was born on October 18, 1953, to Shirl, a
social worker with Salt Lake family services for
three decades, and Irene Sidwell, a school teacher,
in a home delivery that was difficult for his mom.
He was the couple's third child.

Shirl and Irene met at the University of Utah and
married in 1949. She was studying to be a teacher,
and he was taking a string of philosophy courses.

As a child, Brian played Little League and was a
Cub Scout. He went swimming at a local pool and
built toy rockets. The family lived in a 1950s-style
home just a few miles from the base of the Wasatch
Mountains, in a community of low-slung houses
and curving, dead-end streets.

But the Mitchell household was often an unhappy one.

The family initially prayed in the Unitarian
Church, where Brian was baptized, according to
his father. But Shirl said he grew tired of the
"smoking and the coffee-drinking" of the Unitarians, and he couldn't think of a more wholesome
environment for raising a family than the Church
of Jesus Christ of Latter-Day Saints. The LDS

church frowned on smoking, drinking and swearing and taught strict obedience to authority. It urged its members to take part in community activities. Like most organized religions, it was patriarchal, with men holding all positions of power in the church. It taught that a flesh-and-blood God and Jesus Christ came to earth and revealed themselves to the LDS founder, Joseph Smith, in upstate New York, and that its members were to lead humankind into salvation.

The Mitchell family made the switch to their local "ward," the Mormon term for their local church. The Mitchells became longtime members of the Canyon Rim Fourth Ward.

But no matter which church he belonged to, Shirl Mitchell was not a religious man. He confesses that he always questioned the teachings of the LDS church, and preferred his own musings on religion and man's relationship to God.

Five years before he married Irene, Shirl began working on what would become a 900-page thesis on religion and philosophy called "Spokesman for the Infant God or Goddess." The thick text is thoughtfully laid out in two separate volumes, with carefully indexed and numbered pages.

It is also densely written, sexually explicit, and frequently denounces marriage as an unnatural convention that religious institutions—he singles out the Mormon church—force on men and women to the detriment of society.

"The marriage contract is a literal agreement for copulative acquiescence and is an often abrogated agreement," Shirl wrote in the subheading of one chapter. Another declared the "erotic and sexual play of contemporary human teen-agers and adults" to be "maximally contraceptive and minimally reproductive."

The text is accompanied by more than 30 pages of charts, drawn by Shirl, describing the relationships between men and women. Shirl said his writings, which evolved from an earlier work he called "Jack and the Beanstalk," were intended to help men and women understand each other on a higher level.

But his papers were troubling to other members of the ward.

"He thought he understood God on a higher plane than everyone else," said Robert Swensen, an official at the Canyon Rim Fourth Ward, who grew up alongside the Mitchell clan.

Shirl was seen in the neighborhood as moody, unconventional and megalomaniacal. More than one Canyon Rim resident, many of whom have lived there for the last four decades, used the word "weird" to describe Shirl specifically.

Shirl made his family adhere to a vegetarian diet. He didn't socialize with other members of the ward. Shirl Mitchell sometimes flew into rages, shouting at his wife and their brood of six children, all close in age. Irene was often unhappy with her husband.

Neighbors recall Irene kicking Shirl out, only to let him come home a few weeks later. Sometimes he left on his own.

She loved her kids, but Shirl had little interest in actively helping raise them, a difficult burden that increasingly fell solely on her. She was a sweet woman who wanted to keep her family together, neighbors said.

"It was hard for her," one neighbor said.

Shirl, however, was "a little odd," a little stand-offish in the community.

"You had to see things his way," recalled Robert Swensen. Shirl was "intimidating," Swensen said, "very controlling, very domineering."

Shirl admits that he was restless during the marriage, leaving Irene for the first time shortly after they wed. It was before he became a social worker. He took a job at a metal factory in another town, and Irene was alone.

Sharon McGough, a classmate of Brian David Mitchell at the Canyon Rim elementary school, also remembers Shirl as a controlling, domineering force in the family, while Irene was "very meek, very passive," qualities that others would later ascribe to Brian's third wife, Wanda.

Irene was a creative, interesting, and deeply sad woman, others recalled. But it was her husband who was often the subject of chatter among neighbors over morning coffee for his unusual habits, McGough said, including his admitted penchant for peering in women's windows.

McGough recalled a small scandal brewing in the Canyon Rim Fourth Ward after Shirl was caught peeping into a nude neighbor's window.

"I liked looking at naked women, looking

through windows," Shirl admitted later. He said the habit began when he was a pre-adolescent with his friends, and he never shook it.

"It just got to be an addiction," he said.

Neighbors said they remember Irene being physically abused, which Shirl denies, save for one argument the couple had in which he said she charged at him, and he rapped her on the mouth.

He does, however, say he once forced himself on his wife. Their intimate life was difficult, Shirl said, and he once came home and forcefully threw himself on Irene.

"I was all riled up from a Peeping Tom experience," Shirl said. He'd come home, gulped a glass of wine, and "jumped her bones." She later drew a large poster accusing him of abuse.

There were happy moments in the lives of the Mitchells. There were ski trips and family vacations, picnics and summers at a local pool. The abuse that had characterized the early years of Shirl and Irene's marriage had subsided, although they still fought often, relatives said.

Like their mother, Brian's three sisters were loved in the Canyon Rim community.

"Those girls were just wonderful. They were just delightful," said Swensen of Brian's sisters. "They were full of life."

It was the three boys, he said, who "were a problem." In particular, Brian, the third child, stood out. He was the child in the middle, and he often got lost in the shuffle. He was neglected and it stung him. His defense, it seemed, was to emulate his father.

"Of the children that they had, Brian was the most like Shirl," recalled Russell Booth, the family's bishop when Brian was growing up.

At age five, Brian began a rivalry with his younger sister Laurie, who was two years old at the time. The relationship between the two would be troubled for the rest of their lives. According to Shirl, it began as a way for Brian to get attention. He would pick on his sister, then wait for the punishment Irene would mete out. It was negative attention, but it was attention nonetheless, something Brian always craved.

Brian vacillated back and forth from being a sweet, funny kid to a moody attention-getter. He wanted the world to acknowledge him, but he couldn't figure out how to go about it.

Even as a child, there was always a dark undercurrent to Brian, something just beneath the surface that served as a beacon to people who came near him: danger, stay away.

Some neighbors remember a surly, large-eyed boy who spoke to almost no one and often gave his mother fits.

"You know how kids just know about other kids?" said McGough, who was in Brian's grade school class. "He was one of those kids. Other kids just knew to stay away from him. If you were playing tag, you wouldn't want him to touch you."

With pain in her voice, McGough remembers how a young Brian was ostracized by other classmates. In the hierarchy of elementary school, Brian was the odd boy out. He clearly wanted to be liked, and he took part in normal, little-boy activities like Little League. But he never seemed able to make friends.

Instead of finding a way to fit in, Brian acted out.

McGough was seven or eight years old when Brian started lobbing rocks at her on the playground during a recess. Sharon swore at him, and a teacher overheard her. They were both sent to the principal's office, a place Brian became familiar with during his school years.

Sharon's mother was furious at her for cursing.

"I remember having to say to my mother, 'He wasn't just throwing rocks to throw them. It was throwing rocks to hurt someone. He was trying to hit me.'"

He was a poor student and may have had a learning disability. But he was intelligent and crafty. He used the engine from his grandmother's lawnmower to build a go-cart in the backyard. Some relatives remember happy times with Brian growing up. There were moments of lightness, but it clouded over quickly.

Another troubling side of Brian was emerging in grade school. In retrospect, he seemed overly interested in sex. Shirl said he may have inadvertently piqued his son's interest when he showed eight-year-old Brian a medical book with graphic pictures of male and female genitalia, in the hopes of teaching his son about sex. Whatever caused it, the other kids in the neighborhood didn't want to be around Brian.

"The kids would play doctor and the other kids would run home and complain about Brian to their mothers," Shirl said later.

Some of Brian's other relatives believe he may have been molested by someone when he was a child.

"People who molest were molested," said one family member. "And I wonder about that now."

Shirl sometimes used violence to discipline Brian, measures he regretted later. Once, after a toddler-aged Brian smacked another boy with a garden hose while they were playing in the yard, Shirl upbraided him for it.

"I'm going to let you know how that feels," Shirl told his son and smacked Brian with the hose. Another time, Shirl hit Brian hard for accidentally walking into a wall that had just been built in their home.

When Brian was 12, Shirl left him alone in a parking lot and told him to find his own way home. It was intended as a lesson in wending one's own way through the world.

Instead of becoming obedient, Brian acquired his father's strong will. He was growing into a wiry young man with a crown of deep black hair and a voice pitched nearly identically to Shirl's.

Brian always believed his opinions were the right ones. He was fiercely intelligent and liked to win an argument.

"Brian is incredibly convincing," said one relative. "I would never want to enter a debate. Because there's no way to win."

Brian was a growing problem in the Mitchell household. He was almost always in trouble, and he took up a lot of his parents' attention. Irene and Shirl sometimes fought over how to discipline their son.

As Brian found his way through his painful adolescence, the trouble between Shirl and Irene grew steadily worse.

During one of Shirl's separations from Irene, Brian showed up at his grandmother's house, where Shirl was staying. His grandmother let him in, and Brian charged down the stairs to the basement, where his father was lying on a couch.

"You're treating me like garbage," Brian shouted at his father, his fists clenched.

At age 15 or 16, Brian was at home when a young girl from the neighborhood, no older than four, wandered over to the house. Brian exposed himself to her, and she ran back home, terrified.

Her father called authorities, and Brian was taken away for a stint at juvenile detention hall, an experience that Shirl believes scarred him.

When he came back home, he was deeply ashamed and couldn't bring himself to go back to school, Shirl said. School records show that Brian had been a sophomore at Skyline High School. Those records show that he transferred to East High School, although there are no documents showing he actually attended the school.

Other relatives said they had absolutely no memory of Brian being reported to authorities or taken away to juvenile hall.

He became so difficult for his parents to control that they sent him to live with his grandmother. But she was a full-time nurse and had little time to look after him.

Brian started staying in Sandy, a suburb of Salt Lake, with other troubled boys whom he met in detention hall. Brian developed a taste for beer and started using drugs.

According to his father, Brian began experimenting with homosexuality as he ran around with the crowd he'd met in juvenile hall, a "bisexual inclination" that lasted for several months. It stopped when he was called gay slurs by another teen. Brian got into a fight with the boy and walked away from it with a chipped tooth.

"At that time, he was so confused," Shirl said.

Brian was listing, unable to find an anchor. His parents couldn't handle him. He was on his own, fending for himself.

At 19, Brian was leading a fairly rootless existence. He got his high school diploma through a GED program, but couldn't settle on his path in life. He began taking courses at the University of Utah, Shirl said, with the help of a tuition-assistance program. It lasted for only a few semesters.

He started dating Karen Charnetzy, a student at Granite High School in Salt Lake City with mousy-brown hair and a heart-shaped face.

"We went to the drive-in, normal things that teenagers do," Karen would recall later on the TV program "Inside Edition."

She was soon pregnant, and Brian asked her to marry him. The pair wed on August 13, 1973, when Karen was 17 years old. Within months, Brian's first child, Travis, was born.

Brian's marriage to Karen was the beginning of a pattern of reactions within the Mitchell family: Many of Brian's relatives didn't like her, just as they wouldn't like his second and third wives. Karen, like the others, was a bad fit for Brian, they believed.

The short-lived marriage to Karen was fraught with problems and rivaling claims of terrible behavior. Brian wasn't active in the Mormon church and seemed to have no use for religion. He described himself to his wife as an Atheist, and he had a sharp, controlling temper.

He told her she should eat only wheat bread, and yelled at her if he caught her eating candy.

He was also physically abusive, Karen said. She claimed he "forced himself" on her two days after she gave birth to their second child, Angie, and once choked her until she blacked out. Karen said she was in fear for her life.

But Brian's relatives said Karen had struggled with problems of her own. And Brian painted a very different picture of their marriage than Karen later would, when he filed for divorce in 1975. Their troubles were caused by Karen, he said, whom he described as an unfit mother who "had a past history of severe emotional problems" and who had left their children alone "for hours at a time."

Karen admitted to infidelities during their marriage, their divorce records show. Brian fought hard for custody of his kids, and he got it in 1976. The judge gave it a period of a year, and then the issue would be looked at again. But Karen, who remarried soon after the divorce, was awarded custody of Angie and Travis in 1977, after Brian missed a court hearing in the case. Before the children could go live with their mother, though, Brian left the state with the little kids, saying he needed to "protect" them.

At the time, Brian was living with his parents. He wasn't paying room and board. Instead, he bought a nice new car, a Mazda, on which he couldn't finish making payments.

Before he left Utah, authorities came looking for Brian and the children. They went to his parents' home and knocked on the door.

Brian later bragged that his mom had protected him, his second wife claimed later.

"I was at the back door while she was at the front door," he said. By his account, Irene said she had no idea where her son was.

Brian and the kids headed east, living in New York City for several months. They found a home in a tenement in Harlem, where he lived with an African-American woman, a fact his father seems fascinated by years later, calling it "interesting."

In New York, Brian kept up the drug habit he

had developed in Salt Lake City. He had a fondness for LSD.

Within months, Brian went with his children and his girlfriend to New Hampshire, according to Shirl. He spent the next two years there, studying to become an auto mechanic. But he never finished his training.

Instead, he had a vision that he later said changed his life.

"He told me he was using LSD one time while he was in New Hampshire," said Doug Larsen, who befriended Brian a decade later. "And he was in the bathroom, and he looked at himself in the mirror, and he had a vision of himself. And he said he was so beautiful, and he realized then what God wanted him to do."

Brian apparently took that as a sign that he was to turn his life around. A short time later, Brian and his children returned to Utah.

When Brian arrived back home by 1980, he was badly in need of a change. His siblings seemed to be leaving him behind. All five had developed stable lives. The other Mitchell boys, Kevin and Tim, had turned their lives around. They were getting jobs. His sisters were marrying and moving on from their troubled childhoods. Two of the Mitchell children even became marriage counselors.

Brian was still the problem child.

When he came back to Salt Lake City, one of his brothers approached him about his drug habit and urged him to clean up his act.

"He just kicked the habit cold," Shirl recalled. "He went through hell, he just kicked it. So he had willpower, iron willpower. And that's when he got religion."

For the first time in his adult life, Brian showed active interest in the Church of Jesus Christ of Latter-Day Saints. He began going to singles' dances in his ward.

That year was a turning point for the Mitchell family. Irene had finally had enough of her on-and-off marriage to Shirl and filed for divorce. The papers were withdrawn, but eventually reinstated. Their marriage was dissolved in 1982.

"He never forgave her for it," said one family member. Shirl's bitterness would always creep around the edges about his wife, to the point where their children won't have them over for family gatherings at the same time.

While his parents' marriage was falling apart for good, Brian himself seemed happy. He was engaged with his family and interested in making amends for anything he'd done to hurt them. For the first time, relatives recalled, Brian seemed genuinely interested in other people. Instead of the selfishness that had marked his first two decades of life and that would characterize most of his adulthood, Brian was becoming a complete person, his relatives thought. He was fun to be around, and he had a quick sense of humor. His need to get attention, often marked by actions that would have shock value, seemed to be fading.

Brian met Debra Kravitz, a divorcee with three

little daughters, at a lecture by W. Cleon Skousen, an LDS writer who was lecturing on the Old Testament at the time. Debbie was thrilled with the reedy, clean-cut man who seemed to adore her little girls. At that point, he had switched jobs and was working at a Montessori school. He was living with his parents, and seemed to strictly follow the LDS codes. More than anything, Debbie was overwhelmed by the idea of a man who loved children. She wanted someone who would raise her little girls.

Debbie was an insecure, naïve young woman, struggling after a bitter divorce. She was a slightly plump but pretty blond with a breathy voice who had battled her own troubled past. Estranged from her own family, Debbie was eager to become a Mitchell. Her life was her children and her job at the Mine Safety and Health Administration, a unit of the federal Department of Labor.

Their courtship was odd, but Debbie was willing to overlook some of Brian's habits because he seemed like such a catch. He was frugal to a fault, and never took her out to dinner or lunch on any of their dates. Instead, they would eat in his car. Sometimes he would ask her to bring food for the two of them. Other times, he would bring his own, a rock-hard bread he baked himself, using a mash of wheat sprouts he'd grown at home. He would layer apple slices on the bread and offer them to Debbie.

Her colleagues told her they thought Brian acted

odd, but Debbie didn't care. Brian was polite, and courteous, and kind to her girls. He would never kiss her anywhere but on the forehead or cheek, adhering to the Mormon pronouncement about premarital sexual contact.

He proposed to her on a chilly night in November 1980. He came calling to Debbie's house while she was already dressed for bed.

"I love you, and I want to marry you," he said, planting a kiss on her mouth for the very first time. Debbie was elated, but Brian said they couldn't announce their engagement until Christmas day. That week, they went shopping for a ring.

Brian was eager to marry, in part, because he needed to show family court officials that he'd created a stable home, so that he would be granted custody of Angie and Travis, Debbie said.

Once again, Brian's father was disappointed.

"That woman gives me such bad vibes, Brian, you're making an awful mistake," Shirl told his son. Irene also disapproved of the union. But Brian defied his family, and the two married in February 1981.

Again, within hours Brian's wife began to see a change in the man she married.

On their wedding night, they honeymooned in a cabin in Heber City, a rural town about 35 miles from Salt Lake City. Brian told Debbie to bring along some of her two-year food supply, which the Mormon church tells its members to keep in case of emergencies.

Debbie was hungry the whole way there but tried to keep quiet about it.

"If you're hungry, we can stop and get something to eat, but it won't be good for you," her new husband told her. He pulled into a Kentucky Fried Chicken and got a small meal which they shared.

"That was my wedding dinner," Debbie said. They continued to the cabin, and once there, Debbie leaned over to kiss her new husband on the mouth. He shoved her away.

"Don't you dare," he glowered. "Don't you dare be the aggressor. You wait for me to kiss you." Shocked, Debbie recoiled. Looking back, it was a warning sign of things to come.

They made a home with the five children they had between them, and Debbie was pregnant within a year, with her only son, Joseph. A daughter, Sarah, came soon after. Brian wanted Debbie to give birth to their children at home, as his mother had, but she refused. In the couple's daily life, Brian went to church on Sunday and was seen by the community as a solid person, a good father and provider. But at home, things were very different.

He recited scripture from memory, but Debbie doesn't remember him practicing his LDS theology. He would often use fear to leverage power over her.

Months after they were married, Brian left his job at the Montessori school and stayed home with the kids during the day while Debbie worked at MSHA. Debbie was upset that she was working while her husband got to watch the little kids grow up. She cajoled him to get a new job, so she could quit hers and stay at home. Brian relented and took a job as custodian at Churchill Junior High School.

At the same time, a pattern of cruelty was beginning, Debbie said.

Early on, Debbie told Brian about her fear of mice. He came home one night with a live mouse in a jar, with no lid. Debbie screamed uncontrollably.

Another time, as she cleaned the stove one Sunday, she opened her oven to find 50 dead mice, laid out in neat little rows on a cookie tray.

Brian dictated what clothes she could wear—nothing bright, only brown or black. He slung insults at her, he made her feel frightened.

She doesn't remember exactly when the violence started, but she said he once hit her so hard she blacked out. She would have bruises rimming her eyes when she went to church to pray. She said she tried to talk to other members of her ward about Brian's darker side but was told she should stay with him and work things out.

Debbie also told some of Brian's relatives that he was growing abusive toward her. Shirl and Irene didn't believe it, and neither did many of Brian's other relatives. They defended Brian. To them, Debbie was a troubled woman from a broken background who was making up stories.

In 1983, Brian was reawarded custody of his kids Angie and Travis. But months later, with seven children crowding into the house, Brian

placed his kids from his marriage to Karen—
Travis, who was then 10 years old, and Angie, who
was then eight—into foster care. Brian told his
family he made the painful decision at Debbie's be-
hest, because seven kids were simply too many.

That's different from Debbie's memory of what
happened. Angie and Travis never liked her, Debbie said later, and they made that clear to their dad.
Brian decided they couldn't keep living with him
and Debbie, but he felt the only other option was
that they live with Irene, she said.

Brian's relationship with his mother at the time
was perplexing, according to Debbie. He loved her
and protected her, but he also grew angry with her.
He was vexed that Irene didn't like his wife and
urged her to come to terms with Debbie. Brian decided Irene's house wasn't an option, according to
Debbie, and the two kids were put into foster care.

Angie and Travis have defended their father
since. Angie said her father was doing what he
could to save a foundering relationship. The eldest
children of Brian David Mitchell paint a far different picture than his ex-wives and other relatives.
They remember a man who was loving and attentive, a good father locked in a difficult marriage.
The man they remember took them to swim meets
and on fishing trips.

Brian's kids also claimed, when they were children, that Debbie was abusive to them, verbally
and physically.

Whatever the reason for giving up the kids, Debbie and Brian's marriage was headed for an un-

pleasant end. Debbie kept a journal with entries each day detailing how he treated their children. Within months, they'd separated. Brian filed for divorce in 1984.

Brian's version of what went on in their home was drastically different from Debbie's. He claimed in court filings that Debbie was the one who'd been cruel. He admitted that he had sometimes yelled, but insisted he was never violent. It was Debbie, he charged, who had often raged around the children and threatened to turn the kids against their father.

Brian claimed in the court filings that Debbie hurt the children. Their divorce was a messy one, filled with nasty accusations made by both sides. And, as he had when he and Karen divorced, Brian made a strong push to have his children with him.

Nearly a year after the couple split, Debbie began to worry about their three-year-old son, after he behaved in a sexual way with their daughter. When she asked the boy what he was doing, he said he had learned from Brian.

Debbie contacted authorities, who sent the case to Utah's Division of Child and Family Services, the same office where Shirl Mitchell was a social worker.

A police report, dated June 7, 1985, was filed. In it, Debbie Mitchell said she thought "her estranged husband" was trying to teach "her children things to bring about their sexual awareness."

The little boy was interviewed by a caseworker and examined by doctors at a local hospital, who couldn't find any concrete sign that he had been molested by Brian. They said the boy did appear to be too interested in sex for his age, and suggested he have only supervised visits with his father.

However, there was never a prosecution, because authorities didn't think there was enough evidence to move forward.

There was more trouble to come. Debbie's 12-year-old daughter, Rebecca, told her mom around that time that her former stepfather had sexually abused her for four years.

It began when she was eight years old, just after her mother married Brian, Rebecca said. Her stepfather would creep into her room at night. The terrified girl was threatened against telling anyone, because "nobody would believe her," she would later say.

"He told her that if she told anyone, he would do the same thing to her sisters," Debbie said.

Debbie knew nothing of the abuse during their marriage and said Rebecca first brought it up after counseling sessions that began after the divorce. Debbie brought the issue to LDS officials, the second time in three years she said she approached the church about Brian's behavior.

But Debbie said she was discouraged from pressing charges. The church officials didn't lend credence to Rebecca's claims of abuse, and no charges were filed.

Debbie said Brian could have been stopped from harming anyone else back then, had any action been taken.

Debbie's two children with Brian, Sarah and Joey, were kept in her custody, and Brian had no interaction with them. The two remember almost nothing of their father.

Most of Brian's family, having never liked Debbie, discounted what she said. They stuck by Brian's account of the marriage and considered his estranged wife a scorned woman seeking to smear him.

Years later, Debbie said her daughter found a picture in some of Brian's things in their basement. It was a photo of two naked children, relatives of Brian.

Brian was beginning to develop financial problems, a stress that would weigh on him in the coming years. He had worked a series of low-paying jobs during his two marriages—janitor, carpenter, construction worker—and he had little saved to show for it.

He was supposed to make child support payments to Debbie for their children.

He talked about money problems often, Shirl said, and would come to his father for help. "He always sponged off me," Shirl said.

Brian once arrived at his father's house, saying he needed $550 for dental work. Shirl wrote him a check. Weeks later, Shirl got the canceled check back, but it had been signed by Brian. Shirl called the dentist's office and asked if they had received the money. They hadn't.

But during that year after his marriage to Debbie, other relatives said, Brian seemed to be reclaiming the spirit he'd found in the early 1980s, when he was fresh back from New Hampshire. He was light again, relatives said. While he may have been happy, he also sought help. Sometime after he and Debbie separated, Brian went into group therapy.

It was at one of the sessions that he met a bright-eyed woman named Wanda Barzee Thompson, a kindred spirit with a bruised ego and a deep fear of being alone and unloved.

TWO

Wanda Eileen Barzee sat at the piano, sometimes for days at a stretch, her fingers dancing across the keys. She had to get the notes down exactly right.

"She was an extremely talented woman, concert pianist caliber," recalled Cynthia Marsh, who lived in the same ward as Wanda and her family decades earlier. "But manic about it."

There were times when Wanda would practice all night long, driven by a force only she was able to detect. She was thrilled with nearly every piece written by Johann Sebastian Bach, and she studied his work meticulously. Members of her congregation were startled by her nervous energy, even as they marveled at her ability.

In almost four decades, Wanda would go from being an eager, well-coiffed girl peering out of her picture in the 1964 South High School yearbook with a helmet of auburn hair and look of hope and promise, to the leather-faced, haggard woman staring lifelessly from a mug shot in March 2003.

Wanda was usually quiet and prim in public, save for an occasional outburst that seeped with hurt and let others know just how unhappy she was.

She had moments of deep elation, as though she couldn't get enough of life. She would throw her head back and laugh at whatever joke was being told, her mouth twisted into a toothy grin.

There was also an ineffable sadness, a dull ache of memories marked by a terrible marriage and a lifetime of fear.

"Wanda was a follower," said her sister, Evelyn, whose eyes shine behind her round glasses with the same light that Wanda's once held. Like most of Wanda's family, she sometimes speaks of her sister in the past tense. The Wanda they knew growing up seems to have disappeared. The woman who sat behind bars in a prison uniform at the Salt Lake County Adult Detention Center after Elizabeth Smart was found is a stranger to them.

To her friends and even some of her family, there was something opaque about Wanda, secrets she was trying to keep. The one thing she wanted in life that was known to everyone who cared for her, besides her music, was to be protected.

"She just wanted so much to have someone who would love her and take care of her," Evelyn said.

She thought she'd found that when she met Brian David Mitchell in the 1980s, after she left her abusive first husband. She would forgive almost anything he did, just to have someone who said he would take care of her, even if, ultimately, he didn't keep his promise. Wanda thought the best days of her life were just around the corner.

* * *

Wanda was known as one of the "Cackling Barzees."

Born on November 6, 1945, she was the middle of three daughters born to Marvin and Dora Barzee. Wanda and her baby sister, Evelyn, would stay up all night, laughing until their father, a master organ builder, threatened to come up and spank them. The two girls, and the eldest Barzee daughter, Janice, had formed a deep bond.

Wanda was as sunny a little girl as her future second husband was troubled.

Evelyn looked up to her older sister, the gifted musician who doted on her family and prayed dutifully. "Wanda was a very spiritual person," Evelyn said. Sometimes, Evelyn envied the attention Wanda received for her talent. But it was the normal envy between siblings, and mostly they were close friends.

The two would rush home from school to nestle in front of the television, watching "Popeye" cartoons and dunking graham crackers in cold glasses of milk.

Wanda was quite passive. She got good grades, did what her parents told her to do. She was a sweet little girl who deeply craved her parents' love and warmth. Deeply devout, Wanda took her life as a young Mormon quite seriously. She was raised to be obedient, and she excelled at it.

She also may have been a victim early on. Her son, Mark, would later say his mother was molested by her father Marvin, who died of cancer in 1970 at age 54.

In Dora's memory, Wanda was sometimes selfish as a child, particularly when she was holding her dolls. She would carry the dolls around, wrapped in blankets and pressed against her chest. She stroked their heads and whispered to them and was fiercely protective if anyone else tried to touch them. "This is mine!" she would say.

Still, Wanda's family doesn't remember her giving off any signs of the depression that would later haunt her.

"She seemed normal," Dora said.

Wanda's greatest love was her music. She started practicing at an early age, and she was magical at it. She was a natural and practiced for hours when she got home from school. Her parents had to force her away so her sisters, who weren't as interested, could practice. Wanda later trained with a teacher who went on to be hired by the Mormon Tabernacle.

She dreamed of playing before a crowd of thousands, the sound of the music she made filling the theater. She would make Bach come alive, and the applause would be deafening. Mary Ann Hyde, who graduated from South High, remembered going to the Mormon Tabernacle to watch Wanda play the organ while they were still in school. But that was one of the few things Wanda devoted her energy toward.

"I don't remember her ever having a single date," said Hyde. She recalled an extremely quiet young woman who usually spoke only when she was spoken to and who was best friends with her little sister. So Hyde was surprised to learn Wanda had married Talmage Thompson almost straight out of high school, when she was 19 years old.

They met at an annual church conference, while Wanda was sitting with Dora in the balcony. "He started writing notes to Wanda and trying to get a date," chuckled Dora, a widow with piles of pictures of her children around her home. Dora's blue eyes are milky behind her glasses, and she quietly tears up when she talks about her daughter.

Wanda gave birth to her first child, a girl, within the first year of the marriage. She had two more children in the next two years, all born in August. She became deeply depressed after the birth of her fourth child, Derrick, friends and relatives said.

Still, Talmage pushed for more kids.

"If Talmage had had his druthers, he'd have them every year," Dora said. "He thought a healthy woman could have a child every year."

Talmage was an unusual man, and very eccentric.

"He was kind of funny, kind of like a kid," said Cynthia Marsh. "He would show off in front of the boys." Once, when Marsh's sons went to see "Superman" at a theater in downtown Salt Lake City, Talmage was there. Outside the theater, Talmage scrambled onto a large rock that overlooked a mud puddle.

Talmage teetered on the edge of the rock, raised his arms in the air and shouted "Superman!" Then jumped, flat into the mud. Marsh's sons were perplexed.

Talmage was also a tyrant in their home. Marsh

called the marriage "difficult," but Dora was more direct. "He was very controlling, and quite abusive," she said.

The memory of the abuse was burned in Wanda's children's brains. Years later, her son, Mark, would say he could still see Talmage's fists striking his mom.

The neighbors in their Hillside ward also knew of the abuse and felt sorry for Wanda. Her husband was difficult, and so were her sons. The boys were known as troublemakers around the neighborhood.

But Wanda tried to create the appearance that everything was fine. A skilled seamstress, she stitched together suits for Talmage and beautiful outfits for herself and always looked stylish and well put-together—"maybe a little too sophisticated," Cynthia Marsh said—when she was outside of the house. Her poise seemed artificial, almost as if she were trying to prove something. She was too dressed up. Her laugh was a little too exuberant. Instead of distracting people from looking at her life, they only stared more closely.

Marsh had a sense that Wanda was always acting, always on stage. She was playing a part in a drama in which she didn't want to star. Wanda's joy was still her music, Dora said. Wanda took classes at Brigham Young University, where she played an organ for the first time. She was instantly hooked by the rich sound, and later gave a recital at BYU, inviting many of her neighbors. She sent her mother a tape of a recital she gave in 1976.

Back home, Wanda's marriage was plagued by

money woes. Talmage held several low-paying jobs, including gym teacher at area schools. But the money never stretched far, and Talmage liked to live beyond his means, Dora said. He was always looking for the next big thing.

Talmage sometimes disappeared for days at a time, neighbors said. Court papers show a military address for him, and that may have been why he was sometimes away.

"Talmage was always spinning his wheels," Dora said. "He always had them on the move. We could be in the middle of a meal and he'd stand up and use the phone because he got an idea and he had to tell someone."

The last home the family lived in was supposed to have been permanent, Dora said. But Talmage couldn't afford the payments, and they were forced to move. At the same time, he bought Wanda a grand piano, thinking it would please her, along with an organ and a dining room set.

"He was always trying to buy Wanda's love," said Dora. The family eventually moved to the more working-class West Valley City. The organ was absurdly expensive, Dora remembered. Talmage managed to keep it, but only by borrowing money to pay off other costly items, which he would then sell for a new profit.

"It's crazy," Dora said. "It was just crazy how he just kept driving her nuts."

The financial responsibilities of the house increasingly fell to Wanda. She started paying the bills and tried to figure out how to make ends meet.

To help out with the money, Wanda started giving piano lessons. She enjoyed it, and it was a steady source of income. But even that didn't last long. Talmage was so odd that it scared off her students.

"He would come and interrupt the lessons, and she had to give up her lessons because he was so rude with her students," Dora said. "He would just interrupt her."

She later went to work as a beautician and as a cake designer. She made her mother a beautiful layered cake when Dora married her second husband, Glenn Corbett.

But others remember Wanda as distant and somewhat selfish. In the family's living room sat nothing but her organ. There wasn't a stick of furniture.

When Wanda and Talmage were together, there was anger and there were fists. When she was alone, Wanda felt suffocated by the amount of work her family required.

"She wanted help, and she just couldn't seem to get it with her children and her marriage and everything," Dora said. "I think it began piling up so. It was just because of her husband, I think, that drove her to such despondency and so forth."

Her son, Brian, often got into trouble. There was an incident where he vandalized the church, neighbors remembered. The older children were embarrassed by their home life, and they tried to keep friends away, neighbors recalled. Wanda's personality seemed to change as her children got older. Her children remember violent mood swings.

They remember Wanda threatening suicide. In September 1983, she reached her breaking point.

It was the day her baby girl, eight-year-old LouRee, was to be baptized into the Mormon church. Instead of standing by her daughter's side, Wanda abruptly left her family before the service began. She went to stay with her parents, trying to quell a steady wave of fear.

"She was a basket case, really, after going through the divorce," her mother remembered. Wanda was wracked with guilt over leaving her children, but she was in no condition to care for them at that point.

A diligent LDS member, Wanda continued attending church meetings even as she was getting ready to leave the ward. She went regularly to meetings of her ward's Relief Society, a Mormon women's group that does charitable work and is intended to bolster relationships among the people in it. But at one of the meetings, Wanda snapped.

She shouted at the other women that she felt she had been stomped on by the community the entire time she'd been in the ward. Instead of helping her, they'd treated her like garbage, she fumed.

"None of you have helped me," she said angrily.

"I'll never forget it," Marsh said. "Because it was a setting where she was bearing her testimony. But actually, what she ended up doing was telling everyone that she felt like she never had a friend, never had any support. She just kind of let everybody have it."

But Marsh said most people felt as if they had tried to come to Wanda's aid and were put off by the rant. They left the church worried for the woman with emotional problems that were cracking her carefully layered veneer.

Talmage filed for divorce in 1984. He wanted custody of the children. They could sell the organ and split the money. Wanda could keep the piano.

The Thompson children stayed with their father, while Wanda recovered with her mother and her stepfather. While she was struggling to rebuild her life, Wanda suffered medical problems. She had a hysterectomy, and she went to recover in nearby St. George for several months, Dora said.

Dora doesn't remember Wanda being hospitalized for depression after the surgery, but her friends do. Vicki Cottrell, the executive director of the National Alliance for the Mentally Ill and an old family friend of the Barzees, remembers Wanda telling her of a hospital stay for what was then called "a nervous breakdown." She told other friends the same story. Cottrell believes Wanda suffered from a personality disorder and had delusions.

Wanda occasionally kept such details about her life from her mother. It was as though she didn't want her to be aware of the depth of her troubles. She was given psychotropic medication, but she refused to take it. But she did keep up with therapy, something she apparently saw value in early on. It may have been the only time she felt free to talk about the weighty sadness she carried around, which she struggled so hard to keep others from seeing.

Slowly, Wanda began steering her life back on track. She was an excellent typist, something she had learned in school, and got a series of temp jobs working as a receptionist. She got a little duplex near the LDS Tenth Ward in Salt Lake City. She was 40 years old, and she was starting over.

She became a church organist at the Tenth Ward. She made new friends there and became very close with Lee Willis, the church's music director.

In late 1984 or early 1985, Wanda met a young man, devoted to the church, named Brian David Mitchell. After her marriage to Talmage, he seemed like the man of her dreams.

Wanda told those close to her different stories about how she met Brian. Some remember them meeting at a church function. Others were told they met because Brian was "investigating" the LDS church, a Mormon term for exploring the church's beliefs and practices to see if one wants to join.

In reality, they met at a group therapy session, her mother said. Wanda, fresh-faced and well-dressed, went to the sessions to talk about dealing with her divorce and the trauma of her marriage. Brian, eight years younger than Wanda, was also going through a painful separation and was recommitting to LDS church life.

He seemed too good to be true.

THREE

Wanda's family liked Brian. He seemed a little odd, but he also seemed deeply spiritual. He seemed to love Wanda deeply. He was soft spoken, his white shirts were crisply starched and his manner was gentle. He always seemed to be in control, something Wanda craved. He seemed wise beyond his 32 years.

They had a quick courtship, but Brian had concerns before their marriage. He told relatives that he liked Wanda and that they had fun, but that he wasn't sure if he should marry her. She had had problems similar to his, he said, and it might not be a good idea. But he fell in love with her and couldn't help himself.

Wanda was deeply in love, but there was something manic in the way she spoke about him. As she told her friend Lee stories about Brian, he couldn't help but think she was bordering on needy infatuation. She had been hurt so badly before and was just starting over. It would be a shame to throw it all away.

"She wasn't simple, but almost gullible," said Lee. "She was sort of desperate because she really wanted someone to love her. And at all costs, she was going to stick by her man. I think if he'd said, 'Sprout wings and fly,' she'd have done everything she could to make that happen."

For his part, Brian was entering his third try at life. If he told Wanda about his past, she never repeated all the details to her family. The Barzees thought Brian was a "spiritual man," even if he was a little eccentric.

Unlike Brian's other wives, Wanda met with Shirl Mitchell's approval. She was physically strong, moving large pieces of furniture when Brian moved into her home. And she laughed loudly at Shirl's jokes, which helped make her a favorite.

Some of the other Mitchells didn't care for Wanda, relatives said. They didn't approve of her for Brian. She was sweet, but she was very needy. Her emotional issues worried Brian's siblings.

Wanda was also active in the LDS, and, at that time, Brian was immersing himself in scripture, which encouraged the Mitchells. Still, the Mitchells, knowing what Brian's past had been like, were concerned about these two broken souls.

"They clung to each other and they held on all the way," said one relative. But Brian and Wanda seemed thrilled together. Their new lives were well under way.

In late 1985, Brian proposed to Wanda, presenting her with a potted plant with an engagement ring tucked inside.

They were married on November 29 that year, the same day Brian's divorce from Debbie came through. Wanda wore a wedding dress she'd made herself, and a crown of flowers. Brian's mother and brother Kevin were the witnesses who signed the marriage certificate. Brian once again left Irene Mitchell's home, where he had stayed after the divorce, and moved into Wanda's duplex.

Brian was working a string of odd jobs at that point, relatives said, but he always had steady income. After the stress of Talmage's money troubles, Wanda couldn't have been happier. She wanted to be a wife and not to be harried with work outside the home.

"I don't want to have anything more to do with finances," she told her family. "Brian took over even buying the groceries."

Wanda and Brian would go to the movies with Lee and his wife, and they socialized within the ward. Wanda and Brian almost never talked about their pasts. They guarded their histories carefully.

They lived strictly by the LDS teachings. Brian and Wanda abhorred swearing of any kind. They would flip the channel on the TV if any words they considered sins were used, or if sex scenes came across the screen.

Once, while they were at the movies, Brian got up and walked out when an actor cursed. Dora Corbett and Evelyn, both devout Mormons, found Wanda's and Brian's habits extreme.

They had no idea how different Brian was behind closed doors.

Wanda confided to Lee soon after the wedding that Brian wasn't what he'd seemed when they were first together. "There's a change in him," she told Lee. She said her new husband, the one who had seemed so perfect months earlier, had an explosive temper. He threw things, he screamed at Wanda. He didn't hit her, she insisted, but he frightened her.

"I don't know what to do," she said.

"You don't need that in your life," Lee said. He reminded her gently of all she had been through in the past and told her she should leave Brian. There was no reason to be chained to someone who was so troubled.

"I can't do that," she said. After all, she loved him.

At Wanda's urging, Brian agreed to go to couple's counseling. He needed to work on his temper, on not becoming so enraged. Things seemed to be getting better, for a time.

They went to social events at their church. At one costume party, Brian and Wanda came dressed inside a massive shower curtain.

"We forgot our soap!" Brian chirped to a friend, who urged them to open the curtain just a crack so he could videotape them.

Members of their ward liked Wanda and were impressed by her musical talent. They were slightly wary of Brian. He was active in the church, but some members merely tolerated him.

Lee Willis always thought he came off like a salesman, trying to push an unwanted product on people. He was too overbearing. It was like he was running a con, desperately trying to show he was more normal, more of a committed Mormon and family man, than anyone else. But there was only one person who truly bought the impression Brian was selling: Wanda drank in everything Brian said. He took the LDS teachings to extremes, and said he was offended by people who didn't do the same. Wanda was more than willing to go along with his edicts.

There were more problems within that first year. Wanda, always vexed over money, complained to Lee that Brian had lost his job and wasn't bringing in any income. Her last ideal about her new husband, that he would be a steady provider, was quickly fading.

Whether Wanda knew it or not, Brian was also buckling under his other financial responsibilities. Debbie Mitchell said he skimped on six months worth of child support payments for Joey and Sarah.

Dora and Glenn Corbett tried to help Wanda and Brian for awhile. They took the couple on a belated honeymoon in 1986, to the World's Fair in Vancouver, Canada. Wanda adored her stepfather and called him Dad. They were two couples out in a strange town, and they loved it. It was one of the happiest times Dora had with her daughter after she married Brian.

More than a year after they were married, Wanda had reunited with her youngest three children,

Derrick, Mark, and LouRee, and the kids, who had been living with their father, came to live with her and Brian. Shirl said Travis Mitchell, who had been legally adopted by one of his foster families, also lived there for some time, although it was apparently years later.

For Wanda, having some of her children back with her was a gift. She was wracked with guilt over leaving them, friends said later, and this was a second chance at being their mother. The Thompson children moved in with Brian and Wanda around 1987. The memory of Wanda leaving, without saying goodbye, was still fresh. But she and her children were going to try again.

In some ways, Wanda seemed content, normal in her life. She still sent her mother cards every year, on birthdays and Mother's Day, telling Dora how much she loved her. But at some point, she had developed an odd habit of caring for dolls as she had when she was a young girl. She tugged at the blankets she had shrouded them in and propped them up gingerly in chairs. She began carrying them out of the house, taking them with her when she went outside.

Wanda was often caught up in her own world. She was attentive and nurturing to her little dolls, yet selfish and scattered with her kids.

The Thompson children grew wary of their new stepdad soon after they started living with Brian and Wanda. He was "creepy" to Mark, who immediately noticed the emptiness in Brian's eyes.

Derrick, the child whose delivery sent Wanda

spiraling into depression, thought they behaved
normally at first. No one can pinpoint exactly
when the trouble started. But they seem to agree
that the severe changes started in Brian first.

Mark remembered Brian studying hypnotism.
He padlocked the family's television set at night.
He would yell at the slightest provocation. Some-
times, Wanda would yell back.

There were horrible fights. "Get out of my
kitchen!" Wanda would yell at Brian. Sometimes,
instead of raging at his wife, he simply backed
away.

Brian and Wanda shared a sense of isolation, relatives said, but it was often self-imposed. They
seemed to be constantly nurturing an anger over
some perceived slight. Within the first few years of
their marriage, just before a holiday celebration,
Brian and Wanda wrote a blistering letter that they
sent to almost every member of the Mitchell family. They said the family had never accepted them,
had always cast them aside, and that was why they
were skipping the holiday gathering, one relative
recalled. Their relatives were shocked; no one felt
they had done anything to insult the couple, and
their anger seemed to come out of left field.

But to the outside world, Brian and Wanda
seemed to function normally. Wanda still played
her music at church. Brian worked for three years
as a member of the stake council at the Salt Lake
Temple. He was a youth counselor to boys in the
church. He played a range of roles in staged temple

rituals re-enacting characters in the scriptures. Once he played Adam. Another time he played Satan. Church officials told him he had natural acting talent but one thing concerned them.

"They told me I was the best Lucifer they'd ever seen, and could I please tone it down a bit?" Mitchell told a friend, chuckling over the incident.

At home, Wanda's children said they were growing uncomfortable around their stepfather. LouRee, Wanda's baby girl, was 12 years old when she started living with Brian. She was in the throes of adolescence and she didn't like the way Brian behaved around her.

He would hold her and kiss her too long, in ways that didn't feel right. He looked at her the wrong way. He constantly crept into her room at night, trying to tuck her in and press against her with a long hug and a quick kiss on the lips.

LouRee never told her mom what was going on. She knew her mother was struggling with something, but didn't know what. At night, LouRee could hear Wanda screaming from the room she shared with Brian. She didn't know what was happening, but the sound terrified her. She stayed in her own bed and tried to sleep.

Brian also had a brutal side, a sadistic streak that was tinged with violence, LouRee said. For supper one night, LouRee sat down to what Brian told her was a chicken dinner. LouRee polished off her plate. Later, Brian revealed that he had just served LouRee's pet bunny, Peaches. He had killed it and cooked it. When LouRee ran to Peaches's cage, it was empty.

He used to take Mark hunting. Returning from one of their trips, Brian shot Mark's pet dog in the head, killing it on the spot. Brian told the horrified boy that he had done it because the dog had gone mad.

Vicki Cottrell, Wanda's childhood friend, knew Brian had problems. She always believed he was mentally ill and needed help. She remembered Brian's two siblings who were marriage counselors saying they believed he might be schizophrenic, although some of the Mitchells have said since that they never thought Brian was suffering from serious mental problems. He was "weird" but not sick.

But Wanda stuck by Brian. Her own behavior was changing again. She went along with Brian's own peculiar diet regimen of eating mostly organic herbs and vegetables, with little meat. Brian would occasionally describe his past drug use to Wanda's children. He had battled a heroin addiction, he told Mark. He recounted to Derrick how he once ventured into the desert, took 10 hits of LSD, and saw God.

"No kidding, who wouldn't?" Derrick said.

The household was too bizarre for Derrick, who said he moved out within a year. When he turned 18 and was legally an adult, he went to stay with friends.

LouRee stayed awhile longer. When she was about 15, she left the house to move back in with her father. Her mother, whom LouRee had never told of Brian's advances toward her, was devastated. She was hurt, and she was angry. She screamed and kicked her feet. She couldn't believe she was losing her little girl. She said that she considered LouRee dead to her.

"How could my baby do this?" Wanda cried.

Mark was still in the house, but things began to fall apart quickly after LouRee left. Brian and Wanda seemed to grow more fanatical by the day. Mark was awakened once in the dead of night by the excited couple telling him, "We saw angels. They talked to us."

Ironically, Brian had two fewer children to take care of at a time when he was making his steadiest income in years. He had worked as an office messenger at O.C. Tanner, a jewelry-making firm, and he rose up the company ladder to the die-cutting department.

At work, Brian seemed to be the consummate professional. He gave the impression of a man ensconced in the LDS church, one who had faced demons in the past, and conquered them. He became very close friends with Doug Larsen, a colleague at Tanner, with whom he shared similar beliefs.

Brian confided in Doug about his two ex-wives, his past drug addiction and his deep Mormon faith. He even told Doug about taking Angie and Travis to New Hampshire, and about his difficult marriage to Debbie. Brian said he'd met Wanda in therapy, and that she was still struggling with her own problems. He talked about the Mitchell family, warts and all. He told Doug the family had always considered him the odd man out, and about how he was trying to change that. He also wanted to bring his family around to his way of thinking.

"He was, I would say, at the top of his form. He was trying to get his family to be more functional, rather than dysfunctional," Doug said later.

In particular, Brian talked about Shirl. "He used to tell me about conversing with his father and trying to get his father to see the light," Larsen said. "Brian wanted his family to be active in the church, but to all his family members he was just 'poor Brian,' because they remembered his substance abuse."

In Brian's memory, Debbie had often cajoled the Mitchell clan into taking her side against Brian. No one was ever on his side, he told Doug. He was always alone. It was a different version of events than Debbie would tell, or than Brian's father and other relatives would later recount. Most had never liked Debbie and had no memory of falling in line with her against Brian. But Doug wouldn't learn that for another decade.

As for his family, Brian had apparently forgiven whatever transgression had prompted his angry letter, and he and Wanda began seeing the Mitchells again and spending time with his siblings. They loved being around Brian's nieces and nephews. They seemed happy, and that made the Mitchells happy.

At work, Doug enjoyed Brian's company. He

was over-stressed, but he seemed mature, much more so than Doug himself, who was a few years older than Brian. He had been through a lot in his life and seemed to have risen above it. They also saw eye to eye on any number of social issues.

They were both put off by the curse words their colleagues slung around the office. They both voted for Populist Party presidential candidate Bo Gritz when he ran for president in 1992. "We didn't know he was a white supremacist," Doug said. But Gritz was deeply anti-government, and that likely appealed to Brian.

Doug saw Brian get angry several times, but he never actually lost his temper. The dark side of Brian's personality never emerged in all those years working in the small Tanner offices.

Brian often lamented to Doug about money. He simply didn't have enough of it to go around. He complained of child-support payments for Sarah and Joey, and he had mounting medical expenses for Wanda, who was taking antidepressants that cost a fortune.

Wanda was something of a cipher to Doug. The couple seemed happy together, and completely compatible. One afternoon, Doug and his wife joined Brian and Wanda for a picnic in Copperton Park. Doug's wife didn't quite hit it off with Wanda, but Doug thought her a sweet woman, though a little quiet.

Brian grew frustrated, and bored, with his work. His money problems were mounting, and he didn't know how to get out from under them. At the same time, he developed a hatred of people he deemed "hypocrites"—those who said they were committed to the church but didn't practice their faith, and those who were too preoccupied with "worldly things" and material possessions instead of following the word of God. It was likely a way of dealing with his financial woes. Instead of finding a way out of debt, Brian declared a world that wanted his money to be obsessed with the almighty dollar, and therefore sinful.

Brian's views grew more radical. He started attending political meetings of anti-government fringe groups, with beliefs similar to the platform of Gritz, the man for whom Brian had voted. Brian began talking excitedly to relatives about a new discovery—he told his relatives he'd heard income taxes were unconstitutional, and therefore people didn't have to pay them. In fact, he said, there was a legal procedure to be declared exempt from the levy. He tried to convince relatives to do it with him, but they weren't interested.

Brian was also growing disenchanted with the LDS church. He was obsessed with his belief that the church didn't do enough to help the poor, despite its own teachings that the community should take care of the less fortunate.

"He said the church wasn't doing enough to help the homeless," said Gary Shaw, who knew Brian from church. Brian talked about becoming the "prophet" for the homeless.

Brian's family questioned what was behind his

new anti-materialist zeal. Shirl and other relatives didn't believe he was genuinely concerned about church doctrines. Brian wanted to avoid paying the tithes the LDS requires of its members, they said.

Brian and Wanda were about to be on their own for good. Mark Thompson had grown terrified of the couple. At night, Brian would pray for two hours. Their regimens turned more extreme. Brian would circle his bed at night, in some kind of séance. Brian decided that modern medicine was unhealthy, and they used only herbal cures if they got sick.

They were beginning to go "all crazy and homeless," Mark said. With Gritz's words in his head, Brian spoke seriously about cutting himself loose from material existence. Mark, old enough to be on his own, moved out.

Travis, Brian's son from his first marriage, lived briefly with the pair, but it was a short-lived reunion, Shirl said. The three weren't compatible, and Travis was about to become a legal adult.

Derrick Thompson, long out of the house at that point, believed his mother and stepfather were using drugs. He asked her once while they were talking on the phone. Wanda denied it.

Around 1993, Brian took his first step toward viewing himself as a healer. Wanda's stepfather, Glenn, was diagnosed with prostate cancer. One of Evelyn's sisters, who was living in Las Vegas at the time, heard of a natural healer and lymphologist named Dr. C. Samuel West who lived in Orem, about an hour south of Salt Lake.

Glenn and Dora Corbett visited Dr. West, who teaches his patients they can reverse disease through natural practices. When the Corbetts returned home and told Wanda and Brian about the trip, Brian was ecstatic.

"He got all gung-ho on this information, and then he gradually got so interested that he wanted to teach it," Dora said.

Brian had recently read a book called *The Mucus Diet,* and he and Wanda started eating nothing but fruit. The couple decided to live a holistic life. He began to meld the healing techniques of Dr. West with his own religious ideas, which were splintering away from Mormon theology.

"He figured he'd combine his religious preoccupations with healings," Shirl recalled. The couple's church attendance dropped off as Brian complained he was unhappy with LDS teachings. But some relatives believe the real reason for his growing discontent was that the church represented another bill—the tithes the LDS requires of its members, roughly 10 percent of each worshipper's annual income.

Whatever the reason, Brian began shunning the Book of Mormon in favor of Dr. West's texts on healing. He quit his job at Tanner, claiming, Doug Larsen said, that the work was "fatuous." Brian announced that he and Wanda were going to work for Dr. West, selling his books and preaching his lifestyle.

To pay the bills while their new venture was getting off the ground, Brian took a job at an ironworks factory just a few blocks from the Tanner offices. He thought the work presented a better challenge to his creative side.

A few months later, on an evening in April 1994, he and Wanda showed up at Doug's doorstep. Doug was happy to see him, and the two couples sat around the Larsen living room, chatting. But there was something a little off about Brian—an edge to him that Doug hadn't seen before. And Brian's excitement about West's books seemed slightly manic.

But the couple looked healthy and fit. Brian said they had been eating nothing but fruits and vegetables for a year, and exercising more. He told Doug he could achieve the same health and happiness. Handing Doug one of West's books, Brian asked him for a $350 donation. Doug demurred, saying he needed to know more about West before he'd turn over so much money. Brian asked again, and again Doug said no. Disappointed, Brian left Doug with the book and he and Wanda went on their way.

Dora Corbett grew increasingly concerned about her daughter. The laughter had disappeared from her eyes.

"Brian misconstrued everything," Dora said, and other relatives agreed. Brian twisted tenets of the LDS, the words of the Bible and even the federal tax code so that they were more palatable to him. But Wanda didn't want to hear Brian criticized. That year, Wanda sent her mother a card, telling her how much she loved her. It was the last loving card Dora would ever get.

Brian and Wanda began a gradual "sloughing off of worldly possessions," Shirl said. Brian quit his job at the ironworks shop within months. It began with a name change. Brian announced to his family that he was to be called David, the name of the Old Testament king believed to be an ancestor of Jesus. He pronounced it "DAH-vid," and he bristled when people got it wrong. Wanda was to be called "Eladah." Brian corrected Dora anytime she called her daughter by her real name.

Shirl scoffed at Brian's name change. His son talked earnestly about serving as the prophet of the poor, but Shirl saw a more calculated motive. He thought Brian was simply trying to evade tax collectors. And quitting his job at the ironworks factory, the last real work Brian would ever do, would keep authorities from knocking on his door in search of the support payments he owed Debbie for Sarah and Joey.

Brian insisted he was serving the Lord's will to help the downtrodden. The only thing to do now was join his would-be disciples. In 1995, he and Wanda sold off most of their possessions and got rid of their home. They couldn't find a taker for Wanda's $2,000 piano, so Dora bought it from them. They plunked down a down payment for a fifth-wheel trailer and drove south to Heber City, the place where Brian had honeymooned with

Debbie. Wanda's sister, Evelyn, lived there with her own family at the time.

At first, Brian and Wanda were active in the church there. But within months, they stopped going altogether—lifting the burden of paying tithes to the church. Their last financial tie was broken. Brian told Wanda's family that the couple could worship the way they wanted to. They didn't need anyone to tell them how to interpret God's word.

Dora tried to speak to Wanda about the couple's way of life, which contradicted everything she'd been taught in her church and by her family. Dora thought Brian was brainwashing Wanda, and that her daughter, who was always weak-willed, was succumbing to evil. She was living a counterfeit life, Dora told her daughter, worshipping a false God. Wanda snarled at her mother to leave her alone.

In the summer of 1995, she sent Dora a scathing letter, accusing her mother of damaging her life. Dora was responsible for everything that had ever gone wrong for Wanda, she wrote. She called Dora "evil" and "materialistic." She told her mother that she and her two sisters were "Babylon."

Evelyn saw her big sister getting angrier with the world. And she was convinced that Brian was the only one she should listen to.

Brian and Wanda decided to head for Idaho. They had visited the state a few weeks earlier, after a camping trip with Evelyn and her husband, who were thinking of moving there permanently. Brian and Wanda were instantly smitten with the state.

They headed for one of Bo Gritz's survivalist camps, their trailer stockpiled with wheat and fruit. They had to toss their foodstuffs out along the way to lighten the load.

They were in Idaho for only a few months, living in Clearwater. Wanda and Brian were thrilled when they reached Gritz's camp, but the anti-government crusader's followers didn't want them around. Brian's preaching was too radical.

"Brian was accused of being a preacher of hell-fire and damnation," Dora said. "He sounded like a Baptist preacher."

Within weeks, their trailer was repossessed because Brian hadn't kept up with the payments. The couple sold what little else they had, and were truly homeless.

"Where did they go after that? Who knows," Dora said.

Brian and Wanda hitchhiked their way across the country, carrying bedrolls and thumbing rides. They made their way east, a place familiar to Brian from his days on the run from Karen with Travis and Angie. Their hair grew long, and caked with grime. They stayed in homeless shelters and begged for money.

In November 1995, Wanda dropped Dora a line. She said she and her husband had been to Philadelphia, Boston and New York. Wanda had given an organ recital at a church in each city, she wrote. In New York, it had been a Presbyterian church. She and Brian would arrange the impromptu recitals with the churches' musical directors.

They were also sticking strictly to their drastic diets.

They shared a "glorious Thanksgiving" meal, she wrote. It consisted of nothing but fruit. Their next stop was Florida, she said. It was the only time Dora heard from Wanda while she was traveling the country, and she was worried sick about what would happen to her daughter.

The couple went back west, visiting California, and even Hawaii and Alaska. They had made hundreds of dollars holding out their hands for help and doing occasional odd jobs. They had crafted a cart to carry what few belongings they had, and Brian proudly pulled it across the span of the Golden Gate Bridge in San Francisco.

They returned in the summer of 1997, and Dora was thrilled. She agreed to let them stay with her for a couple of months. She and Wanda went shopping together, and took care of the house. Wanda stitched new outfits for herself. But something had changed permanently in Wanda.

Brian, on the other hand, was aglow with his plans. He and Wanda were going to live in a teepee in the Wasatch Mountains. Shirl had bought them the teepee, and Dora offered them wool blankets and a comforter.

Brian also said he'd had a revelation, that he was to begin a new branch of religion. He started drafting a doctrine that would serve as its book of worship. Dora was uncomfortable with Brian writing what she considered a blasphemous book while he was under her roof, but she held her tongue. She didn't make a fuss when she called her daughter by her name, Wanda, and Brian would get angry and correct her. "Eladah," he would say. She gritted her teeth through the couple's daily lectures on religion, even though they exhausted and offended her.

"All that preaching takes its toll," Dora said.

She finally spoke out when she felt he had crossed the line.

Brian came to Dora and Glenn one day, rambling about how he wanted to use their house to begin his church. The house would be the temple for the masses that would follow him. The church would teach a new prophecy, a new version of the Book of Mormon, which Brian found flawed but was going to correct. Dora interrupted him.

"I don't feel right about this, Brian," she said. It was all she said, but Brian flew into a fury. He screamed at his in-laws. Then he turned to his wife.

"Let's get our things and leave, Eladah," he said. Within minutes, they were gone.

That was in late 1997.

Shirl drove his son and daughter-in-law up into the Wasatch Mountains, into a canyon just behind the Federal Heights Ward, in the north part of Salt Lake proper, where Brian set up their teepee. Shirl made several trips with them to get the couple set up. On one of the trips, Brian wouldn't allow Shirl to get close to their campsite, but refused to say why.

When the weather got cold, they stayed with Irene on and off. Then they decided to go to Orem and meet with Dr. West, Brian's inspiration. By then, Brian had changed his named from "David." He had gone by "Shirlson," a reference to his father, for a time, but when he arrived at West's door, he was referring to himself as "Immanuel."

Dr. West let the couple live with him, but Brian was losing control. "I watched these people go down," West said later. "I saw there was something wrong."

Brian answered West's phones and helped him with office work. West subsidized Brian and Wanda while they were with him, giving them meals. West, a Mormon, would have long talks with Brian about the LDS church. West told Brian he should return to the faith in which he was raised. Brian got angry, and he and Wanda left.

They went back to Salt Lake, staying on and off with Brian's mom. Irene felt plagued by her son but incapable of throwing him out. Most of his family, however, had had enough of Brian. They were disgusted by his lifestyle. It was just another example of his flakiness, taken to extremes. And it was getting worse.

Brian declared that he and Wanda should shed their street clothes and wear robes instead. Some were purple, a color that signifies royalty or someone of "exalted" status, and others were white.

Wanda stitched them together on her mother's sewing machine.

They went back to West's house a few months later, before the summer of 1998. He was surprised by their new outfits, but he invited them back to stay. Brian told West he was serving the Lord, helping those who needed it most. Brian sprinkled his sentences with scripture.

"He thought he was representing Jesus out there on the streets," West said. Brian even told West that doing things for him was tantamount to giving to Christ. West didn't agree with Brian's thinking, but he was fond of the couple, whom he called "my little Israelites."

West watched in awe as Brian and Wanda constructed a wagon on his back porch. It had a cover and looked like the ones pulled by Mormon pioneers through the streets of Salt Lake. Brian used two old bicycle wheels to prop up slats of stained wood, about five feet high. It was slightly smaller than a double bed, and roomy enough to store their few possessions and provide shelter. Brian attached two long wooden handles and would pull it behind him as he walked.

By the middle of the summer, West couldn't afford to support Brian and Wanda. West also became uncomfortable with Brian, who grew belligerent when he talked about religion. He constantly criticized the Mormon church and insisted West could be saved if he saw the truth of Brian's beliefs. West asked Brian and Wanda to leave.

Once again, they went back to Salt Lake. They

had a key to Irene's home, and drifted in and out. They also lived on the streets, or camped in the hills that ring Salt Lake County. They would use cardboard boxes, or sleep in their wagon. They became a well-known sight in downtown Salt Lake, where Brian was an aggressive panhandler. A favorite spot was near the Kinko's just off Main Street, at the northern end of town. Another was the Crossroads mall on State Street.

Brian was standing near the mall one day in August 1998, when his old friend, Doug Larsen, came upon him. It took a moment for Doug to recognize him through the stringy long hair, the dirty beard and the flowing robes. But Doug was thrilled. He greeted Brian like a lost brother. Brian ignored him.

Doug tried again, repeating his name over and over again. Brian said that wasn't his name. He was "Immanuel." He eventually walked away from Doug, leaving him shocked and incredibly hurt. Doug followed Brian all the way around the block, trying to get him to admit who he was and that he knew Doug.

"It was a rather disappointing encounter for me, because he was one of my best friends," Doug said. "I had kinship feelings toward him." Doug eventually realized the person in front of him was completely different from the one he'd known. He handed Brian a $5 bill and walked away.

Around town, Brian became known as "the Jesus guy." When he was with Wanda, they were "Joseph and Mary." In 2000, the *Daily Utah Chronicle,* the University of Utah's campus newspaper, featured Brian in a large picture, talking with one of the students. He sometimes wandered onto campus, preaching.

When Ed Snoddy, an outreach worker with the local outpost of the national group Volunteers of America, tried to help Brian, he would end up with an earful of preaching.

He would stop Brian on the street and ask where he was going. "Where God sends me," Brian replied.

"Where have you been?"

"Where God has led me."

Another time, Brian's handmade cart got away from him and it barreled into Wanda, cracking one of her ribs. Snoddy offered to get medical help, but Brian said no, "God will heal her."

Once, Brian tried to enter the William Weigand homeless shelter, but he refused to let go of his wooden staff. Shelter workers told him he would have to leave if he didn't, since it could be used as a weapon. Brian chose to leave.

Brian was a regular on Salt Lake's TRAX system, a criss-cross of trolley cars running through several of the city's major streets. He would use it if he needed to travel a long distance, or if he couldn't hitch a ride.

Pamela Atkinson, the longtime homeless outreach worker who's known as Utah's own Mother Theresa, had dozens of conversations with Brian and Wanda starting in late 1999 or early 2000. She tried repeatedly to bring them into shelters, but Brian and Wanda refused.

"I tried to take him in for an evaluation, but he always, very politely, refused," Atkinson recalled. "My feeling is that he was delusional and mentally ill."

Brian introduced himself as "Immanuel" and his wife as "Eladah." Atkinson never knew their real names. He said they were preaching the word of the Lord. But he also seemed, to Atkinson, to consider himself Christ-like.

Atkinson asked him four times to agree to a mental evaluation. He wouldn't do it, and under Utah law, he couldn't be forced into it against his will. Instead, Atkinson had to settle for giving the couple socks, toiletries and food.

"He needed psychiatric help and medication," Atkinson said. "Whenever I saw him, he did not seem to be on drugs, and you can usually tell which of our homeless are using drugs. I never saw him inebriated, but I do know that he liked his beer."

His wife was a very sweet, very quiet woman. But she was completely subservient to him, and her eyes were a cold, dead stare. She looked defeated.

Brian was an adept panhandler in a competitive field. On any given night, there are between 4,000 and 5,000 homeless people in Salt Lake and the towns around it, Atkinson said. Some 70 percent are pros, who sit on the curb all day, and then get in their cars at night, carrying their signs reading "please help," and drive home. The rest are mentally ill, or drug addicted, and in need of more serious help. The expert panhandlers can make between $300 and $500 a day, she said. Some even have bank accounts.

Brian was extremely convincing, and he could size up the person coming toward him, and their vulnerabilities, in mere seconds.

Rick Jones, a piano teacher in Salt Lake, was crossing the street one day when the biblically dressed pair approached him. The robed man made eye contact with Jones.

"Sir," said Brian. He stepped toward Jones. His voice had an air of authority.

"This woman has lost all her possessions, and she's in need of your help," Brian said, gesturing to Wanda.

Jones was uncomfortable, and baffled. He didn't know what to do. He'd never been approached by the city's panhandlers before, and the man was aggressive. He seemed so authoritative that Jones wondered whether he'd be compromising his soul if he didn't do as the man said.

"Well, how did she lose her possessions?" Jones asked, fumbling.

"Sir, what does that matter?" Brian said forcefully. "The Lord has commanded us to love everyone. What does that matter?"

Jones was uncomfortable and said he couldn't help, but he was affected by the encounter, brief though it was. The man had a point. What did it matter?

Late that year, Brian decided to embrace a facet of LDS life that is no longer sanctioned by church officials. As always, it came in the form of a vision granted from God. But in his writings, he said the revelation came not to him but to Wanda.

Wanda later told her friend, Vicki Cottrell, that the couple both had the revelation, on Thanksgiving Day in 2000. God told Brian that he was the "true prophet." He was Immanuel David Isaiah, and his wife was Hephzibah Eladah Isaiah. The couple was to take seven new brides for Brian, who would be sister-wives to Wanda. Those brides were to be young, so that they wouldn't be "set in their ways."

Brian had never before indicated to friends or family that he approved of polygamy. His estranged wife later saw the vision as fraud, a mask that would let him abuse young girls. Whatever the reason behind it, Wanda and Brian apparently didn't act on their revelation for at least a year.

After the September 11, 2001, terror attacks, there were several months during which Brian and Wanda shed their robes in favor of regular street clothes. Brian trimmed his hair and shaved his beard, looking almost exactly as he had before his revelation that he was the poor man's prophet a decade earlier.

It was a self-protective move. Someone had told Brian, "You look like Osama bin Laden," and he feared a growing backlash against Muslims would prompt someone to attack him and Wanda. He and "Hephzibah Eladah" would return to normal for a little while.

Two months later, in November, Wanda paid a visit to her mother. She needed bus fare, and she called Dora to borrow money. When Wanda arrived, she was wearing a blouse and a skirt, and was wrapped in a lovely cape, which Dora admired when Wanda came in the door. She was pleased with Wanda's appearance and hoped it meant her daughter was returning to her old self.

"She looked sharp. She wasn't wearing robes then, and I think that's why she wanted to come," Dora said. But it was clear almost immediately that it wasn't the old Wanda standing in her living room, dressed in pretty clothes. It was the woman Brian had dubbed "Eladah."

Wanda came in the door with an expensive-looking little doll wrapped in a blanket. She carefully sat the doll in a chair, before she started talking to her mother. They had a pleasant visit for awhile, until Wanda started delving into the past. Then she started preaching her husband's gospel. Dora sat and listened until she got a headache. She tried to answer Wanda, but her daughter wouldn't let her. It was the way things had always been, when Dora thought about it.

"I love you," Dora tried.

"I don't believe you love me," Wanda snapped back.

"She wouldn't let me respond. She gets it all off her chest and then shuts her ears—you can't confront her," Dora said.

She got up to go to the kitchen, and Wanda followed her, still preaching. She picked apart the Book of Mormon, telling her mother everything that was inaccurate about it. Dora ignored her and went to the restroom. Wanda shouted through the door. When Dora re-emerged, she couldn't help herself.

"Are you still a member of the Church of Jesus Christ of Latter-Day Saints?" Dora asked Wanda.

Wanda flew into a rage. "And who's the head of that church?" she shouted.

"You know that Jesus Christ is the head of our church. That's why it has that name," Dora replied. She was shaking. Her daughter's rage was boiling over. Dora said she wouldn't tolerate criticism of her faith in her house. Wanda grabbed her doll and stormed out the door.

It was pouring rain outside, and Dora hated the way Wanda had left. She got in her car and drove around the block, until she caught up to her. Dora rolled the window down and motioned for Wanda to get in.

"She just ignored me," Dora said. "Just kept walking, with that defiant look on her face." Dora gave up and went home. But she called Irene's house, where Brian and Wanda were staying for days at a stretch.

When Brian answered the phone, Dora's stomach braced. She asked to speak to Wanda. She said she wanted to know if her daughter had made it home.

"We have nobody here by that name!" Brian said and hung up. Dora didn't see her daughter again until the spring.

* * *

Over the next few months and through the holidays, Brian and Wanda alternated between camping in the woods around Dry Creek Canyon and other mountain hideouts and staying with Irene. Brian's mother was growing frightened of her son. The preaching was reaching a scary pitch.

Brian was also working on the prophecy he'd started at Dora's house six years earlier. His new religion would be based on a mixture of texts, some ancient and some quite new. One was C. Samuel West's book *The Golden Seven Plus One*. He also was intrigued by a life-after-death book, *Embraced by the Light,* and two books written by excommunicated Mormons.

Brian and Wanda's membership in the church was almost officially over. The church wanted to hold a disciplinary hearing against them, but officials from their ward said they couldn't locate the couple.

On February 15, 2002, Brian's little sister, Laurie, died of a rare cancer, leaving behind six sons and a distraught husband. They lived in Washington, a town in southern Utah, and Irene traveled down there to help Laurie's husband, Scott, with the boys, Dora Corbett said.

Brian knew his sister was dead, but he and Wanda didn't go to the funeral, which was held back at the Canyon Rim Ward, where the Mitchells had grown up. Laurie was the sister Brian had picked on as a child, his foil for getting attention from his parents. Brian's absence was noted by his family.

He and Wanda were still in and out of homeless camps around Salt Lake, occasionally showing up at Irene's house for a few nights before leaving.

Their families sometimes had to use creative thinking for the most basic interactions with the couple. On April 5, Wanda's stepdad, Glenn Corbett, succumbed to the cancer that C. Samuel West had worked to stave off. Glenn's funeral was five days later, at the Westlake Ward.

Wanda's mother, Dora Corbett, desperately wanted her daughter to come to the funeral, or to at least know that Glenn had passed. But she had no way of contacting her daughter or son-in-law.

Her only hope was Irene, but Brian's mother was dealing with her own family death in Washington. Still, Irene somehow got word of Glenn's death through the family grapevine.

She called a neighbor from back home and asked the friend to post Glenn Corbett's death notice on Irene's front door. She was hoping that Brian and Wanda, during their walks around town, would pass by the house and see it.

It was an odd idea, but it apparently worked, Dora said. At Glenn's funeral, Wanda and her husband slipped in quietly, just after the service began.

Evelyn saw them come in, draped in their purple robes among the dark-suited mourners. Wanda didn't smile and tried to avoid eye contact.

"She didn't act like she wanted to talk to us," Evelyn said. "She didn't glow."

Evelyn wanted to talk to her sister and planned

to approach her after the service. But at the very end, Wanda and Mitchell slipped through the door.

Wanda's daughter, LouRee, spotted her mother and rushed out of the church after her. She called to her mother, saying she wanted to talk to her. The robed pair stopped and stared.

"Children of Israel, your time will come!" Brian bellowed.

"Repent!" Wanda screamed.

Then they disappeared into the spring afternoon.

The day after Glenn died, Brian put the finishing touches on his prophecy. Wanda had written out all 27 pages in neat, perfectly spaced calligraphy. Brian called his work *The Book of Immanuel David Isaiah*.

He outlined a new covenant called "The Seven Diamonds Plus One—Testament of Jesus Christ."

The "plus one" was the "inspired sacred music and song and the testimonies of all the humble followers of Jesus Christ by the power of the Holy Ghost." It was likely intended for Wanda, whose love of music was well known to Brian. He even made references in the text to Johann Sebastian Bach, Wanda's favorite composer, as a "servant" who would play for his master.

The text was loaded with references to Brian's and Wanda's dietary habits—wheat and vegetables, and the all-fruit diet that had lasted 14 months. The prophecy said Wanda would be "submissive and obedient unto thy husband."

"Wherefore, ye have my words through my ser-

vant Immanuel David Isaiah, ever my Righteous
Right hand" was another passage.

On page 23 were three sentences that seemed almost like an afterthought. Wanda was to take
"into thy heart and home seven sisters, and thou
wilt recognize them through the spirit as thy dear-
est and choicest friends from all eternity." Those
sisters were to bring Hephzibah "great joy."

Around the time of Glenn's funeral, the doorbell
rang at Dora's house. Evelyn and her husband
were in town, and her husband answered the bell.

On the steps stood Wanda and Brian, carrying
rolled-up sheafs of paper. Evelyn's husband invited
them in, but they refused.

"We can't stay. We just wanted to bring this
book," Brian said, thrusting copies of the 27-page
treatise at Evelyn's husband. He wasn't sure what
to say. He tried to be polite.

"Who wrote it?" he asked.

"He stands before you," Brian intoned.

Dora and Evelyn were dumbstruck, but Brian
and Wanda left, moving on to the next stop on
their delivery route.

"It was just ridiculous," Evelyn said. "I tried to
read it and it just made no sense. I threw it away."

Dora kept hers and tried thumbing through the
pages. But she found it mostly unreadable, and the
sexual references made her so uncomfortable that
she put it down.

Shirl Mitchell found his copy on his porch. It
was well-written, he thought. But it was also "rank

plagiarism, like most of Mormonism." He shoved it in a drawer and didn't pull it out again for another year.

On April 18, Irene reached her breaking point with Brian and Wanda. It began, as always, with incessant preaching, and with Brian and Wanda trying to block Irene from leaving.

This time was different. Irene was terrified.

On April 18, the Salt Lake County sheriff's office was called to Irene's home, where Brian and Wanda were giving her fits. Outside the house, Irene tried to explain to Salt Lake Sheriff's Deputy Troy Naylor what had happened.

She had been trying to leave her house, apparently to get away from her son and Wanda, but they tried to stop her, insisting she needed to hear about his manifesto.

"She states that her son is getting stranger and stranger every day," Naylor wrote in his official report. "He has announced to the family and world that he is starting his own church. He wrote a 27-page letter to everyone about his religious believes [sic]. His wife Wanda is just as bad as him."

Irene explained that she had been getting her "daily lecture" from her son and daughter-in-law when the trouble started.

"They were yelling at her and making comments that they were here to save her," Naylor wrote. "At one point each suspect grabbed one of Mrs. Mitchell's arm [sic] and started yelling for help.

Both suspects let her go. She received no injury or marks from the incident."

After he interviewed Irene, Naylor spoke to Brian and Wanda at the front door of the house, his eyes lingering on their purple robes.

"It was almost impossible to speak with them about what happened," the report said. "Brian just wanted to preach to me. He did say he was moving out. Mrs. Mitchell said he has said he is moving out for the last six years."

That day, Irene started restraining order proceedings against them. In court documents supporting the court order, Irene later said she told her son she had to leave the house.

"Brian and Wanda then stood in front of me each clasping one of my arms very tightly," she said. Furious, Brian and Wanda cried, "You will be destroyed. Your family will be destroyed. Your home will be destroyed."

They eventually let go, and Irene ran to her car and drove away. She apparently came back to meet the sheriff's deputy. Brian and Wanda spent hours packing their things into the wagon, items they'd bought with the money they had earned panhandling over the years. Whatever couldn't be stored, they destroyed. They emptied their wheat supply into the backyard. They bent the tines of forks so they couldn't be used, and they smashed plates to the ground.

Irene secured a restraining order in a default judgment two weeks later, because Wanda and

Brian never showed up to court. They were barred from contacting her in any way.

It was the last time Brian and Wanda were given shelter by their family. When they were forced out of Irene's house by the police, they left their handmade covered wagon behind, sitting in the driveway.

Over Memorial Day weekend, Doug Larsen was downtown and saw Wanda and Brian, draped in their robes. Brian was begging for spare change. Doug was haunted by the memory of the smiling, devout Mormon couple who simply vanished a decade ago.

He had a dream about Brian a year later, just before March 12, 2003, the day Brian David Mitchell's name would become known around the world.

In his dream, Doug stood in a sunny courtyard, and Brian was there waiting for him. Doug approached him tentatively and asked, "Is your name David?" because he didn't want his friend to run from him this time.

"He looked back at me and he said quietly, 'My name is Brian,'" Larsen said. "I wake up thinking about it and I go to bed thinking about it. And I think about it all day."

By that time, Brian and Wanda had been excommunicated from the LDS church, for "bizarre teachings and a lifestyle far afield from the teachings of the Church." Church officials had also become aware of the 27-page prophecy of "Immanuel David Isaiah."

The LDS church excommunicates its members so that they can leave and then come back with a fresh start. It's not a punishment, but an opportunity to begin again, officials say.

Brian and Wanda likely didn't care what their status with the church was. They were staying on and off in the mountains, investigators would say later, constructing a campsite that would soon provide shelter to the two of them, plus one.

FOUR

The panhandler approached Lois Smart as she walked down the busy State Street sidewalk outside the Crossroads mall on a cool day in November 2001. He was thin and clean-shaven, with a crown of dark hair graying at the edges. He spoke softly, said his name was Immanuel. He was a preacher, he said, staying in Salt Lake City with his sister, and could use some help.

Lois sized up the neatly dressed transient with the piercing, blue-gray eyes, then handed him $5. Investigators would later say that some of the Smart children, including Elizabeth, may have been with their mother that day.

Her husband, Ed, often hired the city's homeless to work odd jobs around their home in the affluent Federal Heights neighborhood, northeast of downtown. The Smarts belonged to the LDS church, which encourages members to help the less fortunate and believes that the poor will be better blessed if they work for what they receive. If the man needed work, Lois offered, he could do some odd jobs for Ed. Immanuel seemed eager about the prospect.

The next day, Immanuel made his way up the steep roads to the Smart home. The homes grew bigger, set farther from the road, as he drew nearer the house, which was nestled in the foothills of the Wasatch Mountains. Immanuel knew those mountains well. He had often camped in their brushy canyons, cooking meals on makeshift stoves.

At the Smarts' 6,600-square-foot home, he was quickly assigned tasks by Ed—there were leaky skylights on the roof, weeds festering on the lawn and a yard that needed to be raked.

Ed, a mortgage broker who owned two real estate companies in town, had put the $1.19 million home on the market just weeks earlier. That was his business—buying homes, fixing them, and then selling them.

Ed joined Immanuel on the roof, and they chatted as they hammered. As they kneeled on the roof, just feet apart, the two men talked about religion. Immanuel's only occupation, he told Ed, was spreading the word of Jesus to the homeless. The handyman told Ed he and his sister were just passing through town, staying with friends. Immanuel didn't mention a wife or a family, and Ed didn't pry. They climbed down off the roof, and Immanuel grabbed a rake.

When he'd cleared the lawn, Ed gave him $50 and offered him more work the next day.

Immanuel never showed up. Sixteen months later the Smarts would see him again.

Elizabeth Smart ran along the hills of her tranquil Federal Heights neighborhood, the black and pale blue soles of her sneakers flashing as she chased her latest dream: a spot on the high school track team.

In those first days of June 2002, summer's heat was already bearing down. School was almost over, and Elizabeth and her eighth-grade classmates were about to leave Bryant Intermediate School behind. Their graduation ceremony was just a few days away. She was excited and nervous about her upcoming freshman year at East High School.

Looking to ease the transition, Elizabeth set her sights on a fresh challenge, something that would involve her in her new school, perhaps even forge new friendships. The gangly, athletic teen was determined to run cross-country for the high school track and field team.

A few days earlier, she had met with East's coach, Ben Stowell, who gave Elizabeth a summer training schedule and instructed her to run two miles a day, except on Sundays. Stowell thought his new recruit seemed eager, if a bit daunted, by her goal. Yet in their brief meeting, Stowell picked up from Elizabeth's demeanor something those close to her knew well—the fresh-faced, blue-eyed beauty was sometimes painfully shy, but she possessed a determination and inner strength rare for someone her age.

Born November 3, 1988, Elizabeth was the second of Ed and Lois's brood, and the eldest daughter. At fourteen, she was an adolescent mix of awkwardness and poise, quiet reserve and swift wit, dogged determination and teenaged anxiety. She was dutiful with her parents and respectful of adults. She wrapped herself in the embrace of her sister and four brothers.

"She was a very obedient daughter," her uncle David, Ed's brother, said.

Elizabeth wrote poetry, and she described herself in a poem entitled "All About Me." The twelve simple lines that spoke of mountain air, horseback rides, homemade bread and roasted marshmallows seemed to fit Elizabeth to a tee.

Elizabeth led a sheltered, protected life, friends and family members said. Other teenagers spent their free time at the malls in downtown Salt Lake, and the girls had begun to flirt with boys and experiment with makeup and new hairstyles. But Elizabeth wasn't interested in makeup, friends said, and her older teenaged cousins ribbed her good-naturedly for her modest taste in clothes.

"Elizabeth was guileless," said longtime family friend Missy Larsen. "She was fourteen going on eleven. She was very innocent and sweet, very endearing. She was very sheltered—she didn't use the Internet or have an email address."

Elizabeth was a homebody. She liked to bake cookies and watch movies, and she reveled in the company of her brothers and sister. Her friendships were close and limited to a handful of girls who had formed a tight bond, Larsen recalled.

"She liked hanging out with her family," said Larsen, whose own daughter was Elizabeth's age. "A lot of kids that age wouldn't be caught dead hanging out with a younger sister, but Elizabeth seemed to prefer it."

When she was comfortable, Elizabeth shed her shy exterior. Those who spent the most time with her said they saw her playful, mischievous side. She'd been known to start food fights, and at sleepovers with her girlfriends Elizabeth's quick wit kept them in stitches.

Elizabeth had at least 76 first cousins and was close with many of them. She was particularly close with the daughters of her mother's sister, Jeannie Wright, who were near her age.

In 2001, right before the September 11 terror attacks, Elizabeth's grandparents, Dorotha and Charles Smart, took the family on a trip to the East Coast, including New York, the birthplace of Mormonism. They took the entire Smart clan, Dorotha said, all six of her own children and their spouses and 26 grandchildren.

"We thought it would be a good way to show them some of the places of our church history, and American history as well," Dorotha recalled. One of the stops on their itinerary was New York City.

The kids went swimming in the hotel pool and Elizabeth jumped in, wearing a purple bathing suit. When she got out it had turned pink, bleached by the chlorine. Her cousins erupted in laughter. It was all the more funny because it had happened to Elizabeth, one of the most reserved of the Smart bunch.

Back in their hotel room, Elizabeth and her female cousins bunked together. Elizabeth opened up to her cousins, telling stories and talking nonstop. The giggling started in earnest after bedtime.

"Let me tell you, that little girl is a talker," said Dorotha, chuckling at the memory of the trip. "It was just a big slumber party for the girls. Elizabeth is often a quiet child, but she's got a wonderful sense of humor, and she will laugh louder than anyone in the room. Her cousins always said she was the funniest one of the bunch. She'd get them all going. Her smile just lights up the room."

When the cousins were young, they would play dress-up in Dorotha's basement, with piles of clothes and costumes from a church bazaar.

Every other year, the Smarts vacationed in Montana, at a family homestead. The kids were divided into groups—boys in one room, girls in the other. They stayed up late, giving each other manicures. Often, their chatter and hilarity were so loud they roused the adults sleeping downstairs.

At her fourteenth birthday party, Elizabeth and her friends commandeered the Smarts' newly remodeled recreation room, which had carpeted walls. She had invited 23 girlfriends, the biggest party she'd ever had. They played games, watched videos and laughed so loudly that Lois and Ed could hear them upstairs, the cousins recalled.

But Elizabeth's closest relationship was with her nine-year-old sister, Mary Katherine, with whom she shared a bedroom. Despite the five-year age gap between them, Elizabeth loved to spend time with Mary Katherine. They bickered every now and then, Elizabeth's friends recalled, especially when Mary Katherine's things spilled over to Elizabeth's side of the room. But they would often curl up together in the same bed, and fall asleep holding hands.

In turn, Mary Katherine idolized Elizabeth. Elizabeth was masterful at playing the harp, and Mary Katherine was following in her footsteps. She also joined Elizabeth during her runs through the neighborhood. They would jog together in the foothills behind the house, their uncle, Tom Smart, said.

At home, all of the kids were assigned chores and they worked diligently, helping each other out. Ed and Lois were hardworking themselves, and they wanted to instill the same ethic in their children. The youngest, William, was three years old. The oldest, Charles, was 15.

As the eldest children, Elizabeth and Charles helped care for the other four—William, Mary Katherine, Andrew and Edward—by helping with schoolwork and anything else their parents needed them to do. Elizabeth loved watching over little William, whose shock of blond hair flopped into his eyebrows.

"She was great with the younger kids, very motherly and always looking out for them," Larsen said.

Elizabeth's passion was the harp. She had started playing when she was just five years old. By the time she reached middle school, she was already an accomplished performer. She had talent, but she wasn't a natural, one of her teachers said. It took years of hard work for Elizabeth to get where she was. She practiced three hours a day, her fingers picking out each string.

Her trademark song was one by the Cantina Band, from the movie *Star Wars*. It wasn't a harp standard, but it appealed to her because its difficult composition was challenging, her friends said. Over and over Elizabeth rehearsed, until she played it as perfectly as the classical pieces she'd mastered.

The harp was a perfect choice of instrument for a young girl universally described as "an angel." At her recitals, she wore carefully chosen dresses of velvet and lace, her butterscotch hair in a cascade of curls. Elizabeth blossomed on stage. She loved to perform, her enthusiasm evident and her face aglow as she moved through everything from classical pieces to wedding marches.

"She played that harp like she was born to it," Dorotha would recall. Elizabeth talked with her friends about a dream of going to Juilliard, the prestigious New York music academy.

In her hometown, Elizabeth was already achieving star status. Her talents were recognized and often sought out. Her services were requested for weddings, funerals, and even local concerts. Sometimes she played as a soloist, and other times with a group of other talented young musicians. She was showcased at Christmas shows, a concert in Salt Lake's Capitol Rotunda, and before a Utah Symphony performance. At 13, Elizabeth was invited to perform with 70 other harpists at the Salt Lake Tabernacle.

Elizabeth had a tomboyish side too, her velvet concert dresses replaced by pants and pulled-back hair on weekends and family vacations. She loved horses and was an accomplished, enthusiastic rider, sometimes waking her family at dawn to get out to the barns. Elizabeth was the family's champion frog catcher and wasn't afraid of a little dirt. On one vacation, Dorotha recalled, the kids were making mud pies. "Elizabeth pulled her arms out of that mud, and they came up covered with leeches. The kids love that story."

At school, Elizabeth sang in the Bryant school choir. Her brothers were also musical. The Smart kids would get together and perform impromptu musical skits, Elizabeth and Mary Katherine on the harp and the boys on banjo and piano.

Elizabeth also tried to take on leadership roles. Urged on by some of her friends, she mustered the courage to run for eighth-grade class president—and lost. The brush with defeat, which she hadn't often experienced, left her disappointed. But she bounced back quickly and was on to the next challenge.

The teenager was a favorite of her teachers, the type of student who, if class ended early, would take out her French book and study. In her last year at Bryant, she and a schoolmate labored for hours over a skit on early Mormon history. They stitched together costumes and wrote and starred in their production. The play, entitled "U.S. Reaction to the Early Mormon Settlers," won high praise, even taking first place in a regional history fair.

Lois Francom was in her late twenties when she met Ed Smart—a slight, sandy-haired man with

brilliant blue eyes and an elastic face—at a church
social event for young adults in the 1980s. Ed was
the son of a prominent Salt Lake oncologist. Lois,
the daughter of Myron LeGrande Francom, a
longtime newspaper typesetter, was petite and
auburn-haired. She had an open, trusting face, and
a subtle beauty.

"They were a good match. She was quiet, but
funny—she made him laugh," a friend said. They
were both devout members of the Church of the
Latter-Day Saints. They married in 1986, and their
first son, Charles, was born the next year. By 1999,
Ed and Lois had filled their home with six kids.

Like many Mormons, Ed and Lois were from
large families. Ed was second of six children, and
Lois was one of nine. In the LDS church, a basic
unit of salvation is the family, not the individual,
and Mormons are encouraged to have several
children.

The Smarts' Federal Heights home, where Immanuel worked, is on a cul-de-sac at the top of
Kristianna Circle. The neighborhood sits high over
downtown Salt Lake, in the shadow of the University of Utah, with its enormous "U" painted into
the hills above.

Ed Smart was raised in the privileged neighborhood, a picture-perfect safe haven where children
play in the street and run freely between homes.
People have alarm systems in their homes, but
don't really use them. From their street at the top
of the hill, the Smarts can look down and see their
LDS ward house. A box-shaped brick building set

back from the road and surrounded by a tall black gate and manicured lawn, it is the center of the community.

The Smarts and the Francoms have Mormon roots that run deep, with both families tracing a lineage dating back to the the early days of Salt Lake's 1847 settlement by second LDS president Brigham Young, an apostle of church founder Joseph Smith.

Elizabeth was often at her mother's side during Sunday meetings at the Federal Heights Ward meeting house. They would sit, smiling at neighbors as they passed the sacramental basket filled with torn pieces of white bread, then tipping their heads back to drink water from tiny plastic cups.

Ed and Lois's home seemed to revolve around their faith. Ed worked on building his business, while Lois poured herself into her home and her kids, said those who know them well. Lois had an easy laugh and a subtle sense of humor, but she was also shy and reserved. She was respected by her neighbors, but socialized only with a small group of close friends. She was most at ease with her kids. She helped with homework, urged them on at their music and spent hours shuttling them to their lessons.

"Her children are her world," Ed's brother, David, said. "She's a very dedicated, loving and protective mother. She'd do anything for those kids."

Ed and Lois Smart had few close friends, his sister, Angela Dumke, said. They were happiest in the company of their sprawling, extended families. Neither of them, Lois in particular, was comfortable being the center of attention.

With the school year ending, the Smart family was looking forward to its summer vacation. Most years, they would travel to the family cabin in nearby Brighton, a Wasatch Mountain ski resort town, where Elizabeth and her siblings rode horses. At home, the days were filled with swimming and pick-up games of basketball.

That year, the summer break would also provide a needed respite for Lois. The family's daily life had been tinged with sadness since early spring— Lois's father, Myron Francom, was terminally ill. Nearly every day for three months, Lois would take the children to visit their granddad at his home in nearby Holladay.

With their grandfather bedridden, Elizabeth and the other Smart kids planted a flower garden for him. They raked his yard and tended to other chores around his house. When he died on June 1, Lois was heartbroken.

At his funeral two days later, Elizabeth paid tribute to her grandfather with a harp solo. Her relatives' eyes welled with tears as Elizabeth's fingers moved across the strings. She played "Silent Night," the solemn notes filling the church. Francom looked forward each year to Christmas, when many of his 51 grandchildren visited for the holiday, and the song was his favorite.

On June 4, Elizabeth and her sister set out for a

jog around their neighborhood, police would later say. That evening, the Smarts loaded Elizabeth's harp in the car and headed for Bryant Intermediate School. There was a year-end awards program, and Elizabeth was supposed to play. But the family ran late, and Elizabeth missed her performance. Still, the teen beamed as she picked up honors for her schoolwork and physical fitness.

The family headed home to Kristianna Circle. Ed Smart opened the garage door and hurried out of the car. Elizabeth's harp was heat sensitive and expensive, and he was rushing to get it back inside the house. He would later recall that he'd pressed the button to close the garage door behind him, but it shut halfway and sprang back up again. Something must have blocked the door's sensor, Ed thought as he continued into the house with the harp. He meant to go back out to check it but got distracted.

That night, the family said its evening prayers together at the top of the stairs. It was late, and everyone was tired. They said goodnight, and Elizabeth kissed her father on the cheek as the kids headed to their rooms. Before they turned in, the couple later recalled, Lois asked Ed to check the door locks. Ed suddenly remembered the open garage door and went back downstairs. He checked three sliding doors at the front of the house, and the kitchen door, as well. Out in the garage, he found a tarp blocking the door's sensor. He moved it, and hit the switch. The door swung closed.

Upstairs, only Charles stayed up, studying for a school exam.

Elizabeth, in her dark red satin pajamas, climbed into her bed. Her white Polo running shoes were tucked in her closet. Before dawn, she would be roused from her sleep, ordered to fetch those sneakers and forced to walk four miles up into the dense, brushy canyons of the Wasatch Mountains, spirited away to a place from which she couldn't run.

FIVE

"Be quiet, or I'll kill you."

The man spoke softly. Mary Katherine didn't move a muscle. She pretended to sleep, watching through half-closed lids as the man ordered Elizabeth out of bed. His voice was almost pleasant. He was tall, but not very tall, about the size of her brother, Charles. She couldn't see his face very well.

The man nudged Elizabeth toward the closet. He told her to get a pair of shoes. "Ouch!" Elizabeth cried out, stubbing her toe. That was when he ordered her to stay silent.

"Why are you doing this?" Elizabeth asked. She slid her feet into her bright white sneakers. He steered her out of the room, into the dark hallway.

Petrified, Mary Katherine got out of bed to wake her mom and dad. It was sometime between one and two o'clock in the morning.

When she got to the hallway, the man was still there, taking his time. She saw him looking into one of her brothers' rooms. Mary Katherine padded quietly back to her own bedroom and waited some more, scared that the man was still lurking in the house. She waited for almost two hours. He might have seen her if she got up again. She lay frightened in her bed, not knowing what to do.

Wrapped in a blanket, Mary Katherine eventually walked into Ed and Lois's bedroom. Her mom woke up and looked at her digital clock. 3:58 a.m., it read. Mary Katherine was calm. Elizabeth was gone, she told her parents. A man took her, she said.

The words sounded unreal. Ed sprang out of bed and raced through his house, hoping Mary Katherine had had a nightmare. Ed went door to door, frantically checking the rooms where Charles, Edward, Andrew and William slept. She had to be somewhere. Mary Katherine told him she saw the man with a gun. Ed was in shock.

In the confusion, the family thought Elizabeth might have gone jogging. Ed and Lois went downstairs to look for her. Lois went to the kitchen and noticed that a window screen had been cut. She started screaming.

Those were the painful details of that morning the Smarts would recall in the nine months after the kidnapping.

The call from Ed to 911 came in at 4:01 a.m. Ed made other calls, first to his older brother, Tom, and then to other relatives, friends and members of the Federal Heights Ward.

Suann Adams, who lived down the street from the Smarts, would be one of the first neighbors to

arrive, sometime before 4:30 a.m. Ed then ran out
of his house to the door of his neighbor, H. Brent
Beesley, the head of a bank whose daughter was almost abducted in a ransom plot a decade earlier.
He would know better than anyone in the neighborhood what the Smarts were going through.

Word of the armed intruder spread quickly
across the Federal Heights Ward. Neighbors went
door-to-door, telling parents to check on their
children.

Ed couldn't understand. His daughter had disappeared so stealthily into the night. Ed was a light
sleeper, and he usually awoke when his kids got up
in the middle of the night. But the strain of Myron's death, and his funeral, had left Ed and Lois
exhausted.

The police were on the scene in 12 minutes, but
Ed would say "it seemed forever" because "of the
anxiety." Suann Adams said she arrived moments
later, as did Smart family members and neighbors
from the ward. Soon, the area around the house
was teeming with people. Ed would later say
roughly 40 to 50 friends and relatives came to offer
support and started organizing a search for Elizabeth.

As police were still arriving, more than a dozen
cars lined Kristianna Circle, their headlights shining, ready to comb the area.

By 6 a.m., police were canvassing Federal
Heights, knocking on doors and asking if people
had heard anything unusual during the night. One
neighbor said he had. Around 2:30 a.m., he said he

had heard what he thought was a female's voice crying out. There were dogs barking somewhere in the neighborhood, and he went downstairs to check his own. Finding nothing, he returned to bed. A few hours later, a neighbor came to his house and urged him to check on his children. Then the police came.

The cul-de-sac at the top of the hill was buzzing with activity, but many people were numb with shock. Why? they asked themselves and each other. Why would someone take Elizabeth? The house on Kristianna Circle, where the members of the ward had rushed to the aid of one of their own, wasn't sealed off as a crime scene until 6:54 a.m., nearly three hours after Ed Smart first called the police. It was an oversight that investigators would later acknowledge was a "mistake."

Elizabeth's white sneakers would have flashed in the brush as Brian David Mitchell, a man she would come to know as "Immanuel," forced her to march up into Dry Creek Canyon, a four-mile hike in the chilly night air. He told her he would hurt her family if she didn't do what he said. The hike was about two hours. There was a steep incline before they reached their destination.

The roots of Brian's fixation on Elizabeth were a mystery. Maybe he had focused on her that day in November at the Crossroads mall, when Lois Smart pressed $5 into his hand. Maybe he had spotted her as he raked leaves in the yard. He might have crossed her path downtown, in Salt

Lake, although investigators would later say they had no evidence Brian had had any contact with Elizabeth beyond that day at her family's home, or possibly the day Lois had hired him.

But they believed he had studied the girl. He might have seen her as she jogged with Mary Katherine in the foothills behind her home, a few miles from the camps in Dry Creek and Emigration canyons, where he and Wanda sometimes stayed. However it began, officials would later say Mitchell had spent time preparing an elaborate campsite where he would fulfill the prophecy he had penned the year before.

In the foothills near Dry Creek Canyon was a carefully constructed hideaway, a lean-to barely visible in the dense brush of the mountains. It was about 20 feet long, built over a hollowed-out swath of earth. The logs used to make the roof were camouflaged by mounds of dirt and twigs. Thick plastic garbage bags and a silver tarp were laid under the dirt, keeping it from falling through the spaces between the logs. Nails were driven into some of the cut logs that held up the roof. At their bases, they were wrapped in plastic and duct tape.

Elizabeth would be secreted in the lean-to for coming weeks, investigators said later. It was also the place where, sometime after she was kidnapped, Brian is said to have performed a bizarre ritual, "marrying" Elizabeth to him. Mitchell had anointed himself a priest. At the campsite that morning, Wanda approached Elizabeth and tried to take off her pajamas, court papers said later. When Elizabeth tried to resist, Wanda threatened to have Brian, the man who had already threatened to kill her, do it himself. Elizabeth gave in.

Later on, Brian would tether Elizabeth to a tree, using a cable that he wrapped around her leg to keep her from running. One of her family members would describe her as having been "chained up" in the mountains, day after day. Her home was just four miles away, but it might as well have been four thousand. She had been taken to a different world and was trapped there. That night, Brian would take Elizabeth's red pajamas and burn them. They disappeared, along with a young girl's innocence.

"This is believed to be a child abduction. We believe that she is in imminent danger of serious bodily harm or death."

At 7:21 a.m., Salt Lake residents driving to work heard a bulletin over their car radios. The state's new Rachael Alert, a message system named for Rachael Marie Runyon, a three-year-old Utah girl who was abducted and killed in 1982 after a stranger snatched her from a playground, was activated for the first time on local radio and TV stations. A baritone voice said a young girl was missing, named Elizabeth Smart. Everyone should be on the lookout.

By that time, word was spreading like a brushfire about Elizabeth's disappearance, and a manhunt was in full throttle. Salt Lake City hummed with what would become an unprecedented search.

At 9 a.m., the first of what grew to be about 100 law-enforcement officials and Salt Lake Samaritans took part in the search. They were armed with a description of Elizabeth's kidnapper culled from Mary Katherine's memory—a man, maybe in his 30s, who was about five feet eight inches tall. His medium build was cloaked by a light-colored jacket. On his head was a white cap with a bill. The man was armed with a gun, people were cautioned. The state's helicopter whirred over Federal Heights, looking for any sign of Elizabeth.

Bloodhounds were brought in and they sniffed around the Smart home. One of the dogs caught a scent just outside the house and followed it for several feet, but lost the trail when it hit some bushes. Neighbors organized search groups to head into the hills above the Smart home. They looked around Emigration Canyon and the Bonneville Shoreline.

The traffic around Kristianna Circle thickened. A police trailer and at least four squad cars were parked outside the house. Neighbors flooded the cul-de-sac, with tears in their eyes. They had made their homes in a safe area, and they weren't supposed to have that taken from them.

"To have that taken from you . . ." one woman cried to a reporter, trailing off in mid-sentence.

Ed and Lois's neighbors couldn't understand what had gone wrong. This simply wasn't supposed to happen there. And why the Smarts? There was no one anyone could think of immediately who had a reason to try to take vengeance on Ed or Lois. They were well-off, but not rich, and no ransom demands had come in.

Parents brought their children to help the search, and some of Elizabeth's classmates showed up, trying to do whatever they could.

The police poured their resources into finding the little girl, and tried to make sure the efforts were coordinated. They asked people in the ward to look around their homes and not to travel up to the Smarts' home, to quell a developing traffic jam. It was hot that day, they warned, and people should be careful not to fall victim to heat stroke as they searched the mountains.

Inside the Smart home, the family prayed and fasted. Elizabeth's parents got call after call from people saying how sorry they were, and could they do anything to help. One of them was Elaine Runyon, the mother of the murdered child whose name was used on the state's missing child-alert system. Another was Gordon B. Hinckley, the president of the LDS church who phoned Charles Smart, Ed's dad.

"Charles," Hinckley said, "we're sorry for your trouble. We remember you in our prayers in the temple. Is there anything else we can do?"

Hinckley issued a bulletin to LDS churches in five nearby states, urging people to take part in the manhunt and distribute Elizabeth's photo.

The Smarts reached out to Bob Smither in Texas. Bob and his wife, Gay, ran the Laura Recovery Center in Texas, named for their daughter who was kidnapped and murdered four years earlier. Bob said he would do whatever he could to help. A sister of Dawn Davis, one of Bob's volunteers, lived in Salt Lake, and Bob dispatched her to the search center that was already being set up at Shriners Hospital, down the street from the Federal Heights meeting house.

The woman brought the Smarts a search manual created by the Laura Recovery Center, instructing parents on how to run such an effort. Late that afternoon, Dawn Davis flew into Salt Lake, and she and her sister organized a town meeting to direct the searchers.

Ed was largely relying on his oldest brother, Tom, who had worked for the *Deseret News* for two decades and knew how to organize the media that was descending on the house, as a source of strength. A tall, outdoorsy cowboy-type with a take-charge attitude, Tom knew how to spread focused information about his niece. When they were kids, family members said later, Tom would always get after Ed, teasing his little brother. But on June 5, Ed desperately needed Tom's help, needed him to lead the effort, and the eldest of Dorotha and Charles Smart's children stepped into the role. That day was the first of five straight where Tom didn't sleep.

The Smarts asked police to expand the search area past Utah to Wyoming and southeast Idaho, where there had been recent kidnappings. Police also checked Oregon, where two little kids were abducted in the winter and the spring that year.

Posters with Elizabeth's face were quickly printed up. They were copied at several stores, including the nearby Kinko's, where Ed's sister, Angela, spotted a strange man in robes who asked her for spare change. The Smarts handed out several pictures of Elizabeth in coming days. Some showed her playing her harp. Another showed her with her hair tied back. The different shots would be a good point of reference for anyone who might see her.

The Utah Missing Persons Clearinghouse also rushed into action, sending more than 800 fliers about Elizabeth to law-enforcement officials and school districts in nearby states.

Police looked at a computer in Ed and Lois's home, one of twelve they would look at in the weeks after Elizabeth vanished. Maybe Elizabeth had met someone in an Internet chatroom, and they would be able to flush the person out quickly. But Elizabeth never used the Internet, family friends said later.

The Smarts' house was being renovated as Ed tried to sell it, and several brokers and workers had traipsed through in recent weeks. The police were reaching out to them, while keeping up with hundreds of leads that were pouring in, one a minute at some points during the day. The police issued a $10,000 reward for anyone with information that could lead to the young girl's return.

Dwayne Baird, the burly, salt-and-pepper-haired spokesman for the Salt Lake City police department, fielded dozens of questions from a squad of reporters near the house. In his low growl of a voice, he told them Mary Katherine had watched some of what happened.

The young girl had waited several hours to tell her parents her sister was gone. The man never called Elizabeth by name. They apparently left on foot through a screen door, Baird said, but precious time was already gone. Investigators would later say Mary Katherine heard noises at the side of the house.

"A two-hour window gives anyone the opportunity to be away from this area," Baird said. But while the kidnapper didn't seem to know Elizabeth's home well and they couldn't give a motive, the police made it clear they didn't think it was a random crime. They also said the kidnapper threatened Mary Katherine, a detail that would later prove incorrect.

Those were among the scant details police gave to a media swarm that was already starting to camp out near the Smarts' house. They didn't reveal that a lawn chair had been found against the side of the house, beneath the kitchen window with the cut screen.

The afternoon of June 5, Ed Smart came out of his house and gave the first of what would become twice-daily press conferences through the summer. Ed kept his head down, his face red and contorted with grief. He struggled with his words as he spoke into a crush of microphones and tape recorders.

"Elizabeth, if you're out there, we're doing everything we possibly can to help you," Ed said, choking in sobs. "We love you. We want you to come home safely to us."

He also pleaded with the stranger who had turned the Smarts' world upside down.

"I can't imagine why you took her to begin with," Smart said to the man, whoever he was. "There's no reason that you should have taken her. Please, let her go. Please!"

"Elizabeth! Elizabeth!" The cries traveled across the canyon, voices overlapping. Elizabeth recognized one of them, her family later said. It was her mother's brother, David, calling out her name. But Elizabeth couldn't reply. All around her were hundreds of people, hoping to turn up any clue about where she might be, so close they may have been able to hear her had she been able to call out. She was frightened, had little water and food, and the temperature in the mountains was dropping. Her family would later say she was sleep-deprived. Her uncles and friends, police and total strangers hiked for hours in the steep canyons in search of Elizabeth, pushing aside tree branches and tracking any flicker of movement, hopeful they would find her, frustrated when they didn't. She was there, tucked inside the lean-to, invisible.

Ed Smart was able to sleep for only an hour that night. It was 24 hours since Elizabeth had been stolen, crucial hours in the search for a missing child, the family would hear over and over, in coming days. Most kids taken by strangers are the intended victims of pedophiles, and most kidnappers who plan to murder their prey do it within the first three hours. The Smarts were well past that benchmark. Ed and Lois were puffy-faced, and their eyes were rimmed with tears. But they had a missing daughter to find, and five other children to care for, and so they pressed on.

"Their state of mind, as you can imagine, is traumatized," Salt Lake Police Chief Rick Dinse told reporters at a morning press conference. Dinse had been with Ed during the first news briefing on the abduction the day before. Dinse, a square-jawed former Los Angeles cop, had dealt with high-profile cases before. He had been in Salt Lake for two years, but before that he'd organized Security for the 1984 Olympics in Los Angeles. He had also been in LA during the Rodney King police-beating scandal.

At least twenty-five Salt Lake law-enforcement officials were working on the case, along with the FBI.

That morning, June 6, Ed and Lois announced fresh reward money, $250,000, from private donations. They stopped by Shriners Hospital to thank the volunteers who'd interrupted their lives to look for Elizabeth.

"I know that's how we're going to find her," Ed said, looking at the steady flow of people in and out of the search center. But he was barely enduring. "It's gut-wrenching," he said. "It just seems like a bad nightmare."

Dozens of newspapers across the country had a story about the photogenic missing teen from

Utah that day. The media interest in the Elizabeth Smart case was becoming a frenzy, and Ed and Lois were urged by national networks to feed it, to go on air and talk about their daughter. Such widespread attention could only help them locate Elizabeth. Ed and Lois were exhausted, but they agreed to do it.

Ed declared he had a good feeling that searchers were getting close, that it would be "the day" Elizabeth was found. They made the rounds on the networks, including the "Today" show on NBC. They both cried, begging an unknown man to free Elizabeth. They were as composed as they could be, until Lois hit her breaking point. On "Today," Lois managed to get out only a few words before she crumbled.

With more than a day gone since Elizabeth had been taken, the family was in agony. A faceless villain had targeted them, and they still didn't know what he wanted. Lois simply couldn't understand why someone would cause her family such pain.

"Why would he pick my home?" her brother Mark recalled her asking.

Investigators interviewed Mary Katherine, their only witness, about what she remembered of that night. Any clue could provide a lead. But at home, her family said it was working to keep her from reliving the terror of watching her sister stolen away.

"We are trying not to talk to her about this, so the pressure's not on, so she's not rethinking this over and over, to help reduce the trauma," David Smart said.

The media camped outside the Smarts' home were surprised when Dinse told them that there were no plans to bring in a sketch artist.

"What we might get might not be accurate," an FBI agent with the bureau's Salt Lake office said.

There was also the chance that, with too much questioning, Mary Katherine's memory of the event would become muddied. She might blend what she was being asked or being told with what she actually remembered.

But at some point in the days just after Elizabeth had been taken, Ed Smart, at the urging of a TV news team, put in a call to Jeanne Boylan, the forensic sketch artist whose hooded portrait of the man known to the FBI only as the "Unabomber" helped identify Ted Kaczynski in the 1990s. Boylan's methods were unusual. Instead of simply taking details about a person's face, she focused on the witness's experience of the crime, searching out characteristics of both the suspect and the person who saw him. Ed didn't reach Boylan, but he left a message on her answering machine.

There was still no ransom demand, and police said that if someone took Elizabeth to extort Ed, they probably would have made that clear within two days of the kidnapping. Police thought the kidnapper may have been lurking in the neighborhood for awhile.

The police wouldn't say what their searches were turning up. But no one, not even family members, they said, had been ruled out.

"We haven't been able to focus on any one individual at this point as being a suspect," Dinse said. "At this point it's all speculation."

Elizabeth's middle school held a moment of silence for her that morning. Later on, five teachers were told they could leave school early to go join the search.

There were more than 2,000 volunteers searching the area, and help was coming in from all over. Bob Smither and Bob Walcutt, another worker at the Laura Recovery Center, arrived that day, and the scene that greeted them was slightly chaotic.

"It always is," Smither said. But he marveled at how many volunteers Elizabeth's family and her ward had already rounded up. "It was unbelievable," he said, five times as many as the center's normal search effort. Smither and his workers jumped into action, organizing the effort with military precision. A Salt Lake cop was posted at Shriners Hospital, helping with the effort, but Laura Recovery workers were running the show. People were asked to register, to show photo IDs to guard against the chance that Elizabeth's kidnapper might try to join in. "It's not unheard of," Smither said. Kids under 18 weren't allowed to take part, for fear of the trauma they could suffer if they stumbled on anything connected to the crime, whether it was a weapon, a piece of clothing, or something worse. Instead, those younger teenagers helped watch little kids so their parents could search, and ran errands for the command center.

One team of volunteers signed people in and broke them into groups. Others mapped search grids, starting from the Smarts' house and fanning out for a five-mile radius.

The volunteers headed into the hills with evidence tape and cell phones. They shouldn't touch anything, they were instructed, but they should mark something that looked like a potential clue. If it was a hot lead, they should phone central command immediately.

"They were very capable and very dedicated," Smither said of the search center. He had seen it before, but not to such a degree. "Most people will put their own lives on hold for a missing child," he said.

The searches turned up Band-Aids that had shaken loose, bits of cloth, and pieces of litter. Someone found a roll of duct tape around Emigration Canyon, but it could have been left by almost anyone.

At the end of the day, the volunteers were debriefed about what their searches had turned up. One copy of the reports went to the police, another was kept by the center, and a third was turned over to the Smarts. Bob had no contact with Ed and Lois, and instead worked with Ed's three brothers—Tom, David and Chris. He told them they needed the "triangle of trust."

"The community has to trust the cops, the family has to believe the community is trying, and the cops have to believe the family and the community are working with them," Smither said.

Bob "absolutely" felt such a triangle existed in the Elizabeth Smart case, and things were certainly going well at central command. But that day marked the first in a string of clashes between the Smart family and some of the police running the investigation.

Word began to emerge that the family may have muddied the scene just after Elizabeth disappeared. There were questions about how many neighbors had shown up at the Smarts' house, walking up the front steps and drifting through their rooms. There were suggestions that the neighbors got there over a half-hour before police did. The initial police report said the Smarts "contacted several neighbors" that night, and "then contacted" the cops.

Some reports suggested that neighbors and other people had even walked into Elizabeth's room, the scene of the crime, before police got there.

In the days ahead, there would be questions about the timeframe of the calls to the neighbors and to the police. The initial police report that night suggested that the Smarts had called neighbors before dialing 911. That belief was fueled by the reports in the *Deseret News* that Tom had heard from his brother at 3:30 a.m., a half-hour before the 911 call was recorded. Police would later say they had clarified the issue and that the cops had been contacted before any other calls were made.

Friends of the family said Ed had called a small handful of people in his ward by 4:30 a.m. the morning of the kidnapping. And they were infuriated by the subtle suggestion that the Smarts had done something wrong.

The Federal Heights bishop, David Hamblin,

said Ed had simply wanted to get as many people looking for his daughter as possible. Besides, he said, Ed felt like the police were questioning that Elizabeth had even been abducted, suggesting she may have been a runaway.

Several officials in Salt Lake acknowledge they receive reports of runaways each day, many of whom turn up later, and the jurisdictions have different procedures for dealing with them. There are many categories in Utah of kids who disappear from their homes without an apparent abduction, and teenagers sometimes don't easily fit into any one of them. Elizabeth was right in the middle of the usual age range for teenagers who flee their own homes.

Checking whether Elizabeth was a runaway was routine for the Salt Lake cops, but Ed Smart cared only about finding his daughter, and anything else was a distraction from that goal.

The police re-interviewed Ed and Lois that day. Searchers were poking through the hills into the evening when one of the teams of volunteers thought they had a solid lead and chased it for all it was worth.

During a search in Pinecrest Canyon around dusk, the 22-person search group saw a man wearing what looked like a white T-shirt and a white baseball cap. One searcher saw a tattoo tinged with red, green and blue on his right shoulder. He was pacing back and forth, like he was waiting for something. Another saw him trying to cover his own tracks.

"Hey!" someone called out. The man started to run, scrambling away into the thick brush along a hillside. The searchers heard at least two gunshots. Some said there may have been nine. The man was gone. Some of the volunteers were scared but excited. They thought they were onto something. A few fetched Salt Lake County sheriff's deputies, and search dogs were let loose across the canyon.

A helicopter that used infrared detectors to seek body heat was flown over the mountains, but yielded nothing. It seemed like something promising, but like everything else in the two-day-old search, it just slipped away.

That night, Ed gave in to the exhaustion that had begun even before Elizabeth disappeared, with the death of his father-in-law, and he collapsed. He was hospitalized the next morning. Ed's father, Charles, watched over Lois, who was also showing signs of strain. Ed was scheduled to do a fresh round of interviews, but he sent his brothers in his place so that the family wouldn't lose any chance to get the word out.

In downtown Salt Lake, Elizabeth's picture was taped to utility poles and storefront windows. Buttons were made up with her face on them, the words "please pray for me" in a semicircle over her picture. Her parents often wore them in their television interviews. There was a pall over the city. People broke into tears at work or as they walked down the street and saw a poster of Elizabeth, the word "kidnapped" in bold type printed over her face. Some people compared it to the way they felt after September 11, 2001—sad and helpless. Slips of ribbon in baby blue, Elizabeth's favorite color, began to appear, pinned to people's clothes and wrapped around trees, and on the fences around Bryant Intermediate School, where Elizabeth was supposed to take part in a ceremony marking the end of one phase of her life and welcoming the next.

Instead, school principal Frances Battle set an empty chair where Elizabeth would have sat. There were more than 300 students leaving Bryant Intermediate that day, but everyone's mind was on the one who wasn't there. There was a moment of silence before Elizabeth's brother, Charles, accepted his little sister's certificate. Blue ribbons woven into a heart framed a picture of Elizabeth on the chainlink fence around the school. The ribbons stirred when the wind blew.

Ed Smart went home from the hospital later that day, but he was still recuperating and didn't speak to the media. His sister, Cynthia Smart-Owens, repeated the message that they were certain Elizabeth was still alive.

"We feel urgently that we need to find her," Cynthia said.

Elsewhere, the searchers looking for Elizabeth focused on transient hideouts, often called "hobo camps" by Salt Lake residents, that studded the hillsides. There were camps in dried-out riverbeds, under bridges and tucked into the valleys of the Wasatch Mountains. The camps are mostly used by Salt Lake homeless who refuse to enter the shelter system or have substance-abuse problems. Others become havens for illegal immigrants or transients who work during the day to save money for real housing.

Many of the homeless people in Salt Lake joined the search teams, outreach worker Pamela Atkinson said. They were as moved by the Smarts' dilemma as anyone else, and they wanted to do what they could to help. The search teams were becoming a blend of people, from doctors and lawyers taking the day off to vacationers passing through Utah who signed up at Shriners Hospital. Salt Lake businesses donated food and water for the volunteers. Pilots offered their private planes for the search. Although the LDS church certainly played a role in motivating people to pitch in, Tom Smart said he was amazed at how all walks of life were descending on Kristianna Circle. "We had everyone helping," he said later.

But festering beneath the good feeling over the kindness of strangers was an increasingly desperate push for a good lead.

"Absolutely, I am frustrated," Dinse told reporters that afternoon at the daily press conference. It was the end of the third full day of searching, and so far there wasn't much to go on. The police handed out a detailed description of Elizabeth's size 8 sneakers. They were white with blue trim and suction cups on the soles. Two profilers from the FBI came in from Quantico, Virginia, the day before. They had retraced the crime scene and were going over the tapes of the interviews cops had done.

Dinse said that with the number of different law-enforcement agencies searching for the girl, he hoped to assemble a task force in the coming days. The man who would later lead that group, for just a short time after the kidnapping, was Sergeant Don Bell, a 31-year veteran with the Salt Lake PD who was in charge of the Sexual Assault Unit. Bell had long experience dealing with major cases, including serving as the negotiator during a 1991 hostage crisis at a hospital in Sandy. The case was later turned into a TV movie.

There were questions about whether any lights had been on in Elizabeth's bedroom when the intruder came in, and about whether blood had been found at the crime scene. There were no real tell-tale pieces of evidence—scuff marks or loose fibers—around the window with the cut screen, although officers didn't say that publicly until much later.

Dinse was tight-lipped with most of the information. Yes, police had searched a computer, but he wouldn't say what they'd found, other than that it didn't appear related to the kidnapping.

"We have evidence that indicates there was somebody in the house, we're just not going to discuss what that is," Dinse said. Searchers had looked in the Emigration Canyon area for the man volunteers said they'd seen the night before, but turned up nothing, and police didn't think it was linked to Elizabeth.

Then Dinse talked about the reports that neighbors were in the Smarts' home right after Elizabeth was taken. There were, indeed, people inside before the police got there, he said, and some of the evidence at the crime scene was probably affected. "Obviously that's a problem," Dinse said. Even though he was frustrated, they were making ground in the case.

"The progress we're making is probably more an elimination of things," Dinse said. "We're operating under the plan that she is still alive. That she's still operating under the control of this individual."

The airplanes buzzed overhead, small as flies from the street below. They flew over Salt Lake and the towns around it. There were more than 15 of them, and they were all looking for Elizabeth.

On Saturday, four days after the kidnapping, Ed faced reporters for the first time since exhaustion overcame him, with Lois at his side. Ed again said he knew in his heart that his daughter was still alive, and his brother, Tom, echoed his words.

"It may take awhile," said Tom at the search command center, "but we know in our hearts—and I don't have any evidence to say this or anything like that—she's there, she's alive. Somebody has her. She's somewhere. Check your basements. Check your houses."

Lois, her head bent, spoke directly to her daughter through tears, into the cameras. Her voice broke over her words. She promised Elizabeth that the family would never stop looking for her, ever.

"If you can hear us, we love you Elizabeth," Lois choked. "We haven't forgotten about you. We won't stop until you're home."

The search was still going strong. The Utah Transit Authority started running shuttle buses to ferry volunteers to the search command center, because so many people were heading there the volume of cars created too much traffic.

That morning had brought fresh excitement to reporters camped outside the Smarts' home. At 11 a.m., police gave out a composite sketch of a man who had spoken with Elizabeth at a "social function" shortly before she disappeared, and they wanted to talk to him. Ed and Lois later said they didn't know him or that his description had been circulated. But police said other Smart relatives did know him and they gave cops a description of what he looked like.

He was in his late 30s to 40s, police said. He wore a beret, and his front tooth was missing. He was on a list that members of the Smart family were giving the cops, of strangers who had been around the house or had contact with the family. It included people who had done work for Ed as he renovated the family home, some of whom were transients, police said later.

But by the afternoon, the probe was at yet another dead end. Police had found the man, but they were sure after they talked to him that he didn't know anything about Elizabeth's whereabouts. They located him after someone who'd seen the man's sketch had called police. But he wasn't a suspect, and never would be, they said. They withheld his name to respect his privacy.

The man they'd questioned was a quiet drifter who sometimes popped up around the city. The police were familiar with him before they passed out the sketch.

Dwayne Baird acknowledged to reporters that the man had seemed like a promising development but that he simply hadn't known anything. Police had no better idea of who'd taken Elizabeth than they had before they spoke with him. It was another lead that had dried out.

Pamela Atkinson would later say the man was a transient she knew from her work with the city's homeless. It turned out police were looking in the right direction, but they didn't know it.

The hopes of a city that the missing girl would be found floated over Salt Lake. The relatives of Brian David Mitchell and Wanda Barzee were among those praying for the Smarts. Dora Corbett was touched by the pain of the Smart family, and she prayed for a miracle. Vicki Cottrell went out to join the search effort. They hadn't seen Mitchell and Barzee for months, but they had no way of knowing they should be looking for the couple, as well as for Elizabeth.

*   *   *

That night, "American's Most Wanted" aired its
first blurb on the Elizabeth Smart case, in a three-
minute segment that told the basic details about
the abduction. The show focuses on major criminal cases and kidnapped children, and many in law
enforcement say it's become an invaluable resource
for solving crimes. Its ability to reach into people's
homes with sketches and descriptions of wanted
suspects is unparalleled. The show's host, John
Walsh, exorcises the demon of his son Adam's kidnap and murder in 1981 each week by trying to
bring other people's missing children home. One of
Elizabeth's uncles had called Walsh soon after the
kidnapping, and AMW crews had been taping
around Kristianna Circle all week.

"This beautiful girl was taken from her home at
gunpoint by a kidnapper who went into the house
through a window," Walsh told his audience. The
tips started coming in to the show's phone lines
soon after.

But Walsh's description of what had happened
after the intruder broke into Elizabeth's room was
different from the police account in one respect:
The police had indicated all week that Mary
Katherine had been threatened by the man, which
suggested she had had some interaction with him.
But Walsh said Elizabeth's sister had pretended to
sleep and that the kidnapper didn't know she had
seen him.

Walsh may have been getting his information
straight from the family. That evening's show

wouldn't be the first time he would announce a key detail in the case on-air, before police or the Smarts did. He would become the Smarts' closest ally in the months ahead.

SIX

In the first days Elizabeth was held in the mountains, Mitchell began making what would become occasional sojourns into the valley. He may have gone into Salt Lake City to get a feel for how intense the search for the missing girl was. He was also likely bringing provisions back to the campsite. He wasn't in town as often as it would later seem he had been, but he was definitely there.

Angela Dumke said she saw him outside the Kinko's, and a *Deseret News* staffer told her paper she'd seen a transient in robes trying to rip an Elizabeth Smart "kidnapped" poster off the newspaper's office windows. She asked him to stop, but he said "they found the guy."

Few people know what happened in the months Elizabeth spent in the hills over Federal Heights. Her aunt Angela said she spent 45 days trapped there, but investigators said she was there from June 5 until August 8, during which time her resolve was broken, a process that usually doesn't take very long.

Many psychologists, studying the case from

afar, quickly said Elizabeth was suffering from Stockholm Syndrome, a phenomenon named for hostages taken during a bank robbery in Sweden in the 1970s who began to identify with their captors as they feared for their own lives.

Rick Ross, an expert in destructive cult behavior, believed something different was at work in Elizabeth's case. Though he was not involved in the investigation, he believed Elizabeth was, as her family would later say, "brainwashed."

It began that first night with the abduction, bringing Elizabeth to a place that was isolated from everything she knew, and putting her, literally, in a box, Ross said. It was "standard operating procedure for any would-be cult leader." Once she was stripped of her family, her friends, her home and everything she connected with her life, Mitchell was able to reinforce his beliefs, over and over, until she was reprogrammed, Ross said. The only feedback she got was from Barzee, who was already following her husband's way of life.

It wouldn't have been hard to alter the truth for a young, traumatized girl who was likely exhausted from her ordeal. The difference between Elizabeth's case and Stockholm Syndrome, Ross said, was that the Swedish bank robbers had no interest in converting their hostages to their views of the world.

"Stockholm Syndrome victims don't take on a whole new persona," Ross said. "They are the same people, basically, going into their capture as they are coming out. Elizabeth was not the same person."

Unlike a hostage situation or a kidnapping for ransom, where the captive is the key to the prize, Elizabeth herself was the prize for Brian David Mitchell.

Rowenna Erickson was in her offices a few days after the kidnapping when she got a call from Utah State Senator Ron Allen. Erickson, an executive of Tapestry Against Polygamy, knew Allen well. He had submitted a bill a year earlier to crack down on the practice of taking young girls as brides. Amid opposition from polygamist groups, the bill was watered down, but eventually passed in 2001. Erickson considered Allen a friend of the movement, and she was happy to talk to him.

On the phone, Allen, a non-practicing Mormon, asked Rowenna if she had said anything publicly that raised the specter of polygamy in connection with the Elizabeth Smart abduction.

"No, we haven't," Rowenna replied. The thought hadn't even crossed her mind that the kidnapper wanted a "wife." She told Allen that TAP had gotten some phone calls from people asking if the case might be linked to polygamy, but she had told everyone she'd spoken to that she didn't think it was.

Everything that had been said about the Smart case so far didn't match the usual motives of polygamists, Rowenna said. Polygamists generally look for young women in their communities, and they don't kidnap them; they pressure their families into giving them up.

Rowenna said Allen asked her if the group would give a formal statement saying the Smart case wasn't related to polygamy; her answer was no. There was no clear picture yet about what had happened to Elizabeth Smart, and Rowenna wasn't going to make a public statement disavowing anything. She said he told her he'd been asked by someone to place the call and find out where TAP stood.

Allen, a Democrat in the largely Republican state senate, had a different memory of the conversation. He got word from someone he knew that some people around Utah were growing convinced Elizabeth had been taken by a polygamist and were going to call a press conference. He wanted to warn her that the group needed to be careful and have all its facts lined up before it made such a claim. The group had been important in fighting against polygamy, and he didn't want it to lose credibility.

But Rowenna wasn't the only one whose phone was ringing. In Phoenix, Arizona, Flora Jessop was fielding calls from reporters and members of the general public about whether Elizabeth Smart's disappearance had something to do with an element of Mormon life that stirs discomfort for many in the LDS church. Unlike Rowenna, Flora, of Help the Child Brides, instantly believed Elizabeth was taken by a polygamist. And she said she got calls from some LDS members asking her "to please not associate" Elizabeth with the practice of taking plural wives.

Flora was relying on her instincts. She grew up in Hildale, Utah, one of the state's biggest polygamous communities. The LDS church says there's no such thing as a fundamentalist Mormon, because the church believes in one living prophet—its president—and what he says, members follow. But "fundamentalist Mormons" were what the people Flora was raised by called themselves. The FLDS is its own community that follows early Mormon doctrine. Flora herself escaped a polygamous life, and there was something about Elizabeth's age and her background that set off alarm bells.

"When you're raised in it, you know," Flora said. "She was a perfect victim." It was the deep faith of the Smart home that made Flora think the kidnapped girl could be susceptible to a domineering man. "It's not hard to coerce these girls," she said.

That was the phenomenon Ron Allen saw over and over again as he fought to give polygamy laws some teeth. "Some of these girls plain don't have a chance," he said. The young women who got sucked into a life with so-called "Sister/Wives" usually fit a pattern—easily swayed, and deeply ensconced in a faith where men hold most of the power.

Some estimates put the number of active polygamists in Utah at about two percent of the population. The practice was thrown into the national spotlight when polygamist Tom Green, a man with at least five wives and twenty-seven children who had been a public advocate for plural marriage on television shows, was charged with rape, bigamy and nonpayment of child support in 2000. It came just over a year before the Olympics were slated to arrive in Salt Lake City, and officials were concerned about the message that Green's practices sent to people visiting the state. There was a public push at that time to try to get tougher with polygamists, although some officials say the only way to prosecute them is for other crimes, such as child abuse, welfare fraud and tax evasion.

Even then, some officials say, there aren't enough resources for prosecutors to try all those cases. And in other cases, law enforcement is reluctant to try to shut polygamous communities down, saying it's a personal issue that isn't their business.

Coke Newell, a spokesman for the LDS church, said it never occurred to church officials that polygamy might have played a role in Elizabeth Smart's abduction. "It wasn't assumed that there was any sort of church-specific motivation connected with the abduction," he said. "I don't believe we ever even heard anything to that effect, until after Elizabeth came back."

Elizabeth Smart's family has often called her a "dutiful" daughter, and many observers suggested that obedience made her any easy target for Mitchell. But Ross called it "arrogant" to suggest that the young girl's religion played a role in how she responded to her captor. If anything, he said, her deep faith would have made it harder for

Mitchell to break her down. "She knows that there is only one true prophet, and that prophet is the president of the LDS church—not Brian Mitchell," Ross said.

Besides, Mitchell wasn't associated with any of the established polygamous groups that exist in Utah. Polygamy was officially outlawed by the church in 1890. Since the new, albeit weakened, anti-polgyamy law was enacted in 2001, some of the groups have started to recede, Allen said. There have been reports of leaders of the group preaching to other members against taking child brides.

But Allen said there are still several active clans, most of them known to officials. Some of those groups, such as the one in Hildale, have their own businesses, schools and even a post office. Then there are the others, polygamists who are essentially freelancers blending into the neighborhood, traveling with a raft of three or four women and eleven children behind them as they walk down the street, he said. But as long as they pay their taxes and take their kids to school and obey the law, they don't really call attention to themselves. Allen understands how young girls are drawn into such a life; what he can't comprehend is why an adult woman would help a man do such a thing.

"How some of these guys convince mature, adult women to help them in securing their child brides is still God's mystery," he said.

The position of the church, Newell said, is that polygamy is an offense punished by excommunication. He said polygamy was never a "fundamental doctrine of the LDS church," although it was something that was practiced when the church was established.

Statistics show that most stranger abductions are the work of sexual predators, and the Salt Lake police indicated early on that such a motive was a possibility in the Elizabeth Smart case. But through most of the investigation, police weren't looking for someone who claimed to act in the name of God. They were looking at people who'd worked at the Smart home, and the list, they said, was long.

SEVEN

"The person who has Elizabeth cares for her and doesn't know what to do. The solution is to hold your feelings aside and send Elizabeth back to where she feels most at home," Cynthia Smart-Owens begged an unknown man through the cameras' lenses. It had been five days since her niece disappeared, and Cynthia was hoping the kidnapper was watching.

"Let her walk out to a public place where people will recognize her," she pleaded. The entire Smart family was praying in the hopes that they could soften the kidnapper's heart, and he would set Elizabeth free.

It was the first Sunday since the kidnapping, and all around Salt Lake that morning, pews were full. It wasn't only LDS churches that were packed. Presbyterians, Unitarians and Catholics also lined the pews, their minds on the missing young girl. Many wore their Sunday best, the familiar light blue ribbons fixed to their chests. At the Smarts' Federal Heights Ward meeting house, Bishop Hamblin briefly considered canceling the meeting, thinking it might cut down on the number of searchers.

But the meeting went ahead, and the church was nearly full; down at the search center, volunteers were still out in droves. In downtown Salt Lake, First Lady Laura Bush, in town that weekend to address a community service conference, marveled at the volunteer effort to help find Elizabeth.

At the house on Kristianna Circle that morning, Ed Smart was pulling himself together to face another ordeal. He had agreed to a police request that he take a lie detector test.

"I have nothing to hide," an exhausted Ed later said of the test. The grueling, four-hour ordeal heaped more pressure on a father who, to observers, already had his nerves stretched thin.

Later that night, he and Lois drew some comfort in the throng of more than 500 people settling onto the sprawling lawn of Salt Lake's Liberty Park in a somber candlelight vigil for their daughter. The orange flames flickered in the darkening sky, and soft sobs floated over the park. Ed's voice broke as he offered a prayer for Elizabeth, and Lois told the crowd the family believed she'd come home.

The next few days would bring a flurry of activity. Some would leave the Smarts hopeful, and others bruised the relationships among the two groups of people working hardest for Elizabeth's return—the family and the police.

At Shriners Hospital, the Elizabeth Smart search center was having an effect on normal operations. Business at the hospital, a haven for sick children, was being disrupted by the thousands of volunteers and media camped out on its steps. On Monday, five days after the kidnapping, the operation was moved across the street to the Smarts' church. Bob Smither and his crew from the Laura Recovery Center headed back to Texas, confident that the community had things well under control. Volunteers were still pouring into the search center, but that would change soon.

That morning, police met with Mary Katherine, gently questioning her yet again about the night her sister was taken. The day before, police said they had ruled out the possibility that Elizabeth had run away and faked her own kidnapping. Tom Smart asked anyone with an all-terrain vehicle to band together to search the desert for Elizabeth. Even as he made the request, the police were directing their attention to Tom's alibi for the night of June 4.

In missing-persons cases, investigators look at the family of the victim early on to eliminate them as suspects, and the Smart abduction was no exception. The police were quietly scrutinizing family members for possible suspects. The police went through Elizabeth's male relatives, one by one. Ed took a polygraph, as did Tom and David. Tom's polygraph stretched on for more than seven hours. He was also asked to write out his alibi, and investigators checked and re-checked it.

David Smart was also tested. "I wasn't worried about myself; I knew I didn't do it," Tom said later. "I knew none of us had. I was far more upset about the effect the process had on Ed.

"I realize it is something that had to be done, but the manner in which it was conducted, I had a problem with that," Tom said, his voice rising in anger. "It was just a horrible, hellish ordeal for all of us. Each of us was stretched to our limits, ripped to the core."

"Look," David echoed bluntly, "we would do whatever it took to clear any doubt about us and get the attention focused back on finding who really took Elizabeth. But we got raked over the coals."

Police did not announce publicly that they were testing the Smart men. On June 11, police believed they had identified the driver of a suspicious car that had been cruising the Smarts' street two days before the abduction.

Charlie Miller was making his milk rounds sometime before 7 a.m. that first Monday in June when he noticed a car driving slowly up and down Kristianna Circle. The driver, in what Miller thought was either a Nissan or a Honda, didn't wave back when Miller raised his hand in a gentle salute. That was odd, thought Miller. He'd delivered the milk in the neighborhood for two years and always got a friendly response. The kids, particularly, looked forward to the free milk Charlie passed out as they stood waiting on the corner for the school bus. Miller grew more suspicious when the car began following his truck. Milk drivers had been robbed before, and Miller wasn't taking any chances. He tried to memorize the strange car's license plate, jotting the numbers down on a box he kept in the truck. Miller also noticed something else. The driver was wearing a white baseball cap.

Two days later, Elizabeth Smart disappeared, taken by someone described as having worn a light-colored cap. Miller picked up the phone and dialed Salt Lake Police. The plate number the milkman had scribbled down didn't turn up a match, but the first three numbers, 266, were thought to be correct, and police were instructed to be on the lookout for any plates bearing those digits.

As Mayor Rocky Anderson passed out candles for Elizabeth's vigil Sunday night, police were scrutinizing license plates in the parking lot and surrounding area of Liberty Park. One of them spotted a green, four-door Saturn with plates bearing the 266. There was alcohol in the car. Police staked out the Saturn and when the owner left the vigil, three police cars followed. At one point, the driver pulled over, but as police opened their doors to approach him, he hit the gas and sped off into a side street. Police lost him. Later that night, a little boy playing in a ditch full of cat-tails found abandoned license plates and took them home to his father, who called police. The plates, both numbered 266HJH, had been reported stolen. But police had enough evidence, possibly from fingerprints on the license plates, to come up with a name: Bret Michael Edmunds.

Edmunds had a rap sheet. He was wanted on two outstanding warrants, one for fraud and one for assaulting a police officer. Search dogs turned up Edmunds's scent in the canyons where searches had been looking for Elizabeth. The 26-year-old drifter was known around Elizabeth's neighborhood because he'd done work for some of the families in Federal Heights. But he hadn't, as far as anyone could recall, worked at the Smarts'. And Edmunds was six feet two inches, considerably taller than the man Mary Katherine had described as seeing in her room.

Wednesday, June 12, police went public with Edmunds's name. He wasn't a suspect, they were careful to say, but investigators wanted to talk to him. Police made it clear to the press that they didn't think Edmunds had anything to do with the kidnapping. But his was the first actual name made public and the media ran with it, just as Edmunds was on his way out of Utah. As leads came in, the police were following him across the country. Because of his history of violence with cops, he was considered "dangerous."

The day before the bulletin for Edmunds was issued, Chief Dinse said investigators felt they may have already spoken to Elizabeth's abductor. "We are going to get you," the chief said. While the hunt for Edmunds was under way, police had already interviewed someone else who piqued their interest. He was a local handyman named Richard Albert Ricci.

As 100 investigators followed up leads that were still pouring in, a new round of volunteers showed up to continue the search for Elizabeth. They hoped a fresh team of eyes might spot something overlooked by the hordes of others canvassing the canyons.

Then, on June 13, a bombshell sent the Smart family reeling: "Police Eye Relatives in Probe," blared the cautiously worded front page story in the *Salt Lake Tribune*. The article claimed that cops believed the kidnapping may have been an inside job involving a member of Elizabeth's family. The Smarts were outraged at the story, which the paper said was based on information provided by four different sources on the case, all of whom had asked not to be named.

The article said that police, working on the theory that someone who knew Elizabeth might have taken her, had prompted them to ask certain family members to sit for polygraphs. What's more, the results of one of those tests had raised suspicion about the alibi of someone in the teen's extended family.

Two nights before the *Tribune* story broke, Tom Smart had appeared on Larry King's CNN show. Ed Smart's siblings were already becoming television fixtures in living rooms across America. That night, other guests talked about Bret Edmunds, though at that time the public didn't know his name. Then Tom came on to discuss the family. He talked about Ed's polygraph, and then said that he, too, had been tested. The mention was brief, as if Tom Smart hadn't meant to say it. King didn't press the subject.

Under the sub-headline "Screening the Truth?" the *Tribune* explained that a window screen, seemingly sliced to allow the intruder access to the Smarts' home, may actually have been cut from the inside. The idea, the sources had theorized, was to make the crime look like a break-in. But the screen "appeared to be too small for someone to have climbed through." The cut screen would become a controversial issue throughout the case. Chief Dinse would later confirm that Brian David Mitchell entered the Smart house through that kitchen window.

The article ignited a media firestorm that threatened to rival the one surrounding the JonBenet Ramsey case in 1996. Shortly after the six-year-old baby beauty queen was found brutally murdered in the basement of her family's sprawling Boulder, Colorado, home on the day after Christmas, her mother, father and other family members became suspects in the eyes of the public and in the absence of another plausible perpetrator. As then, the media now scrambled to find out which of Elizabeth's family members it could be, while the public played its own guessing games.

"Between the lines, it's obviously me," Tom Smart told the *Deseret News* two days after the *Tribune* story. That was fine, he said, because he knew he wasn't involved. After Elizabeth came home, Tom talked about the polygraph again.

"Somebody was clearly trying to point the attention on me," he said, anger thickening his voice. "Yes, my polygraph did come up inconclusive. And is that all that surprising, given my mental and emotional state at that time? I hadn't slept—I was at the point where, literally, I was hearing voices." Tom Smart said he had an alibi for the night Elizabeth disappeared. The photographer had shot a Utah Starzz game, gone home and spoken briefly with his wife, Heidi. After that, he said, he took a sleeping pill and went to bed, and didn't wake up until Ed's frantic phone call.

The day the article hit the streets, David faced the media. Cool and composed, his matter-of-fact demeanor belied the anger of the Smart clan. "If the police did not investigate us, they wouldn't be doing their jobs," he said calmly. Tom would later describe the family's reaction this way: "Angry doesn't begin to describe it."

Rick Dinse also spoke to reporters, brusquely stating that police "are not eliminating anyone at this point." There was really no other statement the chief could make—anyone and everyone had to be considered a suspect until more was known. Still, around Salt Lake and the country his words would launch many interpretations.

As the *Tribune* steadfastly stood by its story, Salt Lake police brass quickly moved to do damage control, claiming the inside information did not come from anyone working closely on the investigation. Police Captain Scott Atkinson tried to quell the frenzy by telling reporters the *Tribune* account was "one of many theories." What's more, Atkinson added, Mary Katherine had been extremely forthcoming with anything she remembered about her sister's abductor. "If she had recognized the person and been able to give us a name or recognized it as being a family member, we believe she probably would have told us that."

The Smart family issued a statement challenging the newspaper report as "highly speculative" and urged the public and media to "avoid distraction" from the goal of finding Elizabeth. The statement was also circulated throughout the Federal Heights Ward. "We put no credibility in the story," Elizabeth's uncle, Dave Francom, said.

While the hunt for Bret Edmunds and the *Tribune* story held the public's attention, another behind-the-scenes skirmish was brewing. It pitted the Smarts against a man who seemed a likely ally of the family: child protection advocate Marc Klaas. Klaas became a national figure when his daughter, Polly, then 12, was abducted from her California bedroom December 4, 1993, as her mother slept in the next room. Prior to the Elizabeth Smart search, Polly Klaas's disappearance had spurred the largest manhunt in American history, with thousands, including actress Winona Ryder, joining the search for the girl. Polly was found dead 65 days after her kidnapping, and her murder, by a felon on parole, prompted Marc to become a spokesman for missing kids.

Klaas showed up in Salt Lake shortly after Elizabeth vanished. Handing out business cards adorned with a Michelangelo sketch and the phone number for his nonprofit group, Klaas Kids, Marc offered to help the Smarts with their ordeal. What he failed to mention, the family claimed, was that he was also in town working as a paid commentator for

Fox News Channel. "He came here under the guise of helping us," Tom said. "But his sole intention was to get an 'inside' story. What he did was duplicitous, sick and completely unethical."

Strong-willed and inarguably passionate about the plight of missing kids, Klaas said the family was well aware he was working for Fox. "I was never deceptive with them at all," Klaas countered angrily. "The first thing out of my mouth was not always, 'Hello, I am working for Fox.' It was, 'Hello, I am Polly Klaas's father.'"

Tom Smart and Klaas were at each other almost from the start. Klaas had asked to do an interview with Ed and Lois, and he wanted his crew to film the meeting. Tom balked. Though Ed and Lois would love to sit and hear any advice he could give, the family didn't want Fox to film the meeting. Klaas and his producer were upset, Tom said. Fox pressed the issue, and Tom finally relented. If Klaas's motive was to help the family as he had done with parents of other kidnap victims, Tom said, "I wanted to make sure he had the chance to do that." Ed and Lois agreed to meet with Klaas for fifteen minutes, and Fox could tape for the last five of those.

During that meeting, the reporting team made a request that would drive an immovable wedge between the Smarts and Klaas. The advocate was eager for Ed and Lois to allow Mary Katherine Smart, the only witness to her sister's kidnapping, to meet with renowned forensic artist Jeanne Boylan. Boylan had produced the Unabomber sketch, as well as that of Polly Klaas's abductor, parolee Richard Allen Davis, that led to his arrest. Klaas offered to fly Boylan in, at Fox's expense, to work with Elizabeth's little sister. At Klaas's suggestion, Ed Smart called Boylan and left a message on her answering machine with his phone number. But Tom was against the idea. The family was following the advice of police and the FBI and would let them determine when Mary Katherine should work with a sketch artist.

Boylan happened to call back while Ed was in the hospital, and spoke to Tom. The protective older brother thanked Boylan but said her services weren't yet needed. Boylan would later say she found what Tom said during the conversation "peculiar."

Ironically, the FBI would later call Boylan in to work with Mary Katherine, and the specialist would praise police and the Smart family for how well they helped protect the little girl's recall. "Jeanne Boylan was very helpful," Tom Smart said of the time Boylan spent with his young niece. "We never had a problem with Jeanne—she's the best at what she does. It was Klaas's tactics and motives we objected to."

Klaas admitted he wanted Ed and Lois to "override" police and take his advice. He was livid at what he believed was Tom impeding the investigation in turning Boylan away. "At that time, Mary Katherine didn't even have a clear memory of what the man looked like. But I couldn't say that at the time because I couldn't talk about the investigation. Ed and Lois weren't opposed to the idea in theory—none of us were," Tom recalled. "But we were also taking our lead from the FBI. They told us they had their best resources and were working very hard to make sure that Mary Katherine's memory of that night wasn't compromised in any way. So naturally, we're going to listen to their advice over that of a man, who, no matter how much experience he has in these situations, is asking us to go against investigators."

Early in the second week of the search, Tom was scheduled to appear on Fox's "The O'Reilly Factor." Klaas was also a scheduled guest. Tom Smart cancelled. He was nearing physical and emotional collapse and was running on only a few hours of sleep. "I didn't know if I could take it much longer," he said. His wife, Heidi, put her foot down, taking Tom to Dorotha and Charles's home, putting him to bed and giving him a sleeping pill to make sure he stayed there. "I took an Ambien and she held me while I slept for four hours," Tom said.

In his place, Tom's daughters, Amanda, 17, and Sierra, 21, agreed to do O'Reilly's show. The girls—both beautiful, willowy blonds—are engaging, friendly and well-spoken. Earlier that day on "Good Morning America," they had talked passionately about the search for Elizabeth. Tom said he and the girls were told O'Reilly wanted them on to "spread the word about helping find Elizabeth." But minutes into the show, Klaas and the hard-hitting, argumentative O'Reilly began to discuss the Jeanne Boylan controversy.

"Now, you have recommended to the Smart family certain procedures that they follow," O'Reilly said to Klaas. "Have they followed your advice?"

Klaas answered that the Smart family had been "exceptional" in pursuing his recommendations. But yes, Klaas added, he thought it was "imperative" that Ed and Lois "override the police" and allow Mary Katherine to sit with Boylan.

"There is an image burned on her retina, and that image has to be put onto paper so that we can take a look at it," Klaas told O'Reilly.

"But I understand that the uncle, Tom Smart, Amanda and Sierra's father, is against that, too," O'Reilly prompted.

"Apparently so, because . . . Tom nixed the idea," Klaas answered, adding, "Tom has been a challenging individual."

O'Reilly then turned his attention to Amanda and Sierra. "You just heard Mr. Klaas, who's an expert on this, say that your father has kind of not been on the same page as Mr. Klaas, at least. Do you have any reaction to that?"

"What do you mean by that?" the girls asked in unison, taken aback.

"What I mean," O'Reilly retorted, "is that Mr. Klaas says he's trying to set up an artist to come up there [but] your father doesn't want that to happen."

O'Reilly proceeded to grill the sisters on how involved their father was in the case and whether the family discussed details of the investigation with each other. Amanda and Sierra repeatedly insisted they were not privy to any details.

"O.K.," O'Reilly asked. "How involved is your dad in the case?"

"You know, we don't even know," said Amanda, still holding her composure. "To our knowledge, he's not. He's just another family member." The girls told O'Reilly that, while the family discussed the case in terms of how it was affecting their lives, they didn't have information about the specifics of the investigation, or how it was proceeding.

"It's not really our business," Sierra added.

"All right. But it's a little strange," O'Reilly said. "Trust me, I'm not pushing you, ladies, I know you're here because you want everybody in Utah and across the country to keep an eye out for your cousin . . . But it is a little strange that in a close family like the Smarts', that you wouldn't discuss this case with your dad, in very specific terms."

Turning back to Klaas, O'Reilly observed, "There does seem to be a bit of a problem with the ladies' father. Can you just define it for us as you see it?"

"Well," Klaas answered, "it's almost interference. We've encouraged Ed and Lois to talk to everybody at every possible opportunity. And once we think we're getting towards that direction, Tom then will come in and sort of play things around a little bit so that might not occur. And it just becomes very frustrating. Tom made sure [the meeting with Boylan] didn't happen, and I just find that extremely frustrating."

As the show ended, Amanda and Sierra threw down their earpieces and stormed away. They left in tears. The extended family members who had watched the show were stunned. Their father was incensed that O'Reilly would use his show to "accuse me through my daughters."

At the time, Sierra Smart was taking her last class before graduating from the University of Utah—"Ethics in Journalism." Shocked at what she perceived to be O'Reilly's deceit, she scrawled a note to the cable host, though it was unclear whether she sent it.

"Never have I encountered such a self-centered, heartless human being," she wrote. "I gave you the benefit of the doubt for one reason only—and that was to help get our message out to bring Elizabeth home . . . You deceitfully arranged for my sister and I to appear on your show—but for the most evil reason—I never even knew was possible . . . You mendaciously tried to create a 'sensational' story out of information made up and meticulously arranged to presume my father was trying to hinder the investigation. Worse, you try to put his daughters up against him. Did you not think we are dealing with enough?"

The next day, as police announced they wanted to talk to Bret Edmunds, the entire Smart family kept a low profile. That night on "The O'Reilly

Factor," with few new developments to discuss, Klaas and O'Reilly again rehashed Klaas's clash with Tom Smart over Jeanne Boylan. Klaas also described the run-in he'd had with Tom over the Fox interview with Ed and Lois.

"The day after Ed's collapse," Klaas told O'Reilly, "we were having increasing difficulty getting any kind of access with the family. And then all of a sudden it turned out they were going to be giving an interview to somebody else. I called and asked, 'Why is this occurring? Why isn't it a good time for me to talk to him?' And it just fell apart from there." Tom Smart, Klaas said, accused him of "hostility" and hung up on him.

"Isn't this very, very strange?" O'Reilly said. "We've got an uncle who doesn't want you on the scene, Mr. Klaas."

Again the next night, Klaas was a guest on O'Reilly, and this time their conversation centered on the *Tribune* report, and the suggestions that the family could be involved. The Boylan issue was also a topic, as it had been all week.

"This girl's been missing for a week. There's a good chance she's dead. I mean, what is this guy doing?" O'Reilly asked. "See, I have a problem with this story, Mr. Klaas. . . . It's like the Ramsey case, in the sense that there's crazy stuff coming out of the family. Am I wrong?"

Klaas agreed with his host, telling him that the last time he and Boylan had a "door slammed in our face" was by the family of Susan Smith. On

October 24, 1994, Smith, a young mother from Union, South Carolina, tearfully faced the nation and claimed her small sons, Michael, 3, and Alex, 14 months old, had been abducted by an African-American "carjacker." The thief, she said, stole her car and drove off with the two boys still strapped in their carseats in the back. But nine days after making that claim, Smith confessed to having driven the boys into the John D. Long Lake, purposely drowning them in hope of mending a failed romance.

Klaas told O'Reilly that he didn't want to point fingers at Ed or Lois, but he was confused that Tom, not Elizabeth's parents, was taking the lead for the family in the investigation. Ed and Lois, he suggested, "are so afraid of what's going on here and so desperate to get their child back, I think they're listening to bad advice."

"Does it make any sense for a father not to call the shots?" O'Reilly asked. "You called your own shots, Mr. Klaas, why would Edward Smart not call his?"

"Well," said Klaas, "as I understand it, in the Mormon religion there is a leader of the family [who] calls the shots and everybody else follows suit. That certainly wouldn't have worked in my case, though."

"Is that leader Tom Smart?" O'Reilly asked.

"Apparently it is, sir, yes," Klaas answered.

By the time that show ended, any good will left between Klaas and the Smarts had evaporated. The outspoken Tom was certainly a strong figure in the Smart family, but he was not a practicing Mormon. Before Elizabeth returned home, Tom hadn't been to church for nearly a decade.

"I believe in a higher power, I believe in miracles—but I'm a skeptic, too," Tom said. "I believe in humanism—people should be good to one another. I have a lot of compassion for Marc Klaas. I truly do. He lost his little girl to a monster, and that is a pain nobody should have to endure. But as a journalist, he has to be responsible and I don't think that happened. Who knows how much of what was said on those shows hurt the investigation—not to mention the hurt it caused this family."

Today, the mere mention of the Smart case sends Marc Klaas through the roof.

"The bottom line is, they won. They won the fucking kidnapping sweepstakes and it's still not good enough for them," Klaas stormed. "I never got my daughter back; they did. And I still believe Ed Smart should have been calling the shots all along, not Tom. Ed is the girl's father. If they had listened to me in the first place, and brought in the sketch artist when I had suggested, they might not have wasted so many months trying to find Elizabeth."

After her granddaughter was safely home, Dorotha Smart, the elegant, soft-spoken Smart matriarch, would reveal the pain of those early, trying days of the search. "June 5, 2002, stood by itself as my darkest hour," Dorotha said, her voice quivering with emotion. "But the compounded grief of seeing my children attacked was almost unbearable. When I saw my most important work, my family, being dashed, I wondered if I could go on."

From the start, police "leaks" and misinformation polarized the family and investigators. "It started the very first day," Tom Smart admitted. "When they said Ed called family and neighbors before he called 911. When they said family and friends were at Ed's house before police and ruined the crime scene. When they said the screen was cut from the inside. The investigation started with those lies thrown on the family."

Tom Smart would later say that it was important to stay focused on finding Elizabeth, but acknowledged it was difficult at times. For instance, the family's initial instincts after the glare of media attention swung toward the Smarts in connection with the abduction was retaliation, the *Tribune* would later report. During a family meeting, while the livid brothers discussed lashing back, Chris Thomas, the family spokesman, strode over to a blackboard and picked up the chalk. He scrawled Elizabeth's name, and circled it for emphasis. "We need to find Elizabeth," he told them, quelling, for a time, the brewing storm.

Richard Albert Ricci had "a heart of gold," his wife Angela would say. But he was also a career felon with a 30-year rap sheet and a shaky alibi for the night Elizabeth Smart was taken.

Within hours after Elizabeth disappeared, police had begun checking the backgrounds and whereabouts of various handymen who had worked at the Smarts' house. Ed had been asked if there'd been any unusual activity at the house, and he had volunteered that he'd hired several men at various times to do renovation work. Police were also questioning realtors who might have unwittingly shown the house to the kidnapper, thinking he was a potential buyer.

Police first questioned Ricci, a stocky, balding man with a ring of black hair, on June 6. He'd worked for the Smarts in the spring of 2001, painting and doing yard work, and the Smart kids knew him well enough to call him by his first name. He was a bit undependable sometimes, but Ed thought him "a very nice guy." Still, something about Ricci's account of his time the night Elizabeth disappeared didn't ring true to investigators. A few days later, they called him in again. They were searching publicly for Edmunds, but Ricci seemed interesting, too. The more police talked to him, Dinse said, the "more suspicious" he became.

For the next several weeks, investigators would comb through Ricci's life. His home would be searched, and his family, neighbors and associates would be called in front of a grand jury. Soon, a pile of circumstantial evidence began to build against the ex-con.

Ricci had a history of heroin use, and also battled prescription drug and alcohol addiction. He helped fund his habits by stealing from the homes where he worked, or from those in the same neighborhoods. He would stealthily target children's rooms, perhaps thinking parents would chalk the missing items up to having been lost.

Ricci was 48, a lifetime criminal with a string of convictions ranging from robbery to attempted murder. Ricci was locked up for the first time at 19, and through the years would become a four-time parole violator. At one parole hearing, he was blasted for his repeated "antisocial criminal behavior." But eventually, the parole board always let him back out on the street.

In 1983, Ricci set out to rob a local Salt Lake pharmacy, and the plan would lead him to commit his most serious crime. Salt Lake police officer Mike Hill spotted Ricci running from the drugstore, a sawed-off shotgun bouncing at his side. Hill chased him through an alley and then spotted him in bushes. Their eyes locked, and Hill ordered Ricci to put down the gun. Ricci turned toward Hill, who fired off two rounds. The officer missed his target and dashed behind a parked car. On his way down, a shot from Ricci's gun tore through his hand, shoulder and scalp. Had Hill been standing, he later said, he would have been hit in the face. Ricci wound up back in jail.

Twice in his criminal career, Ricci escaped custody. In 1978, he left Utah State Prison for an Easter home visit, and didn't bother coming back. During another unauthorized leave in 1983, Ricci robbed the drugstore and wound up shooting Hill.

Out of prison, Ricci began working as a handyman. He worked often in Federal Heights, and Ed Smart hired him in the spring of 2001, after a neighbor recommended him. Ricci worked cheap and did good work. But Ed fired him after becoming suspicious that Ricci was stealing from him. He later hired him back, and the two struck a deal that Ed would give Ricci his 1990 white Jeep Cherokee in return for labor around the house. Ricci agreed, and dutifully filled his end of the bargain. The last time Smart saw Ricci was that fall, when Ricci came by to pick up the title to the Jeep.

Ricci went to work at a local nursery owned by Lee Mitchell. The two had met 12 years earlier, while Ricci was in prison for shooting Hill and for robbing a fast-food restaurant. Mitchell had taught a "Green Thumb" class for inmates, and Ricci was an attentive student. Ricci got a botany degree in prison. When he got out of jail, Mitchell offered him work. Ricci was in his element. He was smart, customers and co-workers liked him, and he almost never missed a day of work. Ricci had worked June 4, and had June 5 off, Mitchell said. He showed up for work, on time, at 10:30 a.m. on June 6, and stayed until his shift ended that evening.

Early on the day Elizabeth vanished, Ricci was digging at the side of his mobile home in the Salt Lake suburb of Kearns when neighbor Andy Thurber stuck his head out the door of his own trailer.

"What the hell are you doing?" the neighbor asked, irritated. It was 8:30 in the morning. Covering a hole, Ricci answered. The cats kept getting up under the house, Ricci said, and he wanted to fix the hole to keep them out. By then, both men had heard about the Smart kidnapping and began talking. Ricci mentioned that he'd once worked for Ed Smart. His kids were very nice, and Elizabeth was a pretty girl. The neighbor didn't think much of the comment at the time; he knew people often commented on appearance when they spoke about someone. Ricci drank a beer as he and the other man spoke, and seemed his usual outgoing, talkative self. But something else Ricci said struck the neighbor. Ricci figured he'd be "implicated" by police, simply because he'd worked at the house. Later that day, the two men went to a local pawn shop together. By then, Thurber thought his friend seemed a bit distracted, he told a grand jury.

Ricci's wife, Angela, had been introduced to her new husband by her brother, and it was love at first sight. He was funny, kind and considerate, she thought. In 2001, Angela was involved in a serious car accident, and Richard had refused to leave her side as he nursed her back to health. The pair married on Valentine's Day, 2002, in Mesquite, Nevada.

Their favorite song was "One More Day Together" by Diamond Rio. They lived in a mobile home park right next door to Angela's parents and saw them often. Ricci seemed determined to turn his life around. It broke Angela's heart that nobody seemed to believe her husband was not involved in the kidnapping. He was being railroaded, she would say, based solely on his past record. Angela also

worried about Elizabeth, and admitted she was
"heartbroken" that the attention was focused on
Richard, when police could have been looking for
someone else.

"There's no way he would do this," she said.
Ricci's own nine-year-old son was killed by a drunk
driver in 1985. He might do a lot of things, said
Angela, but kidnapping wouldn't be on the list.
Ricci had been a good stepfather to her 11-year-old
son, Travis. In fact, the night of June 4, the three of
them had sat with Mormon missionaries, cooking
dinner and discussing religion as they prepared the
boy for his First Communion in the LDS church.
The missionaries left around 8 p.m., and the family
spent the rest of the night at home. Angela Ricci
said she'd gone to bed around 1:30 a.m. Though
she had been known to take muscle relaxers for
pain, she claimed she hadn't taken them that night.
Her husband, Angela insisted, had been home all
night.

Other women in Ricci's life quickly rose to defend him. Robin White, his ex-wife, refused to believe Ricci was involved. Though he had a criminal
past, Robin couldn't see her former husband as a
kidnapper. Ricci would never hurt a child; of that,
Robin was certain.

In the days after the kidnapping, the FBI twice
searched Richard and Angela's home. The couple
never demanded a search warrant, and didn't call a
lawyer during the early days of the probe. It was a
move they would later regret, Angela said. The day
after Elizabeth went missing, investigators dug up

a tomato garden in Ricci's yard. In his house, they found jewelry, perfume bottles and a wine glass that had been filled with seashells. Ed Smart was shocked to see they'd come from his home.

The FBI hauled bags of possible evidence from the trailer. Angela's parents, Roxie and David Morse, also allowed agents to search their home. The search would turn up a cap similar to that described by Mary Katherine, and a machete. Both items belonged to Morse, and Ricci hadn't, to his father-in-law's knowledge, used either item. Nevertheless, they were shipped with everything else to the state crime lab, where a team of criminologists, sometimes working overtime, sifted through evidence for clues.

On June 14, Ricci was arrested on a parole violation related to the Hill shooting. Angela and Richard were sitting on their front swing when police came to get him. Richard got up, and one of the six officers handcuffed him. Those moments on the swing would be the last intimate time Angela would share with her husband; because he'd been handcuffed, she couldn't even kiss or hug him goodbye.

An anguished Ed appealed to him through the media: "Richard, please let her go if you've got her."

On what had become nearly nightly television appearances, members of the Smart family seemed hopeful about what the Ricci arrest might turn up, but hedged their enthusiasm. "He's certainly a suspicious character," Ed's sister Cynthia told Larry

King on his talk show. But, she added that the family didn't have access to all of the evidence to make a fair judgment about Ricci. If the police did have stronger evidence, she added, "they would be stronger [in charging Ricci] than they have been already."

Court records show Ricci admitted to stealing from the Smarts and their neighbors. Ricci's lawyer said the theft charges came as a result of things Ricci told police when he was trying to cooperate with the kidnapping investigation. The theft charges, the lawyer said, were the result of police trying to pressure Ricci. Still, evidence against Ricci seemed to be mounting. Many of the investigators were convinced but were still proceeding cautiously. "We don't want to make this another Richard Jewell situation," the chief would tell the *Salt Lake Tribune*, referring to the man who, during the 1996 Atlanta Olympics, was for weeks wrongly targeted as the man who bombed Centennial Park.

Several people were questioned by police and called in front of the grand jury, including Andy Thurber and Angela Ricci. But the person who would wind up dealing the most serious blow to Ricci was his auto mechanic, Neth Moul.

Ricci was usually quite friendly with even casual acquaintances, so when he showed up on June 8 at Neth's Auto Repair in a foul mood, owner Moul was perplexed. Ricci's battered Jeep was covered with mud, the floors were strewn with newspapers, as if to protect them from getting dirty. Ricci barely spoke as he filled two bags with items from his car and removed two seat covers from the back. He grabbed a post-hole digger and, barely saying goodbye, took off across the street to where a friend was waiting to drive him away. According to Moul, there were 750 to 1,000 new miles on the odometer. Moul told investigators Ricci had left with the Jeep May 30, sneaking it off the lot without anyone noticing. Earlier that day, Moul said, a woman claiming to be Ricci's wife had called about the Jeep.

After speaking with Moul, police had hoped to examine the outside of the muddy vehicle, but when they came to inspect it, Moul had washed it clean, thinking he was being helpful. Elizabeth had ridden in the Jeep when her dad owned it, so any evidence found inside wouldn't incriminate Ricci. Police questioned Ricci about the added miles, and he wasn't forthcoming with answers.

Ricci denied he'd taken the car, but Moul was equally adamant that he had. Greenhouse owner Lee Mitchell said his star employee was at work most of the days during that May 30 to June 8 time period. Angela insisted that their Jeep never had seat covers, and that there was another white Jeep parked at Moul's place. Plus, someone had stolen a set of keys to the car, she said. Maybe Moul had confused her husband with someone else. Whatever the case, Angela insisted, she had never called the garage, and Richard hadn't taken that Jeep.

On July 11, district attorney David Yocom filed charges against Ricci. He was charged with felony theft for taking the money, jewelry and other items from the Smarts' home. In addition, Yocom's office charged Ricci with an April 2001 break-in at the home of Suann Adams, the friend and neighbor who was at the Smarts' the night Elizabeth disappeared. Ricci had broken into her home in the dead of night and had awakened a house-guest as he rummaged through a darkened bedroom. The guest, thinking Ricci was a member of the family, suggested he turn on the light. Caught off guard, Ricci coughed in response. The guest rolled over and went back to sleep. The next morning, Suann came downstairs to find a sliding door open and jewelry and about $300 missing.

His longtime record and apparent inability to stay on the straight and narrow had finally caught up with Ricci. Yocom also charged him with "habitual criminal" charges, which meant he could be jailed for life if convicted.

Dinse was careful to say the charges were not connected to Elizabeth's abduction. But Ricci's actions did show that he was at least capable of sneaking quietly into a house, taking what he wanted, and then slipping away again, undetected. "It shows a pattern of conduct," Dinse said. He also said police were "spending more time on him than we are on any one witness in the case."

Over and over police grilled him, but whatever Ricci told them, it wasn't convincing enough. Early on in the Ricci questioning, Ed had implied he didn't think his former worker was a kidnapper. But the unexplained mileage and the thefts had made him suspicious.

Elizabeth Smart "played the harp like an angel." At fourteen, she was already a sought-after player at concerts around Salt Lake City.
Joy Gough/ZUMA Press

Seven months before kidnapping Ed Smart's daughter, Brian David Mitchell spent five hours hammering shingles with him on the roof of the family's $1.19 million home. Mitchell would later hide Elizabeth in the hills behind the house.

Brigitte Stelzer

Salt Lake Police Chief Rick Dinse led the investigation and would later be criticized for mishandling it. *AP/Wide World Photos*

At South High School, Wanda Barzee was a quiet, deeply religious girl whose passion was music.

Brigitte Stelzer, courtesy Dora Corbett

Wanda married Mitchell in 1985. She thought she'd finally found a man who could give her the stable, loving home she desperately craved.

Brigitte Stelzer, courtesy Dora Corbett

Wanda sewed the robes she and Brian wore in the sewing room at the home of her mother, Dora Corbett. Dora said Wanda made the dress she wore when she wed Mitchell. *Brigitte Stelzer*

Brian David Mitchell's father, Shirl, says his son was always troubled but that "what he's done is beyond the pale."

Brigitte Stelzer

Richard Albert Ricci was for nine months considered the prime suspect in Elizabeth's kidnapping. His death in prison in August 2002 jolted the investigators.

AP/Wide World Photos

Elizabeth was forced to veil her face and head in her new life as "Augustine." Mitchell often hid her in plain sight, as he did at this Salt Lake City party.

Anne Elizabeth Maurer/ZUMA Press

Elizabeth and her captors stayed for several days in October at the Salt Lake apartment of Daniel Trotta, a cashier at Wild Oats, where Mitchell often shopped. Trotta said Elizabeth slept in her veil and wasn't allowed to speak to him.

Brigitte Stelzer

After 911 callers thought they'd seen "Emmanuel" on a street in Sandy, Utah, local police officers (*from left to right*) Victor Quezada, Bill O'Neal, Karen Jones, and Troy Rasmussen arrested Mitchell and Barzee.

AP/Wide World Photos

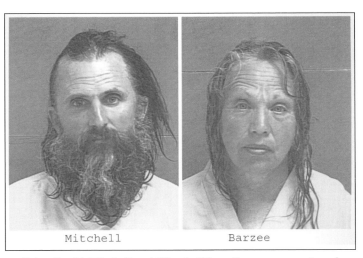

Mitchell   Barzee

Brian David Mitchell and Wanda Eileen Barzee were stripped of their robes by the Salt Lake County sheriff's department after their arrest March 12, 2003.

AP/Wide World Photos, courtesy Salt Lake County Sheriff's Department

Salt Lake County District Attorney David Yocom brought aggravated kidnapping, sexual assault, and burglary charges against Mitchell and Barzee. *AP/Wide World Photos*

Elizabeth's aunt, Angela Dumke, and uncle, David Smart, emotionally greeted reporters after a church service celebrating her return. *Brigitte Stelzer*

A jubilant Ed and Lois Smart thanked their community, and the world, at Elizabeth's homecoming party in Salt Lake's Liberty Park, organized by Mayor Rocky Anderson. *Brigitte Stelzer*

Within hours of Elizabeth's recovery, balloons covered her neighborhood. Her uncles, David and Tom, celebrated her homecoming with Dorotha and Charles Smart outside the Federal Heights Ward church.

Brigitte Stelzer

Ten-year-old Mary Katherine Smart—the only eyewitness in the case—takes a break outside the Smarts' Kristianna Circle home in the days after Elizabeth's return.

Brigitte Stelzer

These are some of the country's most frustrating ongoing missing children's cases. If you have information, please contact your local police department.

Kiplyn Davis
Never returned home from Spanish Fork, UT, high school
Date missing: 5-2-95
Date of birth: 7-1-79
Age at abduction: 16 (photo age-enhanced)
Description: Naturally curly red hair, blue eyes, small birthmark on back of neck

Molly Ann Bish
Disappeared from lifeguarding post in Warren, MA
Date missing: 6-27-00
Date of birth: 8-2-83
Age at abduction: 17 (photo age-enhanced)
Description: Blond hair, blue eyes

Erika Baker
Never came home from walking dog in her Kettering, OH, neighborhood
Date missing: 2-7-99
Date of birth: 6-22-89
Age at abduction: 9 (photo age-enhanced)
Description: Hazel eyes, front teeth are crooked

Jacob Wetterling
Taken at gunpoint walking home from a St. Joseph, MN, convenience store
Date missing: 10-22-89
Date of birth: 2-17-78
Age at abduction: 11 (photo age-enhanced)
Description: Light brown hair, slight build, mole on his left cheek, mole on neck

Ed recalled that, during the time Ricci had worked for him and items started disappearing from the house, he'd confronted the handyman about the missing money and jewelry. "He looked me in the eye and said he didn't do it," Ed said. Now, he knew Ricci had lied. "It can't help but make me feel Richard is involved in the kidnapping," Ed would say.

The day Ricci was charged, Ed snapped. In an uncharacteristic blaze of fury, he demanded Ricci "fully and truthfully" answer police. "This family has been through hell and we want this to end," Ed said in an angry entreaty. "Please come forward. We need Elizabeth back home."

Like police, Ed wanted Ricci to give a plausible explanation for those miles Moul said he'd put on the Jeep from May 30 to June 8. David K. Smith, Ricci's lawyer, said he'd questioned Ricci about the miles, and that his client had given him a plausible answer. But he refused to disclose any details. Chief Dinse said Ricci had given police a statement about the mileage.

After Ed's outburst, family spokesman Chris Thomas said the family desperately wanted Ricci to tell the truth about the Jeep, because time was being wasted if Ricci wasn't involved in the kidnapping. "If he's not guilty, we need to get beyond that," Thomas said. "He is, right now, a roadblock."

Hoping to clear his name, Ricci issued an impassioned statement, delivered to the media by his lawyer.

"First, I want to say I have no knowledge of

Elizabeth Smart's abduction, disappearance or whereabouts. I want to say to the Smart family from my family, Angela, my stepson and myself, that we pray for her safe return," Ricci wrote. "I too lost a nine-year-old son in an accident in 1985 and I know what Ed and Lois are going through."

Ricci noted that he'd been fully cooperative with the FBI, the police and his probation and parole board. He endured 26 arduous hours of questioning and had taken multiple lie detector tests. "I think the reason I'm involved is because of my past," Ricci suggested. But, he said, "I would not nor could not hurt a child in any way." The ex-con insisted he was home with his wife the night Elizabeth disappeared, and woke to hear on the news that Elizabeth had been kidnapped. "I was in shock," he said.

But the circumstantial evidence was damning. He had a devoted wife as an alibi, mysterious miles on a car, he knew the Smarts, and he had an awful track record with the law. One thing he wasn't, at least to anyone's knowledge, was a pedophile—a trait many involved in the case thought could have been a motive. Then again, the chance that Elizabeth had interrupted a robbery attempt, or was taken for ransom, hadn't been ruled out. And the lack of any forensic evidence like fibers, hair, blood or fingerprints linking Ricci to Elizabeth had investigators stymied.

On July 17, just days after the theft charges were leveled, Ricci was indicted for armed robbery. He and two former prison buddies were accused of holding up a Sandy, Utah, bank for $1,713. The two other men had worked odd jobs in the Smarts' neighborhood with Ricci. One of the men would later plead guilty to the crime, and implicated Ricci, as well. As it turned out, Ricci would never have to answer to his alleged involvement in the holdup.

In prison, Ricci was under 23-hour lockdown, with no television or newspapers. His lawyer was the only one allowed to visit. During their meetings, Smith said, Ricci seemed upbeat and prayed that police would eventually believe him when he said he knew nothing about Elizabeth's kidnapping.

For the rest of the summer, Ricci would be questioned extensively, all the while vigorously maintaining his innocence. Ed, Lois and other members of the Smart family were swayed enough by the circumstantial evidence to think Ricci might at least know something about Elizabeth's kidnapping. Mary Katherine apparently was not.

"They don't think it's Richard, do they, Dad?" the little girl asked her father. At that point, she hadn't remembered who it was, said her uncle Tom, "but she never thought it was Ricci."

EIGHT

The daily press conference on Saturday, June 15, brought a new piece of information from police—the cops displayed a replica of the cap worn by the kidnapper. It was a light, golf-style cap, not a baseball cap. It was hardly the "Aha!" that the reporters camped outside the Federal Heights meeting house had been hoping for, amid a growing frustration among the press about the slow trickle of information. It was apparently a new scrap gleaned from the memory of Mary Katherine, although it wasn't clear why it had taken so long to come out.

The daily briefings had become a jousting match of sorts between the police and the reporters, who tried to press for more detail on whatever revelation appeared in print or on TV about the kidnapping. A day earlier, the *Tribune* reported that Mary Katherine didn't get a good look at the kidnapper's face in the darkened bedroom. A few days later, Ed Smart was quoted in a *Deseret News* story talking about the garage door, left open for two hours the night before the kidnapping. The suggestion was that the intruder could have snuck into the house and hidden there unseen.

It was nearly two weeks after the kidnapping when, amid the flurry of reports about what may have happened that night, police decided to clarify the few pieces of information that had already been discussed publicly.

The police had indicated for those two weeks that Mary Katherine was threatened by the kidnapper; if she screamed or made any move, he'd hurt her. The initial police report, compiled by dispatchers based on early accounts that night, said that the youngest Smart child had been threatened. The implication was that she'd had some interaction with the kidnapper. But it turned out not to be true.

On June 18, Police Captain Scott Atkinson explained that, in fact, Mary Katherine had pretended to sleep while her sister was stolen from the bedroom and that the kidnapper probably didn't realize she had seen him. The man "spoke nicely and dressed nicely," Atkinson said. And he had dark tufts of hair on his arms and on the backs of his hands, and wore a light Polo shirt. Atkinson said the information in that initial police report was based on information from the family and that it became clearer after the latest interviews with Elizabeth's sister.

The press was furious, and the muddle only heightened a perception among some of the reporters that the probe was being handled the wrong way. Police Chief Rick Dinse hadn't been at the briefings in days. He was out of town when Atkinson stepped to the microphones to share the new information, and the chief decided to try to take the heat off the department himself. He faced a pack of reporters who were wary of his answers.

"Yes, some information went out. It was not accurate at the time. We thought it was," Dinse said. "We know now that it isn't."

Besides, the chief said, there wasn't a major reason to clarify it until then, and he had to be sure that it wouldn't hurt the probe. The information was coming out gradually, he indicated, through the four interviews the investigators had had with Mary Katherine. But even the number of interviews seemed to change with each new telling, and Dinse's comments met instant skepticism.

"We understand withholding information about a crime scene, but this is information that, had it been released earlier, could have helped us all look for this guy," one reporter said. "How do you defend not releasing that?"

Dinse did not explain why, beyond Mary Katherine's progressive recall, the information had been kept under wraps. He also refused to answer any questions about exactly how much Mary Katherine had seen of the man's face, or whether his voice struck a familiar chord. And reporters were baffled by the idea that she had seen enough of the man to know the brand of his shirt, but apparently not details, such as the hollows of his eyes or the slant of his cheekbones. Everything seemed to be clouded under a layered veil of mystery, and it appeared to be thickening.

*   *   *

Right after the police gave the new information about what Mary Katherine had seen, Dinse put a halt to the daily news conferences. There would be only briefings if there was anything new to report, he said. Two days later, there was big news.

The manhunt for Bret Edmunds had ended, a little over a week after it had begun. The police were chasing sightings that put him as far away as Texas, but he turned up on June 21, a Friday, at a hospital in West Virginia. He had checked himself into the hospital in Martinsburg under a fake name. He was very sick, with an apparent drug overdose that had damaged his liver. Even though he had used an alias, he gave his mom's phone number on an "in case of emergency, contact card," and a hospital staffer reached out to his family in Utah.

One of the relatives called the sheriff's office in Sanpete County in Utah, and the telephone chain was put into place. The sheriff's office called the hospital and got a description of the patient, and deputies were sure it was Edmunds. Federal marshals were sent to the hospital, where they found his green Saturn in the parking lot. They went into the hospital and put him in custody as he lay in the intensive care unit.

Investigators from Salt Lake were quickly flown to Martinsburg to question Edmunds, although he was barely alert that Friday, drifting in and out of consciousness. In the meantime, they towed the Saturn away from the hospital and got a warrant to search it.

Before news of Edmunds's arrest broke that day, Ed Smart pleaded with his daughter's abductor during one of his daily press briefings to bring her home.

"I would do anything to have her back in my arms," he choked. "And please realize how much she's missed. She's missed tremendously."

Later, Ed called Edmunds's arrest encouraging, but the family said the break they wanted was Elizabeth's safe return. At the Smart home, the family was also bracing against another unpleasant report in the media.

The day before police found Edmunds, authorities returned the Smarts' computers after sifting through the hard-drives. The next day, the *National Enquirer* carried a lurid story related to findings on the computers. It was their July 2 issue, and the story, under the headline "Utah Cops: Secret Diary Exposes Family Sex Ring," cited investigative sources, and said that Ed, Tom and David were involved in homosexual activity that their wives knew about.

At the time, the family and the police refused to comment on the story. Ed's siblings said on TV shows that they hadn't even read it. None of the mainstream media picked up details of the stories. A few news outlets alluded to it, but none wanted to embarrass the Smarts, or make their ordeal any harder. The backlash against the *Enquirer* in Salt Lake was sharp. Stores pulled the supermarket tabloid from its stands, or turned the editions around so that the glaring cover couldn't be seen.

Five weeks after Elizabeth Smart was found alive, the *Enquirer* issued a strong statement that retracted information in the July 2 story, acknowledging that it was false, and the tabloid reached a private settlement with the Smarts.

"This information was provided to the *Enquirer* by various unidentified law enforcement and local media sources," read a joint statement from the Smarts and the *Enquirer.* "Although at the time it was legally defensible for the *Enquirer* to publish the information as the *Enquirer* had no reason to doubt the accuracy or truthfulness of the information provided, the *Enquirer* has since learned the information provided was inaccurate and false. The *Enquirer* regrets any embarrassment or harm the article may have caused Ed, Tom and David Smart or their families."

Two days after Elizabeth came home, Tom Smart fumed about the story. He called it "sick," and said he couldn't understand what the implication was supposed to be, other than making the Smart family look sinister. No one ever searched his computer, Tom said, despite what the *Enquirer* claimed.

"About the only thing that was true was that Elizabeth was kidnapped and some computers had been searched," he fumed.

The ugly article sidetracked the attention from finding Elizabeth, he said, and it served only to fuel the family's anger over details about the police investigation that had already trickled out in the two weeks since Elizabeth disappeared.

By Saturday, the day after Edmunds was found, he was alert and able to answer questions put to him by investigators as he lay in his hospital bed. With each hour, it seemed clearer that he knew nothing about the missing girl. For starters, he gave investigators permission to search his Saturn, which gave authorities the sense that he wasn't trying to hide something. Edmunds was later cleared as a suspect. But he was charged later that year for fleeing from investigators at Liberty Park after Elizabeth's vigil, to which he pleaded guilty, but that was the extent of his involvement in the abduction. Within 48 hours of his arrival at the hospital, Edmunds was no longer Salt Lake's most-wanted man. Investigators were already moving Richard Ricci to the top of their list.

On Monday, June 24, Dinse made clear that police were zeroing in on Ricci. That day, Lois Smart went in front of the cameras and spoke out to her daughter as if Elizabeth were right in front of her. She held up a necklace Elizabeth had given her on her birthday. And she reminded her daughter of a time when she was just Mary Katherine's age, riding horseback during a family outing. She got off the horse, but she lost her grip on its reins, and it trotted away, leaving Elizabeth by herself.

"Remember what you did, Elizabeth? You knelt down and prayed," Lois cried. "You are a strong, strong girl."

With few new leads popping up, some of the officials working on the case from agencies outside the FBI and the Salt Lake police were sprung from duty on the investigation. Toward the end of June, Salt Lake City and Salt Lake County had poured a tremendous amount of their resources into trying to find Elizabeth. The tab for Utah law-enforcement agencies that worked on the search had climbed higher than $85,000. About half of that money was spent by the Salt Lake PD. Most of the rest was overtime at the sheriff's office. Salt Lake County Mayor Nancy Workman was authorized to let county employees have up to eight paid hours of work to devote to volunteering in the search effort.

Reporters covering the abduction were growing frustrated with the lack of new information and couldn't understand why certain basics—such as the transcript of Ed's 911 call after he learned Elizabeth was gone, exactly where Mary Katherine saw the abductor in the house and whether she recognized his voice—weren't being released. Dinse acknowledged that police were keeping many details under wraps, but it was to protect the probe, he said. "We're not telling you a lot of things we're doing," he added.

The official task force on the case was starting to shrink.

The volunteer effort pressed on. Ted Wilson, the former Salt Lake City mayor and friend of the Smarts, was coordinating the search effort out of the Federal Heights Ward meeting house. He had set up contacts in all 29 counties around Utah, and he was asking others to join in. David Smart, who owned a software business, had set up a website, www.elizabethsmart.com, with information about who Elizabeth was. The site was updated with new pictures of the missing girl, information for volunteers, and numbers for contacting police.

David had also amassed every scrap of information about the case that he could find and pored through it in his home. He created a computer program that would cross-reference data collected from tipsters with information that had been culled from the search areas during the manhunt.

Only one ransom request had come in by then, police said. It was an email sent to "America's Most Wanted," demanding $50,000. But it called for the money to be dropped off at the "Morman" temple. Police believed it was a hoax, and they didn't take it seriously.

A few days before police went public with Ricci, there was a subtle shift in the investigation internally. Chief Dinse brought Lieutenant Cory Lyman before reporters at one of the briefings. Lyman was to be the head of the task force probing the case.

Dinse didn't say it, but it turned out that Lyman was taking over for Sergeant Don Bell. Lyman, a mustachioed cop with a whiskey voice who'd lost his son in an accident four years earlier, was a twenty-year veteran of the Salt Lake police force, although, like many in the department, he had never handled a case of such magnitude. Bell was still involved in trying to find Elizabeth. But he wasn't taking the lead anymore. Bell would later say he had been pushed out.

NINE

At the beginning of July, the summer heat was becoming oppressive, but people still turned out to put on an orange search vest and look for Elizabeth. Some of the Smarts' neighbors were asked by Salt Lake cops to come to the stationhouse for fingerprinting, possibly to figure out exactly who had been in the house on Kristianna Circle right after Elizabeth was taken, and to identify prints found around the crime scene.

There were also new incentives offered for anyone to come forward. Reporters sweltered at their makeshift camps as Mayor Rocky Anderson stood with the Smarts the day before July 4, to offer a new $25,000 reward for information that would help locate Elizabeth.

Ed Smart made clear that he didn't think his little girl was gone. "We hope this will bring forward people that might not otherwise step forward," he said. "I don't believe in any way, shape or form that she is dead. I still believe she's alive."

In the *Salt Lake Tribune* that day, Assistant Salt Lake County District Attorney Kent Morgan was quoted saying there was "no forensic evidence" yet to link Ricci to the crime, but that investigators were pressing ahead. It was a revealing moment in an investigation that had been marked by a high degree of secrecy. Morgan was telling the truth, but he infuriated Mayor Anderson when he spoke out about the case.

That evening, Ed and his sister Angela appeared on "Larry King Live" on CNN, the latest in a string of interviews they'd done on the show in the weeks after Elizabeth disappeared. King, whose wife is a Mormon from Utah, had steadily kept the spotlight on the case, using panels of experts to dissect information when there was nothing new to report on the search. King wasn't there that night, but his guest host, Nancy Grace, greeted Ed and Angela warmly. The brother and sister asked everyone to pay close attention to their surroundings as they headed off for weekends at their cabins or at the beach for the Independence Day holiday.

Grace asked Ed about a reference that Lois had made the day before to Betsy Ross, the woman who, according to legend, sewed the first American flag. What was the meaning? Nancy asked.

"Basically, the meaning was that Betsy Ross endured hardships, and we know that Elizabeth is out there and she is enduring—I can't even imagine what kind of hardships she is enduring, but we are just asking her to remember how Betsy Ross just stayed true to what she believed, and to tell Elizabeth to stay true," Ed said. "Keep the faith. Know that everyone is out there looking. I have been overwhelmed by the love, the support from the community, from the nation, from the world. We have just—every day we receive letters from people."

In the shadows of the investigation into Elizabeth was a growing unease between Mayor Ross "Rocky" Anderson and the Salt Lake police department. Anderson was elected in 1999, and was facing a re-election campaign in the months leading up to Elizabeth Smart's return. A former defense lawyer with a failed run for Congress under his belt, Anderson won his office after a heated election with eleven candidates. With a shock of silver hair covering his forehead, Anderson was chided by some competitors during the campaign for having no experience managing budgets and for being soft on criminals. But Anderson, who centered his campaign around education and boosting after-school programs, won in a romp. Outspoken and opinionated, Anderson, a former Mormon, tried hard to strike a balance between Salt Lake's Mormon and non-Mormon residents. Anderson was close with the Smarts during the investigation, Elizabeth's uncle would later say. In a memo to Chief Dinse dated July 4 and made public after the abduction was solved, Anderson took the police to task over sensitive information that was making its way into news accounts.

"I have significant concerns about the numerous apparent leaks of information . . . by the Salt Lake City Police Department (SLCPD) during the course of the investigation in the Elizabeth Smart case," Anderson wrote. He singled out two reports: the *Enquirer* story that was yanked off shelves around Salt Lake, and the *Tribune* article quoting Kent Morgan.

"In this case, it appears that unauthorized disclosures of information have either (1) compromised the investigation, as in the case of Mr. Morgan's disclosure to a reporter that there is no forensic evidence relating to Mr. Ricci; or (2) inflicted tremendous damage on members of the Smart family, who are already undergoing the most tragic situation any family could experience.

"When a crime victim, or anyone else for that matter, provides information or property to the police during the course of an investigation, they do so with reasonable expectation that such information (or information garnered from the property, such as computer downloads) will not be the subject of reckless gossip or salacious 'news' articles generated by police officers. That information should be held in the strictest of confidence," Anderson continued. "It should not be disclosed to other officers who have no need to know, to wives or husbands, to friends, to reporters, to hairdressers, or to others."

Then, Anderson described a paper he'd put together in 1994 when he was still a lawyer, a memo that detailed "several botched homicide investigations by the SLCPD. I recalled that my research on behalf of members and friends of homicide victims disclosed not only an astoundingly sloppy investigation, but also, ultimately, corruption in the form of false and misleading information being provided by certain members of the SLCPD to their superiors and to the media."

The mayor singled out at least one Salt Lake PD official. The name of that individual was blacked out when the memo was released. He wrapped up the memo by telling Dinse that he wanted to form a task force to re-open three murder cases from the 1980s that Anderson had worked on as a private lawyer. And Anderson said he'd suggested "two weeks ago" bringing in an independent investigator to take a "fresh look" at the Smart case, "outside, reputable investigators" who may be able to crack the mystery.

While the identities of the people Anderson spoke of in the memo were blacked out, Sergeant Don Bell was widely believed to be one of them. KSL-TV would later report that Anderson acknowledged he had had concerns about Bell's abilities right after Elizabeth disappeared. That was around the time Bell became less public in the investigation. Whether Dinse responded isn't clear. But Anderson's words foretold the recriminations and finger-pointing that would eventually come, once the Elizabeth Smart case was solved.

The middle of July brought almost nothing new in the investigation, and the media attention was dwindling. The family's press conferences were getting shorter. The Smarts were faced with a quandary; they needed to keep Elizabeth's face, and their own, in the spotlight to help find her. But they were carefully guarding the privacy of their home, and of their other five children. They turned down several requests from TV bigs like Connie Chung and Barbara Walters, because the interviewers wanted access to parts of their lives that the Smarts weren't willing to compromise.

The Smarts' media strategy had been a deft one from the start, and keeping the story out there so that someone watching TV or reading a newspaper might realize they'd seen Elizabeth was a challenge. Ed Smart appeared on countless television shows, sometimes with Lois, other times with his brothers and sisters. On one level, the general public felt that they knew the Smarts well. They seemed to be all over television, and they seemed to be revealing a lot about their lives. On July 5, the extended Smarts and Francoms sat with Larry King for a lengthy interview about their ordeal. But it was recorded at someone else's home, a neutral setting that ensured there wouldn't be any intrusions on their private lives. The Smarts were careful to protect themselves, and gave away measured information about who they were, what was happening on a daily basis in the investigation, and how it affected the family. Almost always, what they said was limited to what related to Elizabeth.

Still, they continued their interviews. Many were updates about how the family was doing. Ed would describe the void Elizabeth's absence had created. He and Lois were trying to focus on their five other children, even as their minds were on the one who wasn't there. The kids slept in their parents' bedroom for weeks after the kidnapping, he said. He told the *Deseret News* about a night at the end of June, when he found himself drifting into Elizabeth's bedroom. It was about 1:30 a.m., roughly the time that someone broke into his home and turned the Smarts' world upside down. He couldn't imagine what his daughter, who was taken, and the one who had pretended to sleep, had seen. Lois came into the room about fifteen minutes later.

"We were just thinking about Elizabeth and how difficult the whole thing would have been," Ed said. Elizabeth's father said he knew she was still alive. Every now and then, he allowed his mind to drift forward, to a day when she would come home. It would be glorious, but it would be difficult, as well.

"I feel like if we had her back that I know it's not going to be a cakewalk for her, but I feel the love and support for her in the family. I feel that she'd be able to recover," he said.

After Ricci was charged with stealing from the Smarts and their neighbors, the sketch artist at the center of the feud between Marc Klaas and Tom Smart was brought in by authorities to interview Mary Katherine. Dinse never said why Boylan was brought in, and her role didn't become public until she talked about it on the "Today" show with Katie Couric. But instead of being paid by a TV network, she was working as part of the official investigation, and the Smarts welcomed her.

Boylan, whose background includes psychological counseling, told Couric that Ed and Lois had described Mary Katherine's interests the night before she met the sole witness to Elizabeth's kidnapping. Boylan used Play-Do and fingerpaint. She and Mary Katherine rolled clay over the carpet, hoping to recreate the textures of the kidnapper's skin.

Boylan wouldn't talk about what the session had yielded. She hinted that the public might never see it. But she said she thought the investigation was moving along just fine.

"Typically, I'm brought in to undo damage that's been done inadvertently by investigators through leading questions," Boylan said. "In this case, I was actually fairly stunned to arrive at the scene and find that none of those mistakes had been made. They've done exceptionally well at protecting and preserving Mary Katherine's recall." Her praise, she said, was for both the Smart family and for the investigators on the case.

Boylan's sketch was never released, and no reason was ever given publicly for that decision. Privately, investigators said the sketch wasn't very helpful in terms of identifying any new leads that would point to Elizabeth's abductor. It didn't resemble Brian David Mitchell, one law-enforcement official said. If it looked like anyone, it looked a little like Ricci.

Jessica Wright was asleep in her bed in the middle of the night on July 24, when she was startled awake by the sound of framed pictures that sat on top of her dresser crashing to the floor. She sat up in bed and looked over to her window. Something long and thin was poking through the blinds. All of a sudden it was pulled back and disappeared. Jessica jumped out of her bed like a shot.

She bumped into her dad, Steven, just as she was coming out of her room. He'd also awakened to the loud noise and rushed to his daughter's room. Jessica told him what she'd seen, and her dad sent the family's Labrador retriever out into the yard to try to track whoever had been trying to break in. The Lab immediately ran below Jessica's window and started barking. A chair had been pushed against the side of the house. The sound traveled down their street in the Cottonwood Heights area. Whoever had tried to get in was gone. But the Wrights had a good idea why the intruder had come.

Just miles away, Steven's niece, Elizabeth, had been stolen away by a man who slit a window screen and climbed in, using a chair as his perch. A slit screen and chair were found at the Wrights'. It was too great a coincidence, the family thought. The Wrights felt terrorized, and it was a sickening replay of the morning of June 5.

Wright called the Sheriff's Department, and deputies arrived within minutes. They looked at the window and saw cuts through the screen, vertical and horizontal, as if someone was trying to peel it back. Deputies sent a K9 dog to the back of the house, where it sniffed from Jessica's window to a backyard fence, and stopped. The dog picked up the scent again on the other side of the fence and tracked it to the front yard, but the trail disappeared at the curb.

Steven told investigators who he was, who his sister was, who his niece was. He couldn't think of anyone who could have done it other than someone linked to Elizabeth's disappearance.

"The only indication they made is the connection to the Elizabeth Smart abduction case. Steve informed me his wife was the sister of Elizabeth's mother," sheriff's deputy John Bell wrote in his report.

The deputies stayed at the scene and searched the neighborhood for any clues. The FBI was also dispatched to talk to the family, given their connection to the Smart case. The deputies stayed at the scene for awhile, but they turned up nothing. They kept an open file on the case, but they decided it was probably a prank. Maybe that group of boys from the neighborhood who were already suspected of some recent acts of vandalism.

But Steven was convinced something more sinister happened, and he would be proven right. Brian David Mitchell was looking to steal one of Steven's daughters, investigators would later say, and he could have found out where to go only by forcing Elizabeth to tell him. He had set his sights on Elizabeth's favorite cousin, the one closest to her age. But he'd chosen the wrong window. He wasn't trying to find Jessica. He was looking for her younger sister. The Wrights had redesigned their home, and

Elizabeth apparently didn't know that Jessica's little sister had moved out of the bedroom. The man police privately held as their prime suspect in Elizabeth's case was sitting in a jail cell, and there was no way he was the one who'd torn Jessica's screen.

Steven said later that the cops eyed him suspiciously when they got to his house that night, and it was a hell he couldn't believe he had to endure.

"They were telling me that I staged it," he said, painting with a broad brush the way every law-enforcement official treated him. "They had my wife in tears. It was hell with the breaking in. It was hell with the cops accusing me. It was hell trying to find out who did this."

He said he was forced to take a polygraph test to prove he was serious. Steven later declined other interview requests, but gave his account to the Associated Press wire service, which meant it would go across the country.

The break-in didn't come out in the press until August 9, more than two weeks later. Reporters pressed Ed Smart that day about the eerie parallels between the sheriff's report on what had happened at the Wright home to the night Elizabeth disappeared. But Ed demurred, insisting he didn't have anything to add beyond what the report said.

"We have no idea what the relevance of it is," Ed said. "We don't feel like we can speculate."

Ed was holding his tongue. The family was incensed by their feeling that the police had dismissed the terrifying attempted break-in at the

Wrights' house, and it simply fueled the growing divide. But the Smart clan took two impressions away from what had happened that night.

"Immediately, we knew this was no coincidence," David Smart said. "We thought, 'This has gotta be connected.' That it was one of Elizabeth's closest cousins, near to her age, we just knew Elizabeth was out there. We thought there was a good chance Elizabeth could still be alive. It was a clear message." At the time, the family didn't voice that opinion publicly.

At the time, the Smarts later said, they thought the break-in was as much proof as they could get that Ricci wasn't the man in Elizabeth's room, and that if he'd had a role in the kidnapping, there was definitely someone else involved whom they needed to find.

Ed and Lois Smart, some relatives said later, were frustrated with the investigation's pace at that point, but they were mostly careful to keep their thoughts to themselves. Anyone who has ever had a child abducted, or who works with people who have been through such an ordeal, will say that there is no advantage to criticizing the police, and the Smarts were aware of that. They needed the police. Gay Smither, the co-founder of the Laura Recovery Center that is named for her murdered daughter, said it's always the right thing to do.

"You can't throw rocks at the police. It's not constructive. A lot of times they don't get commended for the good things they do," said Smither. Hindsight, she said, is a "20–20 toss-up."

Ed Smart, the man who faced the cameras daily, always chose his words with care, and the rest of his family followed suit. Only once did Elizabeth's parents give any hint that they were frustrated.

"We support them 100 percent," Lois said of the police. She was speaking to the *New York Times* during one of the interviews that would keep the story going in late July. "It's not going fast enough. I don't think anything they do is fast enough for us."

TEN

The months after Elizabeth's abduction became known as the season of the missing kids. There was a spate of terrifying crimes, almost all involving young girls who simply disappeared on their way to school or from their family's front yard. It seemed like a plague that was striking at random, and no one knew where it would hit next.

In February, four months before Elizabeth's disappearance, seven-year-old Danielle van Dam was taken from her family's home in San Diego. Her broken body was found about three weeks later, and a neighbor who lived two doors away from the van Dams was arrested and found guilty of the murder. In July, in Orange County, California, five-year-old Samantha Runnion was snatched from outside her mother's house on a quiet street in a residential neighborhood where she was playing with a friend. She was found murdered the next day, and police believed she was sexually abused. A man named Alejandro Avila was arrested and is awaiting trial. A week after Samantha was killed, six-year-old Casey Williamson was stolen from her dad's home in a working-class area in St. Louis, Missouri, and murdered. A 24-year-old named Johnny Johnson, a drifter with a rap sheet, was charged with the crime.

Then there were the lucky ones. Seven-year-old Erica Pratt chewed through the duct tape that bound her hands and feet after she was taken off the street near her home in a low-income Philadelphia neighborhood by abductors in search of a ransom. After more than 24 hours hidden in a basement, she escaped. In Lancaster, California, teenagers Tamara Brooks and Jacqueline Marris were abducted as they sat with their dates in cars parked on a secluded drive. They were saved by sheriff's deputies who shot and killed the kidnapper after a car chase.

The cases, all of which were high profile and documented by the national press, suggested an epidemic. In reality, officials said, "stranger abductions" were on the decline that year. In 2001, there were fewer than 100 children kidnapped by strangers, according to FBI statistics. The National Center for Missing and Exploited Children also said that the number of stranger abductions—the rarest and most potentially dangerous category— hovers around 100 each year, down from 200 to 300 in the 1980s. About 40 percent of those children are murdered, 56 percent are recovered, and the others are never found. About 800,000 go missing each year, according to the National Incidents Studies of Missing, Abducted, Runaway, and

Thrownaway Children. Most of them are runaways, or are taken by a family member. The statistics on kids who are taken by strangers vary, depending on how different states report the cases. Advocates believe many of those cases are initially ruled by authorities as runaways, and once that happens, it's hard to get the classification changed. Some advocates put the number of stranger abductions at more than 3,500 a year.

The cases of Danielle van Dam, Samantha Runnion and Casey Williamson all made headlines, but the Elizabeth Smart abduction garnered the most attention. Part of the reason was because she remained missing, while the three little girls were found murdered within weeks of their abductions. There was a resolution in those cases, terrible though it was, while the Smarts were still searching for their daughter. The Smarts also learned quickly how to keep the media interested in the story for the purpose of finding their daughter.

But while Elizabeth, Danielle, Samantha, and Casey made headlines from coast to coast, others did not. A month before Elizabeth Smart was kidnapped, seven-year-old Alexis Patterson vanished as she was on her way to school in Milwaukee, Wisconsin. Her stepfather said he dropped her off at her school. Her family said she was last seen walking in the playground. She was about four feet tall, with a red pullover jacket and light blue jeans, and she was black.

Alexis disappeared May 3, but her case received scant attention outside of Wisconsin, save for a

segment on "America's Most Wanted" and some
briefs on a few national networks, until the *Milwaukee Journal Sentinel* ran a story on June 15.
The story questioned why the Elizabeth Smart disappearance was getting wall-to-wall coverage,
while no one in the national press seemed interested in the search for Alexis. Within a week of the
article, most of the national networks ran stories
on Alexis, in some cases for the first time. But
many of the pieces focused on why it was that she
got less attention than Elizabeth. In effect, the
press that hadn't covered the story was dissecting
its own motives.

Part of the perception at the time was that Alexis
received less attention than Elizabeth because of
the color of her skin. However, there are a number
of factors that play into how an abducted child's
case is covered—not the least of which is the perception of the family. Runaways and family abductions have a lower priority in the press, and the
interest seems to fluctuate depending on how old
the child is, how long the child is missing, and the
socioeconomic standing of the family.

John Walsh, the missing-child crusader, said as
much in an interview with Larry King.

"Alexis Patterson is a tough case because we got
a stepdaddy who says he brought her to school,"
said Walsh. But he dismissed the idea that race was
a factor.

"This is one that some people in the media are
saying that black children don't get the same coverage as white children. I don't believe that,"

Walsh said. He pointed out that there might be an issue with Alexis's family.

"Nobody can verify that this stepfather brought Alexis to school that day. Nobody saw him. Nobody saw Alexis . . . So when it's a little dicey like this, the—you know, it doesn't get attention."

But Walsh had choice words for the media, too. "It's pack reporting. They're all out—everybody's in Salt Lake City right now because this little girl got abducted from a million-dollar home."

Laura Recovery Center's Gay Smither said there are indeed economic issues that affect the way a case is covered and how much time people can devote to a search effort.

"We've done searches where nobody comes out to look. It's heartbreaking, and we go out ourselves and beat the bushes," Smither said. "Some of these kids come from communities where people can't afford to take off work if they wanted to. Some of them could lose their jobs. Many of the parents don't have the financial means to support the search effort."

Patty Wetterling, whose son, Jacob, was abducted at gunpoint in 1989 in Minnesota and remains missing, said the media often zeros in on families who "play well on television."

"Sometimes, if the media feels the family won't look good, they're not interested," said Wetterling, who helped found Team Hope, a national telephone support group for parents whose kids have disappeared. Families need to be able to delegate someone to speak for them if they aren't "TV-ready," she said. "There is no reason why one child should get more attention than any other. And the media and the community at large need to be made aware of this."

Many parents aren't as good at dealing with the media and targeting their message of finding their missing child as the Smarts were. They had help coordinating their search effort from the LDS church. They also had a full-time spokesman and media strategist early on. Within the first few days, the family got help from the Intrepid Group, a public-relations firm in Salt Lake City. Tom Smart was friends with one of the people who worked there, and one of the firm's founders, Missy Larsen—the daughter of former Salt Lake City mayor Ted Wilson, who coordinated the search— had known the Smarts for years. Chris Thomas, another member of the firm, was brought into the Smart case a few weeks after Elizabeth disappeared, and he became the family's watchdog. He helped track their course and their strategy for keeping word about Elizabeth's case alive. The family kept pictures of Elizabeth circulating, fresher ones over time that kept the media interested. The press, especially the TV networks, took the images of the blonde, photogenic teenager and aired them constantly. The Smarts held briefings even when there was nothing new to report, and they didn't turn down many chances to talk about the case on television.

The nature of the way Elizabeth was taken was also unusual, since most stranger abductions occur on the street or somewhere outside the home. A child stolen from her room is the most chilling scenario imaginable for most parents. The Smarts also had the strong support of their local government and the local police. In many cases, police, however well-meaning, don't respond immediately to reports of missing children, Smither said. Despite a 1990 federal law that requires law enforcement to immediately enter a missing child into a national database, it doesn't always happen. Smither urged parents not to take "no" for an answer, and to find someone who can vouch for the missing child. And the first three hours are crucial.

The amount of resources put into the Smart search was attention-catching, and TV ran reels of footage of searchers in the Wasatch Mountains, some of them Salt Lake County employees who were given a day's pay while they volunteered.

The Smarts also had the benefit of a relatively slow news cycle at the time Elizabeth was kidnapped; the amount of coverage nationally depends on what else is happening in the world in deciding the importance of a story.

The controversy over an imbalance in the coverage also played out closer to the Smarts' home. Several people in Salt Lake and the areas around it called TV stations and wrote letters to newspapers saying they sympathized with the Smarts but were curious about the attention it was getting.

A day before the *Journal Sentinel* ran its story on the scant attention paid to Alexis, the *Salt Lake Tribune* published a long article about Kiplyn

Davis, a 15-year-old girl from Spanish Fork, Utah, who disappeared in 1995.

For the first three weeks after Kiplyn, a happy teenager with red hair, went missing from her high school, police believed she had run away. The FBI offered to help, but local police said no. The case was eventually classified as a kidnapping, but it garnered few headlines. Kiplyn's parents, Tamara and Richard, knew just how the Smarts were feeling. But they couldn't relate to the intense interest in their plight.

"How come we didn't get all this publicity? How come I didn't have 40 FBI agents and 60 law-enforcement agencies out looking for Kiplyn at the time?" Richard Davis asked the paper. "We know it's a lot different. Elizabeth was taken out of her home. But my daughter was taken out of her school."

Davis remembered the first days after Kiplyn disappeared, when the police said she was probably at a friend's house. When children go missing, families are often told by experts to run their own search, parallel to the police investigation. But Davis didn't know how to go about coordinating it. He handed out fliers and searched the streets, but that was all.

"We weren't running an investigation because we didn't know how to," he said. "We did that finally, two weeks after she disappeared. But they should have done that right off the bat. They should have been hitting the canyons, just like they did with Elizabeth."

Richard Davis said that a year before Elizabeth vanished, his wife had tried to get a local store to post a flier about her daughter, but workers refused. But Tamara saw Elizabeth Smart's face in the same window the week after June 5.

Richard Davis said he was still searching for his daughter. Her picture was on websites that feature missing children's fliers. He had kept the light on his porch burning since she disappeared. Neighbors would sometimes knock on the door, telling the Davises that the light had burned out. "We'll never turn if off until we find her," he said.

The Davis family's situation is often the rule. For children who are stolen, the attention paid to their cases can make the difference between life and death, between being found and having families left with a lifetime of unanswered questions. It was a fact that would prove true in Elizabeth Smart's case, as well.

ELEVEN

Ed Smart strode into the hearing room at the Third District Courthouse. It was the last day of July, and the man who might have helped steal his daughter was due for an appearance. Across the courtroom was Angela Ricci, Richard Ricci's wife, who had come to support her husband. The judge entered an "innocent" plea for Richard, who was in shackles with four guards surrounding him, and the hearing was over.

An emotional meeting came right afterward. Ed met with Angela and her father for about thirty minutes, and said he begged her to help him get information from Richard.

"I don't need any more lies," Ed told reporters afterward. "I pleaded with her to please ask Richard to tell the truth."

Richard needed to clear himself as a suspect in Elizabeth's disappearance, Ed said. The handyman hadn't been forthcoming about where his Jeep was when Elizabeth was kidnapped. He hadn't explained the mysterious 1,000 miles that were put on the car. And he hadn't said who picked him up from Neth Moul's auto shop on June 8.

"If it's Richard, he needs to let us know where she is," Ed said sharply. "If it's not Richard, he needs to get out of the way."

And if there was anyone who could get Richard to talk, it was Angela. But Angela left the courthouse maintaining Richard's innocence. Her encounter with Ed was dramatic, but it didn't bring forth any new information.

August would bring a jolt to the case, although it wouldn't come until the end of the month. The news of the break-in at Steven Wright's house hit the newspapers in the second week of August. The story appeared on August 9 in the *Deseret News*, which, at the time, was an evening paper that went to press in the afternoon. The *Salt Lake Tribune*, a morning paper, carried the same story the next day. The Smarts were still organizing searches, asking people to show up at spots where there had been suspicious sightings that could be linked to the abduction.

On August 1, Ed went on television and said that Mary Katherine thought the kidnapper's voice sounded familiar as he spoke to her sister the morning of the abduction. She thought she'd heard it before but couldn't pinpoint exactly where, the family said the next day. She only knew that it rang a bell.

The Smart family normally spent summers at their cabin in Brighton, but that August they were in Federal Heights, enduring days without answers. Ed Smart scaled back his daily briefings to three a week. He told reporters that he and Lois were focusing on life with their other kids, but they hadn't given up looking for Elizabeth. They were convinced she was still alive.

In town, well-wishers started scrawling messages of hope about Elizabeth on a kiosk that had been used to sell snacks during the Olympics. Some people taped the missing teenager's flier to the structure, while others wrote notes in black marker.

Ricci sat in his cell, waiting for his next court date, scheduled for August 27. A few days after the reports of the Wright break-in surfaced, Ed Smart told a handful of reporters who came to one of his thrice-weekly briefings that there may be more than one person who was involved in the kidnapping.

"We feel that our lead suspect is in custody, but we feel that other people were involved but we haven't been able to find those other people," he said, referring to Ricci. Ed spoke directly to the kidnapper, as he had before, pleading that he get in touch with him, and he told his daughter to stay strong. "Elizabeth, wherever you are out there, know that we are not giving up in any way, shape or form," Smart said.

The pleas for someone else to come forward were intensifying. At their next briefing, Ed and Lois Smart released an open letter to whoever took their daughter. Ed read the letter at one of his briefings, crying as he spoke:

"To the holder(s) of Elizabeth Ann Smart and Friends Throughout the World," the letter began. "It has been several weeks since our daughter Eliz-

abeth was awakened during the night and taken
from her home by force. Every minute of the day
we continue to search for her, pray for her, and
yearn for her to come home. So many of you have
joined us in our search and our prayers. Since we
last saw Elizabeth on the evening of June fourth,
we have not received any communication from her
or from the person who took her. We continue to
eagerly await information about her location."

The letter thanked people around the globe who
had prayed for the family, or tried to help them
find Elizabeth. "We believe that through awareness
of this terrible tragedy in our family many children
throughout the world will be saved."

Then, the letter spoke directly to the kidnappers:
"As the authorities continue to piece together a
puzzle, we still are only interested in one thing—
finding Elizabeth. We believe that she is still alive
and wants desperately to be returned to us . . .
Whether or not you are the person who took her,
we are pleading with you to do the right thing and
let her come home."

The letter was signed, "Anxiously awaiting,
Ed & Lois Smart."

Ed took questions after he read the letter, and
the frustration was etched on his face. He wanted
his daughter home, he said. He wanted her to begin her year at East High School. By that time, Ed's
other daughter had turned ten years old, a mile-
stone birthday without her sister, and the lack of
answers was torture.

Ed told reporters that day that he was growing

more convinced that Richard Ricci had something to do with it, and suggested the ex-con had an accomplice who was working with him.

"The information that has come forth regarding Richard," Ed said, "makes me feel he was certainly in on it." There was probably "someone out there holding her now."

Dell Blair's wife came home one day later that summer. She'd been in downtown Salt Lake, just a few blocks from their house. They chatted, and she told him that she had seen the guy they called "Joseph"—the one with the flowing robes who begged for money with a woman standing next to him—while she was walking in town. There was something different this time. He had two women by his side.

"Joseph has a new Mary," Dell's wife said. All she could see of the new one was her eyes.

It's unclear exactly when Elizabeth started walking around her hometown with Barzee and Mitchell, her face cloaked by a makeshift white veil. But the three remained at the lean-to campsite in the hills from the night of the abduction until August 8, and it was sometime in August that Salt Lake residents first remember seeing "Joseph and Mary" with a girl shrouded in smudged white robes. They were on the streets, at strip mall restaurants, and occasionally on UTA buses. More than once, they were seen walking by stores with Elizabeth's face taped to the glass, the words "kidnapped" alongside the picture. Brian carried a sack over his shoulder, and the three walked in step, a tight group that seemed a little odd, certainly, but not odd enough to prompt people to linger on them. Sometimes they stood on street corners while Mitchell spoke what he considered God's word and asked people to give them money.

Nine months later, reports of missed chances to have helped Elizabeth Smart poured in, creating a picture of a girl who was literally under everyone's noses. In truth, the trio was in town for only a few weeks, and not every day. Their trips into the valley were sporadic.

Still, they were sometimes in plain sight, with dozens of people passing by them. None realized that the girl whose parents had been begging people on national television to help find her was right in front of their eyes. And as strange as their habits were, the three seemed just another set of drifters passing through Salt Lake before moving on to another town, and then coming back again. They seemed to be following some religious doctrine telling them to wear the robes, and people were tolerant of what they thought was simply another faith. Their robes were dingy, but they may have just been down on their luck, and while people wanted to help, they didn't want to pry into their lives. Besides, "Joseph and Mary," or "the Jesus guy" and his female follower, had been a presence on the streets of Salt Lake for more than two years. That there was now a third person, this one wearing a veil, didn't weigh on anyone's minds.

The three were usually seen at all-you-can-eat

restaurants or food fairs, where meals were in great supply and didn't cost much. They went to places Brian and Wanda had frequented before June 5, places they had mostly stopped visiting in the weeks after the kidnapping, but where they were already a common sight. The Souper Salad chain had been a favorite of the couple's through most of 2001, and they started visiting the restaurants again that month. Toward the end of August, they walked into the Souper Salad in Midvale, about 10 miles from Salt Lake. The restaurant was in a strip mall, wedged between a children's toy store and a Chinese restaurant. An all-you-can-eat meal cost about $5 at the Souper Salad, and that was probably one of its draws for Brian and Wanda. "Jesus and Mary" were familiar to the wait staff. The couple had been coming in, on and off, for about a year, dressed in robes and spouting scripture. They were often caked with dirt, but they were harmless. They spoke only a few words to each other during their meals, and would thank the wait staff with a "God be with you" or "God bless you." Once, sometime in the fall of 2001, they came in dressed in everyday clothes, prompting raised eyebrows among the waiters. Raeonna Perez remembered someone asking the pair why they had changed their style.

"Because God told us to," the man replied. When they left the restaurant, it was always on foot. Sometimes, Raeonna saw them outside the store, making a slow pilgrimage up State Street.

When they came in with a second woman, employees were surprised to see them—not because they hadn't come by for awhile, but because of her covered face. Barzee wore a veil as well, and the Souper Salad staff had never seen her do that before. The sight of the women's eyes peeking out over the edges of the white strips of cloth made the waitresses uneasy. The three gobbled up as much as they could from the buffet, as if they hadn't eaten in days. Elizabeth walked up to the L-shaped buffet counter to get her own food, and then sat back down. She never gestured to employees or cried out. She simply ate, saying a few words to Mitchell or Barzee in a whisper. They left after about two hours, passing by an Elizabeth Smart poster on the door.

Another time, Mitchell took them to a Crown Burger. Barzee and Elizabeth sat at a table right by the window, while Brian got their food. Sometimes they would shop at little supermarkets in town, where Brian would buy supplies, including the beer he seemed to crave.

They also liked to visit the Wild Oats market, a health-food chain with a store right in downtown Salt Lake. The three would often come by in the late morning, piling their plates with salads, and sometimes pizza, which was served in boxes that the three would save. Others in the store occasionally caught a glimpse of Mitchell stuffing fruit and vegetables into the boxes and then sneaking the purloined food out of the store.

They were apparently still staying in the mountains, using the lean-to campsite and a second one closer to the base of the mountains. Hikers occasionally saw them in the valleys of the Wasatch, but didn't think anything of it. A man riding his bike in Dry Creek Canyon crossed paths with the trio once, but they seemed personable and polite. The cyclist kept moving through the mountains.

Some people said they saw the three hitchhiking around Salt Lake County. One woman swore she saw them riding a UTA bus, sitting down among the commuters, late at night.

On some days, Elizabeth was in plain sight, but she went unseen by everyone—those who knew her before, and those whose jobs were closely involved with her case. Russell Banz, who worked at KSL, a TV and radio company owned by the LDS church, fell into both categories. Banz was a member of Elizabeth's LDS stake, and he had seen her any number of times before the kidnapping. He knew the details of the case all too well. Banz told his network that he was at a restaurant with his parents one night that month when he saw a veiled girl. She walked by his table three times, her robes brushing against his chair. She seemed to be doing something strange with her eyes, almost as if she was trying to hold his gaze. But then she passed him, and that was that. He went back to his dinner.

All around town were the blue ribbons and balloons that went up in the early summer, after the kidnapping rocked Salt Lake. The ribbons had grown dingy, but they were still there. Elizabeth's parents would say later that she had seen the blue ribbons and balloons around town but hadn't known they were for her.

John Walsh would later say Elizabeth's uncles told him she had tried to escape at least once. She made it about ten feet from Mitchell and Barzee, approached a woman, and told her she was Elizabeth Smart. But the woman didn't recognize the name, and Elizabeth's captors came and grabbed her away.

But those who saw Elizabeth during that time said she never tried to approach them, and the question of why she stayed silent while she was in plain sight was repeated around the country.

Several observers believed the girl had been completely brainwashed by then. She was stripped of her identity, said cult expert Rick Ross. "The change in clothing adds to the breakdown—and the isolation," he said. "The robes were another way of putting a wall between them and everyone else."

Patty Hearst, the magazine heiress who absorbed a new identity after she was kidnapped by an extremist group three decades earlier, also offered an explanation for the transformation Elizabeth likely endured during her months with Mitchell and Barzee, which she based on her own ordeal.

"You're not even thinking about trying to get help anymore," Hearst told Larry King on CNN. "You've, in a way, given up. You have absorbed this new, you know, identity that they've given you. You're just surviving. You're not even doing that, really. You're just living while everything else is going on around you."

At Kristianna Circle, the waiting for answers was excruciating. The Smarts knew Elizabeth could have been anywhere, and they urged hunters that month to keep an eye out for their daughter while they were in the woods.

The phone calls from psychics offering to help locate Elizabeth hadn't stopped. Police took their calls and checked out what they had to say, keeping thick logs of their tips. John Walsh, the "America's Most Wanted" host, had become close friends with the Smart family, at times talking to Ed every day, he said later. Walsh said he'd told the family that psychic tips could be important because they may have been in touch with someone who had information but didn't want to come forward. Cops said they agreed with that theory and tried to chase down leads generated by psychic tipsters, even though they were sometimes a drain on the amount of people working the case.

In late August, psychics from PSI Tech in Seattle descended on This Is The Place State Heritage Park in Emigration Canyon, behind the Smarts' home. The park has a vault that serves as an American Indian burial ground, and some of the company's psychics had had a "vision" that Elizabeth was inside it. They had pinpointed her location in midsummer, weeks after they reported on their website that Elizabeth wasn't alive anymore. They also said they were contacted by David Smart about looking into the case. When PSI Tech's psychics showed up at the crypt, state archeologists wouldn't let them in. Authorities were called, and they came and checked it out. Elizabeth wasn't there.

The national attention that had swirled around the case had died down somewhat by the end of the summer. On August 21, Ed Smart took up a national cause and stayed with it in the months ahead. His family urged Congress to pass a national AMBER Alert system. The acronym for America's Missing: Broadcast Emergency Response, AMBER is a rapid response system that uses TV and radio stations to alert people to missing children and their suspects. The alerts give descriptions of the child and any pertinent details. The system—which is similar to the Rachael Alert that was used in Utah for the first time during Elizabeth's abduction—is named for Amber Hagerman. The nine-year-old from Texas was abducted in 1996 while she was riding her bike around her neighborhood. The AMBER Alert bill was going into the Senate, and Ed said he wanted to stand behind it.

As it turned out, Ed's AMBER Alert push came shortly after a new horror in Salt Lake County that frightened the valley all over again.

An eleven-year-old girl in the town of Midvale had been taken from her home, raped, and then beaten in her family's backyard. A concerned neighbor called police when she heard odd noises in the neighborhood. The girl lived, and the neighbor's call was what saved her. The rapist took off when police arrived, but they quickly caught up to him. Salt Lake police wanted to talk to the man because the crime was somewhat similar to the Elizabeth Smart case, although there wasn't any obvious connection. Still, Ed Smart heaped praise on the neighbor who had helped stop the little girl's ordeal. The rapist was off the streets, but the crime was a chilling reminder of what had happened just months earlier in Federal Heights.

The excitement that always comes with a new school year was buzzing around Federal Heights. The Smarts had four children preparing for the fall term, but this year would be different. Across the country, relatives of victims of the September 11 terror attacks were preparing for the first anniversary of the blackest day in the history of the United States, and they were painfully aware of the voids left in their families. At Kristianna Circle, the feelings were similar. Ed and Lois Smart talked publicly about the hole in their daily lives. But they also had to prepare their eldest four kids for the coming year, especially Mary Katherine, who was entering the fifth grade. Investigators described Mary Katherine as their "touchstone" throughout the summer. Everything in the investigation centered on her memory.

The police didn't think Mary Katherine's memory of the event would be tainted by being around other kids. But her parents said they were worried that her classmates would ask her about the case, meaning no harm, but that such questions could make her feel guilty about what had happened that night. Her mother said the girl was worried about being asked questions about the ordeal. "We're hoping she's strong enough," Lois told the *Deseret News*. "I believe she felt she was protecting the rest of the family and saving Elizabeth from being shot." At that point, the belief was that Elizabeth had been abducted at gunpoint.

"I just want her to know she did the right thing. She was so brave," the girl's mother said. "I can't even imagine lying there, watching someone with a gun in your sister's back."

In the future, the kids would be shuttled to school by their parents. The kids' schools tried making life easier for them, watching out for any incidents with schoolmates that could be upsetting. Life went on, but the pain was always there.

Richard Ricci could barely catch his breath. He was in his cell at the Utah State Prison, and he felt like he couldn't get air in his lungs. It was just around 7:30 p.m. on Tuesday, August 27. Ricci had been in Third District Court that morning for a hearing on the burglary charges, a hearing that was literally seconds long, with Ed and Lois Smart looking on from the gallery. Ricci didn't lock eyes with either of the Smarts when he came into the court, but he did fix his gaze on his wife Angela for a moment. Ricci had also been indicted in federal court for a bank hold-up in November 2001. But there was no sign earlier in the day that anything was wrong.

Ricci pushed the call button in his cell to ask for help. A guard asked over the intercom what was wrong. He was having trouble breathing, Ricci replied, and he had a bad headache. Guards showed up at his cell two minutes later and watched as Ricci tumbled onto his bunk. The paramedics that were called in tried to revive him with mouth-to-mouth resuscitation, but the prisoner was unconscious. He was brought first to the prison infirmary, and then he was taken in a helicopter to University Hospital. He was put on life-support, and it seemed unlikely that he would make it through the night.

Prison officials were baffled by the mystery illness. Ricci had a history of drug use, including system-damaging narcotics like heroin, and he had also been busted during a past jail stint for using while he was behind bars. But when prison officials searched his cell, they turned up no evidence that he was high when he collapsed. Angela Ricci was allowed to be by her husband's side, even as several police and FBI members stood guard at the hospital because of the high-profile prisoner.

Cory Lyman was with his family that night when his cell phone went off. Ricci was in the hospital, comatose, Lyman was told. The Salt Lake captain was dumbfounded. There had been so many strange turns in the case, but no one foresaw this one. "What else can go wrong?" he asked himself.

By the next morning, Ricci had gone through four hours of brain surgery to remove fluid on his brain.

The surgery brought a slight glimmer of hope that he would come out of it. He was actually doing better than he had been, according to officials.

But Ricci's illness left the police and the Smart family reeling. He was the prime suspect in connection with Elizabeth's case, and he was literally slipping away, taking with him whatever information he might have had.

Dinse joined the Smart family at their news conference later that afternoon and admitted the thought of losing Ricci was troubling. "If he does not survive, it would be a big impact on our case," the chief said.

Officials had chased down thousands of leads so far, but Ricci was still at the top of the list of possible suspects. If Ricci didn't make it through his ordeal, he may never be completely cleared of the crime. But if he came out of his coma, he may be more amenable to telling what he knew, the chief said.

Ed Smart, who stood with his mom and his sister while the chief talked, was clearly stunned by the latest twist in the search for his daughter. "This is the most bizarre thing I could have imagined," he said.

"We're at a very critical point in the investigation," Smart said. "I'm asking everyone to pray that the Lord will help us bring this to some type of resolution. We really feel it's in the Lord's hands."

By the next day, doctors had diagnosed Ricci's ailment: He had suffered a brain hemorrhage, a rupture of a vessel that caused a clot. He wasn't conscious, but he also wasn't brain dead, hospital officials said. But that evening, the prognosis wasn't good. Ricci had brain damage, and Angela decided the next day to take her husband off life support. Ricci was raised Roman Catholic, but Angela was a Mormon, and her husband was given an LDS blessing before he stopped breathing. It was around 7:30 p.m., almost 72 hours to the minute when he had first started gasping for air in his cell.

Angela Ricci, who had maintained her husband's innocence in the Elizabeth Smart case to the end, gave a statement that evening saying that she knew he wouldn't have wanted to be kept alive by machines. "Six months ago when we married, saying goodbye was unthinkable. Like other new brides I had planned a life with the man I loved," she said.

"I know that the world will never know the Richard that his family and I knew, but I will always remember him as a kind and gentle man who was a loving husband to me and a caring father to my son."

While Richard Ricci was in his final days, Ed Smart was asked to go on national TV shows to talk about the strange development in the case and what impact it could have on finding his daughter. As always, Ed never said that he believed Ricci was the man in his house or pointed the finger straight at Ricci in any way. He said he believed Ricci was somehow involved, but because he never opened up to investigators, Ed may never know how. He told the "Today" show he believed there were "other people involved with Richard. I had placed so much hope in him coming forward. There is a potential that we might not know because we haven't been able to get anyone else to come forward with information."

He told Larry King that he desperately wanted to know with whom Ricci had left Neth Moul's shop back in June. King asked how the Smarts were holding up, and Ed said life was difficult, with the family hurtling toward the three-month anniversary of Elizabeth's disappearance. Then, King asked Ed if he was "happy with the police work so far, or is 'happy' the wrong word?"

"You know, I feel that they have been very diligent, along with the FBI," Ed replied. "You know, at different times we're at odds. But we—you know, I feel the only way this is going to be solved is by cooperation of everyone's help. And I am so grateful to them and the FBI for their help. I may have words with them at times, but I truly and sincerely am very, very thankful for them."

When Ricci died, the Smarts extended condolences to his wife. Around that time, the family was recruiting forensics expert Henry Lee, a regular on TV expert panels, to come in and take a fresh look at the evidence police had gathered. Dinse said he had no problem with that, as long as Lee would agree to keep confidential the details of what he'd reviewed, in order to avoid harming the case. Without credible fresh leads and with the prime suspect dead, the probe was in desperate need of a new break.

* * *

The day Richard Ricci was pulled off his life-support system, Ed Smart revealed a key piece of information about the night of the kidnapping. He told the *Deseret News* that a wrought-iron chair was moved from the family's patio and was found by police beneath the kitchen window with the cut screen. It was information that hadn't come out publicly before, and Ed said he thought the evidence was important because it was similar to what had happened at Steven Wright's home a month earlier. The sheriff's office still believed the Wright incident wasn't connected to the abduction, but the Smarts thought differently.

What was happening behind the scenes, Tom Smart said later, was growing upset among the family over how the incident at the Wright house was being treated. The Smarts thought it was definitely connected to Elizabeth, he said, and authorities were brushing it off.

"We felt the break-in was a significant development, and people—the police—just summarily dismissed it. Played it off," said Tom. "The police wrote it off as a prank."

Ed said he was putting up a new $3,000 reward for information that could answer two questions: Who picked Ricci up at Neth Moul's shop, and who tried to force their way into the Wright house? Ed Smart wanted to bring as much pressure as he could to solve those puzzles. His daughter had been missing for too long.

TWELVE

Each time Dorotha Smart pulled into the drive at Kristianna Circle, she could picture her granddaughter on the stone walk.

"I expect still to have Elizabeth come bounding down the front steps," Dorotha said. It was September 3, three months since Elizabeth had been spirited away from her bedroom. Dorotha and other members of the family stood with reporters, some of them wiping tears, as they marked the emotional date. Ed and Lois, needing a break, had taken the children out of town. But the rest of the family kept the daily press schedule.

Dorotha talked about how she wanted the world to know more about Elizabeth, her aspirations for making the track team, her dream to attend Juilliard. The stoic Smart family matriarch read Elizabeth's poem, "All About Me," in the hope it would give people more of a sense of the little girl who had been ripped from her family's lives. Dorotha talked about her granddaughter's "quiet ways," and told reporters "she had a real flair."

It was a quiet, almost solemn beginning to a week

that, before it was over, would bring new questions about the probe into Elizabeth's disappearance.

In the first few days of September, Sergeant Don Bell was sitting in a meeting with the Elizabeth Smart task force when he got so sick he had to leave. Bell was diagnosed with pneumonia and had to take leave from his job. When he finally returned awhile later, he was no longer on the task force.

On September 7, police found themselves in the same position the Smarts had been in back in June: on the defensive over a newspaper report. The *Deseret News* ran a story under the headline "Smart scene unsealed for hours." It recounted allegations of sloppy police work the night of Elizabeth's abduction.

Dinse, the story said, had admitted to an "oversight" on the part of his officers, who waited nearly three hours to seal off the Smarts' home that night. The mistake, he conceded, could potentially have muddied the crime scene. The story put law enforcement in an uncomfortable position. Their prime suspect, Richard Ricci, was dead, and so far, investigators had not uncovered enough evidence to charge anyone with Elizabeth's kidnapping. The suggestion that potential evidence might have been ruined in an unsecured scene didn't help matters, especially when there was an anxious family waiting for answers.

Investigators were "very upset," according to task force leader Cory Lyman. "It was a pretty big issue," he told the paper. Lyman said the patrol officer who first responded to Kristianna Circle did the right thing in making a search for Elizabeth his first priority, because sealing off the swath of land around the Smarts' home would have taken four or five men. However, Lyman told the paper he couldn't give a justification for why the scene wasn't cordoned off in the first 15 to 20 minutes.

Ed Smart estimated there were probably 40 to 50 family and church members in his house in the first hours after the abduction and suggested police should have taken action. "I wanted all the help I could get to find her," he said. "I wasn't thinking about contaminating the scene . . . Looking back, I would think that [police] would have said something to me because there were a lot of people there."

Deputy district attorney Kent Morgan was also concerned about the possible destruction of evidence. But he seemed to try and spread any perception of blame more evenly. "It was the ward function of the year where everyone was trying to help," he reasoned. "By the time police got there, they had to undo the chaos before they could begin reasonable forensic procedures."

The story highlighted the strain between the Smarts and the Salt Lake police. It also was part of a pattern that began that summer and continued through the duration of the case. Early in the probe, leaks to the media by members of law enforcement had drawn the ire of mayor Rocky Anderson and the Smart family. After Anderson's blistering memo to Chief Dinse, those leaks seemed, for the most part, to stop. In their place was a new round of information that appeared to come from outside law enforcement.

By the end of the month, with the Smarts sometimes outnumbering reporters, the family dropped its press conferences to once a week. But they hadn't given up, and neither had police.

Ed Smart stepped up his pressure on Congress to pass the AMBER Alert. He became an active supporter of the bill until it eventually passed, weeks after Elizabeth's ordeal was over. But it also gave him a chance to keep his missing daughter's case in the spotlight. The day before the anniversary of the September 11 terrorist attacks, Ed spoke to reporters of the importance of homeland security. "There is nothing more important," Ed said, "than our personal homes and the security of those homes."

Investigators went back to the basics, returning to the Smarts' neighborhood to look for more clues and re-interviewing the family. Lois Smart sat with police for more than two hours. She carefully reviewed and rehashed an extensive list of family friends, acquaintances and handymen—trying to come up with names of anyone who might have been at the house. There was a handful of people who police hadn't yet tracked down.

Lois Smart wriggled through the crowd of people surrounding George W. Bush in the ballroom of the Ronald Reagan building until she stood in front of the President. Bush warmly clasped her hand in his as she and Ed introduced themselves. "God bless you," the President said.

On that early October afternoon, the Smarts were only two people in a fraternity of anxious parents searching for missing sons and daughters. The Smarts, like hundreds of others, had been invited to Washington for the President's first White House Conference on Missing, Exploited and Runaway Children. They wore ribbons and "Have You Seen Me?" buttons, and carried photos of their missing kids. Bush unveiled a series of new federal measures to heighten protection of children from predators, and he repeated his commitment to creating the national AMBER Alert system.

The Smarts had dinner with families of other missing kids, some of whom had gone agonizing years without word or new developments in their cases. Their ongoing sense of hope, Lois would later say, bolstered her strength to keep searching for Elizabeth.

While her parents were at the White House, Elizabeth was in downtown Salt Lake, likely staying in a small studio apartment just one block from the city's police station. During his frequent trips to the Wild Oats market in the months before the kidnapping, Mitchell had befriended Daniel Trotta, a twenty-four-year-old cashier at the store. One day near the end of September, Mitchell showed up at the shop and asked Trotta to meet him outside after work.

"He was waiting for me when I went out, and he asked if I had a place they could crash," Trotta later said. "I told him they could stay with me for a few days. He was always very nice and friendly, and I figured, why not?"

For nearly a week at the beginning of October, Trotta said, Mitchell, Elizabeth and Barzee moved into his small apartment on Oxford Place. Mitchell did most of the talking as the four of them sat around a round wooden table in the small, cluttered kitchen. They played music and ate, and Mitchell drank beer. During the stay, Trotta said, he tried to draw Elizabeth out, but when he asked her name, Brian interrupted and said, "Just call her My Joy in Her." If Trotta was out late, the women sometimes fell asleep on his bed, with Mitchell taking the couch. But as soon as their host arrived home, all three would move to the floor. Elizabeth, he said, always slept with her veil covering her face.

During their stay at Trotta's studio, Mitchell asked his new friend if he might be able to help them find a house in the city, the host said. They normally camped in the hills, but winter was coming and they wanted something more permanent. Trotta asked around but couldn't come up with anything.

"He said it was okay, that they were just going to head to California," Trotta said. Months later, Trotta would recognize Mitchell when his picture was shown on "America's Most Wanted." He said he immediately called police, who examined the apartment for evidence and dusted for fingerprints. Investigators would later say they suspected Trotta had embellished portions of his tale about the robed houseguests, but several people in the apartment complex said they had seen the three coming in and out of the building and believed they spent a handful of days there.

Mitchell made several trips around town before the stay at Trotta's place—some with Barzee and Elizabeth, others alone.

Nanda Sookhai spotted the trio one day as he walked through Liberty Park. Intrigued by the three robed strangers sitting at a picnic table, he trained his video camera on them. "They stood out," Sookhai said. But they didn't seem to notice people staring as they ate and spoke among themselves. Sookhai was intrigued, and he thought about approaching them to ask about their lifestyle. But they seemed so relaxed, and Sookhai didn't want to intrude. He left them alone to enjoy the waning summer day.

Those that did try to strike up conversations with Elizabeth or Barzee while they roamed town were quickly shut down by Mitchell. He did the talking and deflected the questions. It was around midnight on a September night when the trio appeared at a party at a house at the corner of 10 East and 2 South. Residents of the house were mostly college students, many of them in the theater department, and their large parties were well-known in the neighborhood.

No one seemed to recognize the three people draped in what looked like white sheets, but the revelers were welcoming. They thought the new guests were in costume, a group of eccentrics bringing a personal flair to the gathering. A few people who'd brought cameras that night snapped pictures of them. Mitchell introduced himself as Immanuel and almost immediately launched into conversations with other partygoers about religion. Barzee and Elizabeth stood nearby, staring blankly out at the crowd. Mitchell grabbed a beer, hoisting the dark can to his mouth, but no one remembered seeing him give anything to his companions. A few people tried to talk to them, but Mitchell promptly stopped them.

"Don't talk to her," he told several people who approached Elizabeth.

Another guest came near. "What's your story?" he asked the women. They mumbled and averted their eyes.

Benjamin Crane thought there was something surreal about the women, particularly the younger one. He was one of the party's hosts, and he had never seen these people at other bashes he'd thrown. All he could see were the young girl's eyes, and they looked flat. He tried to meet her gaze, but she looked away.

The three stayed at the party for about an hour, until Mitchell's pontificating reached a loud, fever pitch. He had spent the entire time in the house telling people his religious beliefs, at one point shouting, "Jesus lives!" His rants became belligerent, and some of the guests were getting uncomfortable. A few asked him to leave.

Pamela Een was one of them. She escorted Mitchell to the door, but the women, for some reason, didn't follow him. When they got to the front of the house, Mitchell began shouting at Pamela, who was focused only on getting him to leave. Once he was outside, Pamela turned her attention to the two veiled women standing in the hallway.

"Are you okay? Do you need help?" Pamela asked, sensing something wasn't right. The women didn't answer. They turned and followed Mitchell, who stood outside the house, waiting. When all three were gathered together, Mitchell began what some guests at the party called a "chant." He was screaming for people to repent, that the house would be brought down, destroyed in some horrible way. The guests were spooked by the rant. But Mitchell suddenly stopped, and the three walked off into the night.

The friends and family from the life Mitchell had just a decade before would often see him downtown over the years, after he and Barzee had taken to the streets, but he never acknowledged them. That fall, one of Mitchell's relatives saw him drifting through the Crossroads mall, the shopping center he had been standing near when Lois Smart gave him $5 four months earlier. The relative called out to him, but he simply kept walking.

Doug Larsen, Mitchell's friend from his days working at O.C. Tanner, saw him near the mall one day. It was September 27, and Brian was wandering around. They locked eyes for a moment, but Mitchell kept walking.

That same day, Mitchell walked into Albertson's supermarket on 200 South. He picked up a flashlight, batteries, gum and beer. His odd dress and scraggly appearance caught the attention of a store clerk, who watched as Mitchell tucked the pilfered goods into his backpack. The employee summoned the manager, who called police. After a search of his pack, Mitchell was arrested for stealing $52.39 worth of merchandise. When police officer Robert Randell asked his name, Mitchell replied, "Go With God." He also gave the alias "Lueal." His birthdate, Mitchell told Randell, was "sometime after Christ."

On the way to the police station, Mitchell finally gave police his real name. He listed his mother Irene's phone number as his emergency contact. The driver's license he produced listed his address as "homeless." Mitchell was issued a citation and given a court date, which he later skipped. It was the first time he would be in police custody during the coming months, without anyone knowing they had Elizabeth Smart's abductor in their grasp.

A few days later, Pamela Atkinson saw Mitchell on the street in Salt Lake. He was alone, and he was panhandling. She realized later that the man whom she had tried for three years to steer toward social services was probably raising money for a trip to the West Coast.

Midway through October, the Smarts summoned the fresh set of eyes they had been seeking to Salt

Lake. Weeks earlier, they'd spoken with Henry Lee, the forensics expert who had consulted on the Chandra Levy case, JonBenet Ramsey's murder and the O.J. Simpson trial. Investigators had agreed to share information with Lee in the hope he might be able to spot something they'd missed. The scientist would spend a day and a half reviewing the crime scene and looking at evidence in the state crime lab.

"I'm very hopeful he can bring light on something or recommend something we can do," Ed said. The family was anxious to see what Lee would come up with, added family spokesman Chris Thomas, even if "he just sees that everything has been done correctly."

Though the move to bring Lee in was perceived by some to be a slap in the task force's collective face, the team seemed to welcome him. They weren't expecting him to crack the case. But Cory Lyman appeared open to the help, saying, "We're going to see if he has any suggestions that we should look at."

Lee took his time going through the house on Kristianna Circle. He combed Elizabeth's bedroom and examined the kitchen window where the cut screen had been, replaying the crime in his mind. Lee also sifted through evidence that had been collected. He spent time with the detectives, who turned over copies of their investigation reports to him. During his visit, Lee also had dinner with the Smarts, police and FBI agents. Lyman wouldn't divulge the results of the forensic expert's visit, and Lee had signed the confidentiality agreement that police asked of him. He said he wouldn't discuss the case with reporters or even the Smart family. But Ed said the scientist did say "he was very impressed with the people and the FBI and the way they have run the case."

The Smarts marked the kick-off of Utah's 2002 general rifle buck deer hunting season with an appeal to the state's 250,000 hunters to be on the lookout for Elizabeth. At a press conference with police, family members held up a pair of burgundy pajamas and Polo sneakers like those Elizabeth was wearing the night she disappeared. They handed out fliers printed with photos of the shoes and vital information about the missing teen. "Please keep your eyes open," David Smart urged, asking that special attention be paid to cabins or other shelters where Elizabeth could be hidden. "Call out her name . . . she could be inside."

By the time the hunters took to the woods, Elizabeth was in California.

"Dad, I think I know who it is."

They were the words that the Smart family would later recall Mary Katherine telling her parents sometime in October. She had been leafing through a *Guinness Book of World Records*, when something jogged her memory and the gears locked in place, her parents said. She put down the book and went into her parents' bedroom.

"Who? Who? Who is it?" Ed recalled wondering. "She said 'Emmanuel.'"

His ten-year-old was talking about the man who had been at the house almost a year earlier, Ed said. The man had pulled weeds and worked on the roof.

It had seemed inconceivable, the Smarts would say later. "Emmanuel" had been at the house for just a few hours of work, and didn't come back the next day, even though the Smarts had offered him another opportunity to make some money. But "Emmanuel" was the only person, at that point, whom Mary Katherine had singled out, the Smarts said later. And, her uncle Tom would later point out, she was the only eyewitness.

Exactly what happened between October and January was unclear. The Smarts said that Mary Katherine came forward with the epiphany, and that the following months were spent creating sketches and pressuring the police to put them out.

After Elizabeth was found, Dinse said investigators first learned of the roofer on October 13, and that he was on a list of potential leads that half of the task force was chasing. Other investigators said he surfaced the same week that Lois Smart sat down with investigators to once again go over a list of potential suspects. On October 15, Dinse said, Mary Katherine, her memory having been tapped throughout the probe, was interviewed at the Children's Justice Center. It was a sort of safe haven and neutral setting in Utah, where children are sometimes questioned in cases involving traumatic memories and where juvenile specialists conduct the interviews.

Between October 21 and November 18, Dinse

said, the police tried to track the roofer at homeless shelters around Salt Lake, but had no luck. During that time, they also checked videos from the Crossroads mall, because they'd heard the man they were looking for sometimes drifted through there. Security officials at the mall pointed to a man they knew as "Emmanuel," he said, but it wasn't the right person.

Other investigators said that Mary Katherine had indeed remembered something in October. Still others said officials didn't have the name of the roofer early on; he was known to them only as a worker who had come to the house. Later, there was confusion about the name, Tom Smart and law enforcement said. It's unclear what caused it, but investigators were working with the wrong name. They were looking for a man named "Manuel," not "Emmanuel." It wasn't until later that it was clarified, they said.

After Elizabeth was home, Cory Lyman said in an interview on ABC's "Primetime" that Mary Katherine had provided the name "Emmanuel," and she said he could be the kidnapper. But Lyman said that when he entered that name into the department's database to search for the files for anyone using that name or alias, he spelled the name with an "E" instead of an "I." When Mitchell was busted for shoplifting in September, the officer put the alias down as "Immenuel." Lyman didn't say in the interview exactly when that happened, but he said that since the spelling was off, Brian David Mitchell's arrest record never came up.

On the Elizabeth Smart task force, many investigators were still convinced that Richard Ricci was the prime suspect.

Salt Lake PD Sergeant Don Bell, the man who led the Elizabeth Smart task force during the first month after the abduction, later told the *Deseret News* that he was skeptical that someone who'd been at Kristianna Circle for such a short time could know the layout of the house well enough to come back and kidnap Elizabeth. In his mind, as far as suspects were concerned, "Ricci is number one, and there isn't even a close second." There was nothing about "Emmanuel" that would "elevate him above the many, many others." Bell, who had been taken off the case in September, later said that he spoke because he had been caught off guard by a reporter's call. But, as it happened, his words summed up the sentiment of many investigators. Until something seemed to elevate "Emmanuel" above other suspects, investigators weren't comfortable putting out a name or sketch.

It would be December before the public would learn of the existence of the roofer.

THIRTEEN

Mitchell, Barzee and Elizabeth arrived by bus in Lakeside, an unincorporated town in San Diego County, in the days soon after they left Salt Lake City. The small town is twenty-five miles east of the heart of San Diego, one of the original cowboy enclaves in the old West, rimmed by dusty hills. Right in the middle of the town is Lindo Lake, the only natural water besides the San Diego River that runs through Lakeside. The town is less than an hour's drive from the Mexico border. It abuts the city of Santee.

Lakeside residents call their town an unusual place, where different types of people coexist without paying much attention to each other. Bikers live alongside deeply devout churchgoers, store clerks alongside the vagrants who drift into their shops. There is also an active transient community in Lakeside, and some investigators early on thought that might have been why it appealed to Brian Mitchell. He and Barzee may have heard about Lakeside during their two years traveling across the country.

"How we got picked out of every community in the world is a mystery," said Captain Glenn Revell of the Santee outpost of the county sheriff's office. But Revell had one theory.

"This is pure speculation on my part, but we're within walking distance of another country with no extradition treaty," Revell pointed out. "In our line of work, I've had people say, 'How come she didn't just leave?'"

On at least one occasion, Elizabeth was away from her captors for hours and didn't run. But she was in a strange place, filled with people she didn't know if she could trust. And she had already spent months being held against her will, and that alone could explain why, Revell said. "If I tell you, 'You leave, and I'm gonna go back home and kill your family,' you begin to believe that that's entirely possible. That's the really frightening part, but it also sheds some great clarity on why a person doesn't just run away."

By the middle of October, the trio was becoming a common sight around Lakeside. Unlike Salt Lake, where Mitchell and Barzee were familiar faces for more than two years and had become part of the tapestry of the homeless network, their presence in Lakeside was felt, mostly because of Mitchell's preaching.

The sheriff's office first became aware of him in the last week of October, when they got a call complaining about a man in robes standing on the corner of Winter Gardens Boulevard and Woodside Avenue. He was spouting religious jargon, and the merchants nearby were being driven crazy by it, the caller said.

A sheriff's deputy who was normally assigned to the nearby town of Santee but who was working overtime in Lakeside, went to check it out, and found the man, dressed in white robes, with two women by his side. The women stood off to the side, their faces covered, while the man loudly preached to passersby. The deputy told the man that he was bothering storeowners, and would he please move along.

"Of course," Mitchell replied, surprising the deputy, who was expecting a challenge.

They talked for another 10 minutes or so with the deputy, who recognized strains of LDS church teachings mixed in with the man's words, asking about his beliefs.

"Is your preaching from the book of Mormon or the Bible?" the deputy asked. Mitchell explained that he had rewritten the book of Mormon, "correcting it" in places where it erred, the deputy would later recall.

Toward the end of the conversation, the deputy turned his attention to the veiled women. He tried to speak to them, but Mitchell stopped him. He didn't let them speak to anyone, he explained to the deputy. And he covered their faces "to cloak them from the atrocities of the world."

The deputy looked closely at the women's eyes, searching for any glimmer, any sign that they were looking for his help. But there was nothing, just blank stares over their masks. The deputy lingered a moment, but they didn't seem to need any help. He never wrote up a report on the encounter with the three, one of the many "contacts" that law-enforcement officials in Lakeside have with the homeless, because there was no criminal activity. It was something that essentially amounted to a noise complaint, and it had been resolved. The deputy moved on with the rest of his shift.

By that time, Mitchell had apparently begun setting up the campsites that investigators believe the three stayed in for most of the next four months. One was a ramshackle, abandoned trailer left in the middle of a green field on a hill overlooking El Captain High School at the northern end of the town. The white paint had peeled off the outside, and the interior was filthy, the tile floor strewn with glass, strips of wood, nails, and broken cabinets.

At some point, Mitchell also built their main camp in an area known to Lakeside residents as the "river bottom," in a clearing no more than a mile away from the trailer. Mitchell hollowed out a brushy area, about 20 feet by 30 feet, and created separate compartments where they slept. He apparently used duct tape to tie branches of trees together to build the frames for the little compartments.

"I guess that's their condo," remarked one sheriff's deputy after he viewed the campsite months later. But residents of Lakeside said the "condo" was actually the trio's main living quarters, an elaborate set-up stocked with provisions. There were about five rooms, one of them quite large, and it was well-stocked with provisions. There was a mattress and bedding in one section. There was also a little cooking area, with cans of sterno fuel and a little grate. There was a small washbasin for cleaning. Mitchell had put effort into making the huts, and it showed. He also built a makeshift altar where he and Barzee would pray. They called it "Golgotha," the name of the spot where Christ was crucified.

Within weeks, the trio became regulars around Lakeside, with Mitchell sometimes standing on the streets handing out religious pamphlets, possibly versions of his own prophecy. They also resumed the panhandling that paid for all of their meals. Unlike the high earnings that some of Salt Lake City's panhandlers make, the homeless population of Lakeside doesn't fare as well, Revell said. Those who beg for change won't make enough to get a hotel room, but they will have enough at the end of the day to buy food.

The three made daily public appearances, immersing themselves in the self-described cowboy town where no one was looking for Elizabeth Smart. They became regulars at grocery stores around Lindo Lake, at the town's center. Mitchell went almost daily to the KK Market across from the lake, where he'd buy a 99-cent can of Steel Reserve, a malt liquor. Then, they would go next door to Wrigley's market, where Mitchell would walk through the aisles in search of snacks, the women following close behind. Only Mitchell would pick items off the shelves—snack bars, chips—while Barzee and Elizabeth stood next to him, silent. He would always ask about prices, putting back anything that seemed too expensive. The extent of his conversations with clerks were usually, "How much is this?"

Mark Arabo thought they seemed strange when they first started coming into the store in early November, not because of their clothes or Mitchell's long hair and gnarled beard so much as their demeanor. He was struck by the way the women acted, almost zombie like, following the man around the store. They behaved that way every time they came in, which was about three times a week for most of the winter. Once, the store's butcher chuckled about what he thought were "costumes," and Mitchell clearly took offense. Another time, a clerk asked why he wore robes, and Mitchell replied that all people are naked in heaven.

They occasionally frequented the Sunburst Laundromat. Other times, they sat at picnic benches in the parks around Lindo Lake, eating fast-food lunches. Barzee and Elizabeth would slip the food beneath their veils, leaving their face covers intact.

The way of life in Lakeside is generally "live and let be." But in a town where most people fit into a pigeonhole of cowboy, biker or businessman, the religious wanderers stuck out. Most people didn't approach them, and the few who did were told that the three were ministers of the Lord, carrying out his word. Residents mostly thought they were creepy and stayed away.

Robert Smith, a handyman, saw them almost every day. They used the stretch of road that ran by his house, Wildcat Canyon Road, on the march to their "condo" almost daily. He would wave to Mitchell and the women. Out of curiosity, Smith eventually approached to ask who they were.

"We're from Heaven. We were sent here by Christ to do his work," Mitchell replied. He never gave his name, and said the women with him were his wife and daughter. Smith once got so curious about where they were going that he followed behind them and watched as they disappeared into their campsite. It looked like "a house without walls," Smith said. Where the brush covering the hideaway was thinnest, Mitchell had hung dark blankets. Smith knew the river bottom area well, but even someone who had walked through that brush a hundred times could have passed by the huts without realizing they were there.

A pastor's wife drove by the three while they were walking near Main Street. They looked cultish, she thought, and the women's apparent leader resembled Charles Manson. The two women walked several feet behind but kept pace with him. She saw the three again a few weeks later when they stopped at an Arby's restaurant.

Robert Smith saw the three board a bus to downtown San Diego nearly every day, where they took to the streets before a bigger audience of passerby with coins to spare. They also rode the trolley system that ran through Santee, a town just four miles east of Lakeside.

Mitchell didn't give his name to many people, although one man who ran into the three while Mitchell was passing out leaflets asked if they were Muslim and struck up a conversation with him.

They talked about what the name "Immanuel" meant, and the man pointed out that it translates to "God is with us."

"Yes, I am that person," Mitchell said.

As they had in Salt Lake, the three often headed for places with free food. On Thanksgiving Day, November 28, they caused a mild stir at a dinner for the homeless hosted by the Salvation Army at Golden Hall, one of the city's conference centers. There were trays of steaming turkey, mashed potatoes, green beans and stuffing, and they nestled in at a table with several other people. But in a sea of a thousand downtrodden faces, the three seemed out of place.

"They just stuck out like a sore thumb because of their outfits, and they were very quiet," recalled Tom Kovacs, a volunteer who helped with the dinner. The women slightly lifted their mesh veils to eat, but never showed themselves, and never spoke to anyone, or to each other. The man, on the other hand, chatted throughout the dinner. He looked like someone from the band ZZ Topp, Tom thought. He told people the women couldn't speak

under the doctrine of their faith although he never
said what religion they practiced.

Ed and Lois Smart said the days leading up to November 3, Elizabeth's fifteenth birthday, were spent
poring over pictures and looking at videotapes of
past celebrations, listening to their daughter's voice
trill from the television. The couple met with reporters to talk about the day, and Ed again pushed
for the AMBER Alert bill to move ahead, after it
had stalled in Congress. He took note of the sniper
shootings that had terrified people around Washington, D.C., through October. As tragic as the attacks were, Ed reminded the press, children are
abducted every day.

To mark Elizabeth's birthday, Ed and Lois took
William, Andrew and Mary Katherine to California, and to Knott's Berry Farm. Their eldest son,
Charles, had a dance that weekend, and decided to
stay in Salt Lake. But the rest of the family was
headed to Disneyland. It was one of Elizabeth's favorite places, they said, and if she couldn't be with
them, they wanted to be somewhere that would at
least bring happy memories.

The evening of Elizabeth's birthday, Ed and Lois
sat for an interview with Larry King on CNN.
King still used his show to keep the story going,
and he spoke with Ed and Lois about the difficult
benchmark.

It was hard, a "huge void," to be without Elizabeth, her mother admitted. "She needs to be with

us," Lois told King. "But we also realize that our other children need a life. And so, to remember and celebrate happy times, we wanted to do this." She smiled as she recounted the happy scene of Elizabeth's previous birthday.

King asked Ed if there was anything new to report on the search for his daughter. Ed told him about the visit of Henry Lee, the forensic scientist who had been brought in to review evidence in the case. Because Lee had signed a confidentiality agreement, the family wasn't privy to all of the expert's findings, Ed said. But he was encouraged that Lee agreed with things that were "kind of conclusive" in Ed's own mind. One of those issues, he said, was that Lee felt that whoever took Elizabeth knew the Smarts' house.

"The other thing was that Henry Lee concluded that our police and FBI are doing a terrific job. They're doing the best," Ed said. Some people, Smart told King, had questioned why the family had thought it necessary to bring in a private investigator. But it gave Ed and Lois "great comfort" to know Lee thought the investigation was being handled well.

Ed also talked about possible motives for his daughter's kidnapping. "Whether it ended up being a ransom that did go bad, I mean, because of the media attention . . . or some person having a fixation on Elizabeth. You know, those are the only type of scenarios."

As King and the Smarts began to discuss progress in the case, the conversation turned to

Richard Ricci. The Smarts told King they thought their former handyman had information about Elizabeth that he hadn't divulged before he died.

Ed said the fact that investigators believed the kidnapper knew the Smarts' house made the light "shine brighter" on Ricci as someone who could be involved.

"So you think Mr. Ricci was involved?" King asked.

"I think he had something to do with it," Lois said.

"But not—you don't think he acted alone and took her and killed her and then eventually died himself?" said King.

"That I don't know," Lois answered. "But I think there was someone there waiting for him to take him someplace when he dropped his Jeep back off. There was someone else that knew something."

Ed told King of his frustrations with Ricci, how he had never given them answers to their questions. And it was clear, on the day he appeared in court on the burglary charges, Ed said, that "Richard was not going to give us any help."

Soon, the conversation drifted to Mary Katherine and how she was handling her sister's absence.

"How about the younger sister coming forth somewhere to tell about the night?" King suggested.

"You know, it's been very traumatic for her," Lois said. "And to have to keep reliving it over and over—I mean, she was nine years old when that happened. It was devastating to her." Her younger daughter "seemed fine," Lois offered, adding that with the support of school friends, teachers and neighbors, Mary Katherine was "moving ahead." But Lois acknowledged that she couldn't surmise what went through Mary Katherine's mind when she went to bed each night knowing that Elizabeth wasn't there.

"She will bring up what she wants to bring up," Ed added, but talking about the night of the abduction was still painful for Mary Katherine. One night, after their kids had returned home from a counseling session with a therapist, Mary Katherine's anxiety was evident. "Mary Katherine says, 'Dad, do I have to talk? I just—hate talking about it. I just hate it,' " Ed remembered.

Elizabeth was never far from her family's minds as they traveled around Disneyland. They had no idea how near she really was. One hundred miles away, Elizabeth was marking her birthday with her captors, surrounded by strangers in a town she didn't know.

"She would have been in San Diego that day—I don't even want to think of what might have been going through her head," her grandmother, Dorotha, recalled later, her eyes welling.

The month of November marked nearly 4,300 man hours spent on the search for the missing teen by authorities, many of them consumed by wild-goose chases that went nowhere.

In September, police had received a tip that a man had been seen digging in the canyons near Manti, about a hundred miles south of Salt Lake.

He was spotted by hunters, who said it looked as if he were digging a grave. The man had claimed he was digging a pit to roast a pig, but the hunters noticed he was awfully close to the brush. Concerned, the hunters scrambled to town. When they arrived back at the spot with police, the man had vanished. One of the hunters drew up a sketch and it was quickly circulated. In the end, the lead turned up nothing.

Another tip that turned up nothing was delivered to Ed Smart in July. It was a single-page, typed letter from someone claiming to be in touch with Elizabeth's abductor. The kidnapper, the writer said, wanted to work out terms for the teen's release. The letter had been sent to one of Smart's neighbors, who faxed it to police and delivered the original to Ed and Lois. Ed went public with the information in the small hope that, if it were legitimate, the sender would contact him again. He never heard back.

Just after noon on a hot day in late August, a short, well-groomed man in flip-flops and denim shorts walked into Rocky Anderson's office and nervously asked to see the mayor. He claimed to be from a courier service and held a large white envelope in his hand. Told that Mayor Anderson was out, the man offered the envelope to an office worker at the desk and said, "If Mayor Anderson wants information about Elizabeth Smart, tell him to go to the Soup Kitchen at 1 p.m."

Summoned out of his meeting, Anderson went to the St. Vincent DePaul soup kitchen, where he was given another envelope. Inside was a letter. The writer, who claimed to be a substitute teacher, said Elizabeth had been spirited away by a boyfriend who had helped her escape a bad home life. The writer provided the name of the purported boyfriend, along with a phone number that turned out to be nonexistent and an address on a street that didn't exist in Salt Lake. The writer claimed to have given the same information to police in June.

Another letter followed and was quickly traced to a man named Phil Mokate, who claimed he was setting up a nationwide, fee-based program to find missing children. He offered to solve the Elizabeth Smart case as "the one free case that is being offered to Utah." Mokate was quickly dismissed as a crackpot. In a memo to Police Chief Dinse, Anderson's sharp wit and sarcasm was evident:

"You will be pleased to learn (as was I) that Mr. Mokate left a message for me today that the Lord has told him that we are to disregard the information he has provided. He also stated (apparently not realizing the internal inconsistency) that the Lord has told him that the Lord only speaks to one person, Gordon B. Hinckley. (He also added that he and his mother will, therefore, be getting baptized as soon as possible.)"

Not all correspondence could be so easily dismissed. From mid-October to November 4, a man claiming to be Elizabeth's kidnapper deluged investigators with forty emails, demanding a ransom of $3 million for Elizabeth's safe return. Using the name "elizabethsmartkidnapper," he used the Internet to contact the Salt Lake Police and the Royal Canadian Mounted Police, and even sent a handful of emails to Elizabeth's uncle, David Smart, who was manning the website set up to track his niece's case. Hoping to spare them more pain, David didn't divulge the full contents of the notes to his brother and sister-in-law.

"TELL ED TO GET 3 MILLION DOLLARS AS SOON AS HE CAN BECAUSE THIS THING HAS GONE ON LONG ENOUGH," one of the notes threatened. The sender gave instructions for a drop-off, writing "if theres [sic] other police or anyone else there or you try to stop my friends from leaveing [sic] then the snipers will be called in to clean up the mess."

Through online conversations with the sender, investigators quickly established that he didn't know details of the case that he should have, were he truly the kidnapper. But while he wasn't a suspect, the interstate threats were still a serious crime. The emails were traced to South Carolina, and on November 6 federal agents swept into the home of Kenneth Holloway, an 18-year-old part-time cleaning man who lived with his parents. There was no evidence of a connection to Elizabeth, but police confiscated Holloway's computer, some of his writings and four rifles. Holloway was later charged with interstate extortion and threatening communications. He was later expected to plead guilty.

Police were openly frustrated with the lack of

progress in the case. Still, most of the players, including the Smarts, continued to indicate publicly that they thought Ricci had held the answers they needed to unlock the mystery.

Task force leader Cory Lyman, who by then had been promoted from lieutenant to captain, hadn't often been quoted in the press during the probe. But in November, he embarked on a media push, issuing an open appeal for more clues. "We are working very hard right now to make our own luck," the investigator said.

Insisting the probe was still alive, Lyman said police had a list of suspects that fluctuated between three and five different names. And despite Ricci's death, the ex-con still topped the suspect list. During his media rounds, the investigator revealed that, in addition to the jewelry, perfume and cash stolen from the Smarts, Ricci also took some "trinkets" from the home. He wouldn't, however, disclose what those items were, or say whether they were important to the investigation. Police also remained skeptical of Ricci's alibi that he was home with his wife all night when Elizabeth disappeared.

Despite a shortage of solid leads, Lyman said task force investigators had plenty of theories, although they were the same ones they had been working with for months: She could have been taken for ransom, or she could have interrupted a burglary and been kidnapped by the thief after she spotted him. Or she may have been abducted by a sexual predator, Lyman said. Within the group of three Salt Lake detectives and two FBI investigators, opinions varied. Lyman considered this "healthy," an indication that options and possibilities were being kept open.

As her family suffered through a birthday without her, Elizabeth became a fixture in Lakewood. Out of Salt Lake, Mitchell seemed to become less furtive. The trio lived almost openly, sometimes in a decrepit, abandoned trailer and other times at their campsite. Several people saw them at stores and on the street, or heading toward their campsite at the end of the day. But, just as in Salt Lake, curious locals didn't question the three.

Each fall for seven years, Elizabeth Smart had performed in the annual harp concert at Utah's Capitol Rotunda, and her absence at the 2002 recital was palpable. The concert was dedicated to the missing young harpist, whose picture adorned the front of each program. In tribute, a light blue ribbon was attached to each of more than one hundred harps. Mary Katherine Smart took the stage in a black dress, wearing a pair of her sister's ballet shoes, and played Elizabeth's harp. For the grand finale, a videotape of Elizabeth played against a backdrop of string music. Part of the video showed Elizabeth playing her pedal harp, and it almost seemed as if she were there, playing along with the others.

The adults in the extended Smart family found themselves on an emotional "roller coaster," David Smart recalled. Lois still jumped when the phone rang, her heart filled with hope that it could be somebody telling her Elizabeth had been found.

But sometimes, family members said, hope was hard to come by. "There were days when it was hard to maintain hope. You know, the phone would ring and the police would say they found a body—we'd have to go see if it was Elizabeth. It was tough sometimes, because the reality is, it could have been her. Have we doubted? Yeah. But doubt and faith are very involved with each other."

During the course of the investigation, police called the Smarts "at least three times" when bodies of young women had turned up, Tom Smart said. "You just can't imagine it. Even when it didn't turn out to be Elizabeth, you know that you're looking at some other family's pain."

At some point, Tom recalled, "Ed had to consider, 'What is the worst thing that can happen?' If his daughter was being tortured at the hands of a madman, wouldn't he rather have her gone and at peace? And he said, I'm just selfish enough that I want her back with me."

Throughout the search for his daughter, investigators said, Ed Smart held steadfast to the belief that Elizabeth was alive. That dogged faith was echoed in the actions of his other children, who continued to mark their sister's absence with their own special plea to her abductor.

"Every time we had a meal with those children, one of them would end the blessing with: 'and please keep Elizabeth warm,'" her grandmother, Dorotha Smart, recalled. "They never faltered in their faith—they just knew she was out there, somewhere."

At a family dinner at an Asian restaurant in town that fall, the family paused before opening the fortune cookies delivered to the table at the end of the meal. As they began to crack them open, Dorotha said, "One of the children said, 'I think we all know what our wish is.' These children, they are just incredible. Their faith is such an example to us all."

The kids stockpiled gifts for Elizabeth's return, saving first her birthday presents and other trinkets, and later adding her Christmas presents to the growing pile. "They saved everything," said Dorotha, smiling at the memory.

At the end of the month, there seemed to be little new to go on in the hunt for Elizabeth. But the next eight weeks would put the investigation on the path to closure.

It was sometime in early January when Robert Smith noticed that Mitchell was suddenly walking alone on Wildcat Canyon Road without the two robed women. He was alone for so many days straight that Smith approached Mitchell one day. "I don't see your friends anymore," Smith said.

"They're staying with other disciples," Mitchell replied, adding, "We've got hundreds all over the United States."

Where Barzee and Elizabeth were during that time is known only to them and to people close to the case. But, as had been the case for some of their time in Salt Lake, Barzee was the person with whom Elizabeth spent more of her time while she was captive. Barzee would later tell a friend from her jail cell that she "loved" Elizabeth and would have done nothing to hurt her. She either didn't realize, or didn't want to realize, what she had become part of.

Ed and Lois Smart stood with Rocky Anderson at a Friday press conference. Elizabeth's parents wore their lapel pins with blue ribbons and their daughter's picture. They were making a new push for information about Elizabeth, and Anderson was upping the reward he'd offered months ago from $25,000 to $45,000. It had always been separate from the $250,000 that the Smarts had offered on their own from donations, and from the $3,000 Ed had offered at the end of August for answers about Ricci and about the Wright break-in.

There was a new qualification for getting the reward. Instead of being only for information that could help arrest and convict whoever was responsible for the kidnapping, it would also go to anyone who could help find Elizabeth's body.

"Someone out there knows something," said Ed. "I know that person will do the right thing and come forward. We look forward to having this come to an end."

Ed still felt his daughter was alive, but the announcement of the new reward was sobering. It acknowledged a statistical reality that was hard to accept. "It has been difficult to talk about the possibility that Elizabeth might be dead," Chief Dinse admitted because he didn't want to make the Smarts' ordeal harder.

But the lack of any resolution so far was frustrating, he said, and he wanted to see it figured out. Sometimes posting a new reward with a new condition could shake something loose. Maybe someone who had been afraid of speaking out would do it now.

Mary Katherine sat on a couch, her face cloaked in shadow. Jane Clayson sat across from her talking quietly. Clayson, a reporter with the "48 Hours" news show on CBS, had once worked for KSL-TV, the Utah station owned by the LDS church. She was the only reporter who ever landed an interview with Mary Katherine. The piece aired hours after the new reward money was announced, but it was taped soon after the family had returned from Disneyland in November. Mary Katherine's parents had shielded their daughter and their four sons from the press until then, although there had been many requests. The piece revealed a surprising new detail. Mary Katherine, her mother said, had thought she heard the kidnapper say he was after a ransom.

Clayson was prohibited from asking the Smart children, who were also part of the interview, certain questions. She couldn't ask Mary Katherine anything about what she saw when her sister was taken, but she could ask the little girl general questions about her sister.

With her scratchy, cautious young girl's voice,

Mary Katherine said she missed her sister and wanted her to come home. "It makes me sad to know that people in this country kidnap children and take them away from family and people who love them," she said.

Elizabeth's siblings said they would write notes to their sister. One of Mary Katherine's was, "Elizabeth, I miss you playing the harp, playing games with me, reading to me and sleeping with me." When Lois was on camera, she praised her little girl's bravery through the horrible early morning of June 5. "I want the world to know how brave and courageous she was. Because in a nine-year-old's mind, it could have been her whole family gone and she was the only one there," her mom said.

"And she absolutely did the right thing. And I want her to know that. That we are so proud of her, she did the right thing," Lois added. Ed also said his daughter had done the right thing. "She was worried that he saw her, and she hopped back into bed and just stayed there . . . Had she, you know, come running in or yelled, you know this, this person could have killed the entire family," he said.

"I think she has actually encased this little situation and probably put it somewhere for the time being," said Lois, about how Mary Katherine was enduring the weight of her experience. "But I do believe that at some point in her life, she'll want to deal with it and talk about it." Elizabeth was often the focus of family conversations, Lois said. It might have occurred when they went to the store and saw something she would have liked. "This is Elizabeth's favorite cereal—let's buy that one, Mom," she said, giving an example. "Or, 'She loves grapefruits. We've gotta buy some of those.'"

Ed and Lois mentioned that all five kids had gone to therapists soon after the kidnapping. But they didn't want to keep going, and their parents agreed to let them stop, taking comfort in their family instead.

Elizabeth's older brother, Charles, who was then sixteen years old, said the family knew they'd been through something horrible, and that it wasn't a normal occurrence in people's lives. "But we need to start making our lives normal and stuff so that it doesn't affect us more than it has to," he said.

The report swung around to look at the probe, and Cory Lyman walked Clayson around the Smarts' house, showing her the window where the screen had been cut. It was a ruse, Lyman believed, intended to mask how the kidnapper actually got inside and throw investigators off his trail. He said the kidnapper could have come through the back door, and might have had a key.

That matched something Ed Smart had said months earlier, when he announced the additional $3,000 reward for information about who Ricci left Neth Moul's shop with, and who had broken into his brother-in-law's home in July. Smart had said that some of the workers at his house had had keys, and someone could have made copies.

The piece also featured Angela Ricci, who had never wavered from saying her husband was innocent, and again said he wasn't involved.

The revelation that Mary Katherine may have heard a ransom demand was surprising, since it had never come up publicly before, and while police hadn't ruled out a kidnapping for money, no ransom demand over seven months had been real. Investigators later said that it hadn't come up in earlier interviews. She told it to her parents, who passed it on, they said.

"That's a possible piece of information," Dinse said in the *Deseret News*. "We're looking at all of that, although it's sometimes hard to determine when somebody remembers something after periods of time. You can put some weight behind it, but you can't be absolutely sure that that was accurate."

The Clayson piece brought in more than 100 phone calls from possible tipsters, and police went through the information one by one. The cops were also checking out an anonymous letter, claiming that Elizabeth was living in Seattle, with a whole new life. But there didn't seem to be anything to it.

The rest of the month seemed to pass quietly. But there were a series of talks about how to proceed with the "Emmanuel" information, and there wasn't much agreement. At that point, the name still hadn't been released, and the three sketches were a subject of debate. Some characterized the talks as "discussions." Others said there were tense disagreements.

Tom Smart said later that the police were dismissive about pursuing "Emmanuel." "The attitude was, oh, they're desperate. This 'Emmanuel' homeless person is one of the latest of fifty suspects they've asked us to try,'" he said. But investigators insisted they had, in fact, been searching for him.

Pamela Atkinson, the homeless outreach worker, said she didn't get any calls about "Emmanuel" and a connection to the Elizabeth Smart case. "If we'd only known last fall that we were looking for a man named 'Emmanuel,' we could have helped," she said.

"To us, he was known only as 'Emmanuel,' so our homeless friends would have known instantly who police were talking about. If police, or somebody, had called us and said this is the man, I have no doubt the Salt Lake homeless community would have found him. They regularly help turn up runaways, they have a tremendously strong grapevine, and they can reach people in places the police can't."

Within the next few weeks, the Smarts started a new search effort. This time, they were looking for their own prime suspect.

FOURTEEN

Ed and Lois Smart flew to New York in mid-December for an appearance on John Walsh's new daytime talk show to try to keep interest in Elizabeth's case alive. Walsh and Ed Smart had been in touch throughout the summer and fall, sometimes talking every day. Walsh later said the Smart case got into his system, and when he saw that Ed and Lois were struggling to keep the case going in the press to help find Elizabeth, he tried to help as often as he could.

Publicly, there seemed to be little movement in the case that month. Bret Edmunds, the target of a nationwide manhunt early on but who quickly fell off the list of suspects, was sentenced to up to five years in prison for fleeing from cops after he showed up at the candlelight vigil for Elizabeth right after the kidnapping. He had pleaded guilty two months earlier.

There was also some interest in finding out whether a terrible murder-suicide case in Arkansas could be linked to the Smart case. A 47-year-old man from California had killed a 13-year-old he met on the Internet, and then himself, and police found their bodies outside of Little Rock. The man had been a Salt Lake City resident decades earlier, and might have family still living in Utah. But it would take weeks to figure out where the man had been at the time Elizabeth was taken. Publicly, those seemed to be the only new potential leads.

By then, the investigation was six months old. Many involved were convinced Ricci was either the kidnapper or that he'd helped out in the crime. "If we weren't looking for Richard Ricci, we were looking for someone like him," a law-enforcement official said shortly after Elizabeth Smart was found. And at that point, most believed they were looking for a body. But Ed, investigators said, wasn't among them. He never thought Elizabeth was gone.

Throughout the late fall and early winter, the sheriff's department in Lakeside, California, had several contacts with Mitchell and his two companions, usually because someone had complained about the noise level outside their shop, as the self-proclaimed prophet preached on the street. Each time, the deputy told Mitchell that there were services to help the homeless, and that he might want to use them. Each time, he refused.

It was December 8 when a very different Brian David Mitchell appeared at the Santee Third Ward of the LDS church on Lake Jennings Park Road. Instead of his robes, Mitchell wore jeans and a blue checked shirt. His beard was tied in a rubber band, and his hair was slicked back in a neat ponytail.

He was "dressed like a normal Westerner," said Virl Kemp, a ward official who eyed the stranger as he came into the meeting house. The stranger gave his name as Peter, no last name, and then began asking questions about the faith, as if he were looking to join and wanted more information.

"He didn't make any odd comments, he didn't act out of place," Kemp said. "He just seemed like somebody a little out of place, but not terribly." But Kemp couldn't help feel the man was hiding something. It began when Mitchell took part in some of the church meetings and knew the words to every hymn. He was clearly someone familiar with the LDS church, and yet he asked questions that suggested he'd never been part of the faith before.

When Kemp left for the day, he got into his car with two missionaries he and his wife, Peggy, were hosting. They spotted Mitchell slowly walking along the street. Peggy nudged Kemp, saying they should invite the stranger home for dinner. Mitchell happily accepted the invitation.

At the Kemp home in Santee, Peggy had made a meal fit for a king. They had pork chops, chicken breasts in a cream sauce, and vegetables. There were two desserts, an apple cake and a Swedish almond cake made in individual servings. Mitchell polished off his plate and asked for seconds of everything. He washed it down with a scoop of ice cream.

The chatter around the table centered mostly on

Mormon theology. Kemp did what he could to make headway with his guest, who asked questions, and never mentioned that he had started his own splinter faith. He said he was from the East Coast, but he gave no hint that he had other people with him. Kemp talked about his family and might have mentioned that his wife's daughter from a previous marriage wasn't home. At the end of the meal, as the guest was getting ready to leave, Kemp gave him two gifts. One was a copy of the Book of Mormon.

The other was a beautifully bound copy of the Bible that the LDS church had spent hundreds of dollars printing. Kemp tucked in his name and address, telling Mitchell to get in touch if he ever needed anything, and offered him a ride back to Lakeside. Mitchell kissed Peggy's hand gallantly before he left, and they drove back to Lindo Lake. Mitchell got out of the car and walked away into the park. Kemp never saw him again.

It was nearly five months later when Kemp got a call from a reporter for the *Deseret News* in Salt Lake City, asking how he felt about the fact that Brian David Mitchell had tried to kidnap his stepdaughter. Kemp was stunned. He'd heard nothing about any kidnapping attempt from authorities, and he hadn't seen Mitchell since that one time at his house. The reporter said that Barzee, imprisoned in Salt Lake City, had told authorities that Mitchell had targeted the 12-year-old to add to his group. Kemp felt sick. He called the FBI for answers, but they couldn't give any. The reporter said that Mitchell had tried breaking into Kemp's home over the winter but left when he found it locked up tight. None of Kemp's neighbors had seen anyone strange lurking around the house, and he'd found nothing that was out of place. He wasn't sure whether to believe what he was hearing, but he was rattled by it. He felt as though the world had suddenly shifted on its axis. He made sure the windows and doors of the house were locked that night. And he believed that Mitchell's problems were, in part, because he'd left the LDS church.

"I know something about people who have once been members," Kemp said. "They tend to lose an awful lot when they leave. He's really living proof that you go way off the deep end. It keeps me on track."

The Wasatch Mountains were snow-capped two days before Christmas, and Salt Lake was awash in holiday spirit. Elizabeth Smart was still on people's minds around town, the "missing" posters with her picture still taped to store windows. Shoppers thought about the Smarts spending Christmas without their daughter, what was likely to be the first of many. Friends of Elizabeth's came by the Smarts' house with letters, talking about how much they missed her. Their words broke Ed Smart's heart. They showed how much Elizabeth was still on the minds of everyone who knew her.

On December 14, John Walsh aired another segment on "America's Most Wanted" about the Elizabeth Smart case, updating his viewers that the girl remained missing. Except for Walsh's shows and the Utah papers, the case had lost its hold on the media, and Americans were turning their attention elsewhere.

The weekend before Christmas, Dorotha and Charles celebrated their 50th wedding anniversary with a trip to the Homestead, a resort in the Heber Valley, a much-needed break after another season of heartache. Their children, Tom and Angela, had taken scads of family photos and looped them together in a video. The reel was studded with pictures of the grandchild who wasn't there. "It was very intense," Dorotha said. "There were lots of pictures of Elizabeth and it was just so overwhelming, an emotional time. We have so much, but we were missing so much, too, with her gone."

Her son, Tom, gave the family prayer, "and it was beautiful," she said. He talked about how hard a year it had been, and how "we were grateful for this chance for celebration, but that we miss Elizabeth every day." The Smarts took a round of family photos, and Ed and Lois posed for several shots with their five children, Dorotha said, recalling that Lois later approached Tom about whether there was a way to graft Elizabeth's image onto the pictures.

In late December, the sheriff's department suddenly stopped getting reports about Mitchell, Barzee and Elizabeth on the streets of Lakeside, and authorities thought they might have left the area. Some people saw them turn up in nearby Santee, Revell said, but officials couldn't find evidence of a campsite there. They may have gone there to panhandle and then commuted back to Lakeside to the "condo." But Santee is tougher on panhandlers than Lakeside is, Revell said, and Mitchell likely found it to be a difficult place to raise money. By that time, Mitchell was growing familiar with the area and could have found any number of spots that were more agreeable.

Wherever they were spending their days, some investigators said Elizabeth might have spent Christmas at the campsite. She had been away from her family for 203 days. Investigators had begun to believe she was lost forever. Instead of being known as Elizabeth Smart to everyone around her, she was simply the girl with the white veil, following the odd man with the beard, always just a few paces behind.

Two things happened on December 23, the Monday before the holiday, both related to the Elizabeth Smart case. The first was Captain Cory Lyman acknowledging he was leaving the Salt Lake police department to become the chief of police in Ketchum, Idaho, a resort town in the heart of the state.

By then, the Elizabeth Smart task force that Lyman was in charge of had shrunk from 100 police officers and FBI agents to about five. Ed Smart had nothing but praise for Lyman. The detective was the "epitome of what I would hope for in a policeman," he said. Lyman was their "Johnny-on-the-spot," Ed said, the family's go-to guy who'd kept the Smarts apprised of what was happening in the search for Elizabeth.

"I feel like I am abandoning you," Ed recalled Lyman saying, but Ed simply wished him well. Lyman's leaving, however, prompted immediate questions about what would happen to the investigation.

Nothing, the Salt Lake cops insisted. Ricci was gone, but they were still actively pursuing a number of threads that could unravel the mystery of Elizabeth's whereabouts. One of those leads was about to become known to the entire country.

That night, Larry King had John Walsh on his CNN show. There was no fresh kidnapping or crime that the two were discussing, and the interview started with easy chatter about Walsh's new daytime talk show, the search for terrorists involved in plotting the atrocities of September 11, 2001, and the number of criminals that "America's Most Wanted" had helped put behind bars.

They were about halfway through the segment when King asked Walsh how the investigation in Salt Lake was going. As it happened, Walsh said, he had just the day before been with Ed and Lois Smart.

"I said, don't give up hope. Justice delayed isn't justice denied," Walsh said.

Walsh had just had Ed and Lois on his new daytime show, in New York, to keep the focus on the story. They hoped that information about where

Elizabeth was hadn't died with Richard Ricci. The Smarts, aching from the lack of any information about their daughter, were bracing for the worst. They were frustrated that the case was slipping from the media spotlight, concerned it would hurt the search. Walsh promised them he would keep it alive. Then, Walsh casually mentioned the new mystery lead in the Smart case. He described it as one that could knock Richard Ricci from the top of the list of potential suspects.

"Their young daughter has now said that she believes that Ricci wasn't the guy in there that night, that it may have been another guy that did some work on their roof, an itinerant guy that worked at a homeless shelter, and he may be a suspect in this," Walsh said. "And I don't want to give away a lot of breaking information here, but 'America's Most Wanted' is going to take a look at the Smart case, because I know one thing—we have been able to solve crimes after ten years."

Walsh had first discussed the new suspect with Ed and Lois the week before, when they were in New York for the taping of his talk show, he said. But Ed chose his words carefully when he talked to reporters about the mystery suspect.

After the show, an Associated Press reporter cobbling together a piece about the new scrap of Mary Katherine's memory reached Ed, who said he was surprised by what Walsh had said. Ed didn't deny the lead, but he almost seemed to distance himself from Walsh speaking out so publicly on a piece of information connected to the case, and he made a point of saying the family was working with the investigators to solve the case.

"I didn't know he was going to do that," Ed said. "We're working with the police." He said it was so dark in his daughters' bedroom that night that he couldn't yet say exactly what Mary Katherine had seen, but that he hoped to be able to give a pretty detailed account soon. He never let the name "Emmanuel" slip from his mouth.

The next day, Chris Thomas said that Walsh spoke "prematurely," and that the family would give more information in the next few weeks. As for the Salt Lake police, they acknowledged that they had known about him for awhile and they wanted to talk to him, but what Walsh said shouldn't be taken as a huge break in a case plagued by dead ends. The unnamed man wasn't much different from any other lead, and he may not have even been around Salt Lake the morning of June 5. Ricci was still at the top of the police list of suspects. And nothing about what Walsh said suggested that Mary Katherine's story had changed.

"We would like to talk to him to clear up that lead," Salt Lake Captain Scott Atkinson said. Police were trying to find him, but they had only a single name and a description to go on. The man had been at the Smarts' house only that one day, and it was a long time before the kidnapping, Atkinson said.

The news was covered by the local papers and on the AP wire, but there was no national media stir. It was the holiday season, a time when news slips through the cracks, and the man police had said for months was their top suspect was dead. The story disappeared into the winter air. But Ed Smart's comments belied the tense back-and-forth between his family and the police over the new lead.

Four months later, reporters who covered the Smart case for the Salt Lake papers told the *Salt Lake City Weekly* media writer that they had started hearing about the roofer in December. One scribe said he learned from a Smart relative that "Emmanuel" was someone they wanted to locate. But both reporters opted not to write about it because neither the family nor the cops had talked about it publicly. It wasn't until the Larry King interview with Walsh that any newspaper made mention of the one-day handyman the Smarts had hired more than a year earlier.

The Smarts and the police both said later that there were three sketches made of a potential suspect in those days. The Smarts said they believed one of them was the closest match, but police said there didn't seem to be a clear consensus on the sketch, and without that, they were reluctant to release it. There had been a few other sketches made public before, and none had turned up any good leads.

Walsh later said the Smarts first told him about the roofer in December. "Early December, I get a call," Walsh said. "It's Ed. He said, 'I had a guy that Lois brought to the house to do some work

for one day and she thinks that this is the guy.' "
Walsh asked the Smarts for a composite and promised to feature it on his show.

Ed spoke with Walsh again about the roofer after he and Lois appeared on Walsh's talk show on December 20. Ed later suggested that police were refusing to put out the new lead because they wanted to handle it their own way for the time being. Law enforcement later said they were hesitant to release information because they had no idea what kind of person they were dealing with. If the man indeed had Elizabeth, they were afraid of scaring him off. Until they knew more, investigators said they wanted to tread carefully.

FIFTEEN

"Put it out, or we will."

Tom Smart would later recall that as the sentiment of the Smart family by February 3, when Elizabeth's parents held a press conference to announce a new reward in the case for anyone who could definitively show that Richard Ricci had nothing to do with the kidnapping, and to release a sketch of the mysterious roofer.

After weeks of debating what to do about "Emmanuel," the Smarts decided to tell reporters that Monday about him. Tom said the family told the police, who were still reluctant to put out something that they feared would spark a string of bad leads and bogus tips, that they were going public, with or without investigators, who then agreed to release the sketch.

Ed and Lois Smart addressed a relatively small group of reporters, compared to the crews that had flocked to the press conferences for any hint of news in the case over the summer. Two days earlier, the space shuttle Columbia had crumbled into pieces during its descent to earth. The national press was also heavily focused on the disappearance of a Modesto, California, woman named Laci Peterson, who had been close to her due date with her first baby when she vanished. Still, the Smarts tried to keep their message focused and said they were looking for the nation's help in finding a handyman who'd worked on their house for about five hours. He had his own interpretation of the word of God, and he went to different homeless shelters around the country preaching it, he told Lois. He said he was from "everywhere."

"He seemed like an awfully nice person," Lois said. She'd hired him downtown, near the Crossroads mall. He'd never given many details about his life.

The family said Mary Katherine called "Emmanuel" clean-cut, like the man who took her sister, and noted that she'd never said that about Richard Ricci. Ed said he hoped someone could come forward to prove Ricci was innocent.

"If somebody knows and can clear Richard Ricci, I would love nothing more. I would like to have Richard out of my life," Ed said.

Lois couldn't say at the press conference precisely how Mary Katherine came to realize that "Emmanuel" looked like the person who had taken her sister. But her children didn't have much to do with him that day, she said.

The Smarts later said they sometimes hired drifters to do work on their home, although Ed said he usually went through the Traveler's Aid Society, a social services group that has been renamed The Road Home. They work with the Utah Department of Workforce Services to place Salt Lake's homeless in jobs, both temporary and permanent. The DWS program involved background checks for permanent workers, but not for the temporary ones, who usually were placed in jobs much like the one "Emmanuel" did for the Smarts. Still, the officials at DWS were familiar with the group of transients that lined up at their offices each day, and could often vouch for them. Many people in Salt Lake use the service. Homeless outreach workers said it's uncommon for people to hire someone outside the DWS program, although they credited the Smarts with being generous.

Angela Ricci made clear that she was unhappy with the idea that her husband had to be cleared of something. She gave a statement saying she didn't think it was necessary to "exonerate" him for a crime he hadn't been charged with. People are innocent until proven guilty, she said.

"Emmanuel" was never described as a suspect during the press conference. Police said at the time that he was one of a handful of people who'd worked at the Smarts' home that they were still trying to track down, to see if they knew anything about the kidnapping. He was a "person of interest," but Richard Ricci was still at the top of the list.

The day after the press conference, Ed went to Washington, D.C., for a news conference with a handful of congressmen who were pushing for an

AMBER Alert law. They wanted a new bill in the House of Representatives, after another one had died months earlier. But the Senate had already passed its version, and Ed said he was hopeful that the House could do the same. Utah Congressman Jim Matheson, a Democrat who lived near the Smarts' home, said he couldn't give a good answer when his neighbor asked him why the measure hadn't yet passed.

"I don't know of anyone who doesn't think this is a good idea, and I am a little surprised we're back here again," Matheson said.

They'd heard Emmanuel might live in the camp-sites in the mountains, Tom Smart said later. He had been trying to find the drifter on his own, wandering around town asking about someone named "Emmanuel." But a problem for the family and for investigators was that the "Emmanuel" they were looking for was physically different from the "Immanuel" known as the "Jesus guy" to people around Salt Lake. He was clean-shaven and well-kept when Lois Smart hired him in November 2001, because that was during the time he'd shed his robes for fear of anti-Muslim attacks after September 11. "Emmanuel" was soft-spoken and nice, while "Immanuel" was known for preaching loudly at anyone who would listen. It was as if the Smarts were describing two different people.

The phone rang at the Salt Lake police department on February 8. On the line was someone who said they thought they knew who the man in the Smarts' sketch was. The relative told the officer who answered that the description sounded like one of their family members. The officer passed on the message, and someone on the Smart task force called back.

The call came days later because the relative hadn't seen the local news the evening after the press conference, but instead had been looking through archives of the *Deseret News* on the Internet. It wasn't the sketch that made the relative believe the person the Smarts wanted was Brian David Mitchell. It was the description: a roofer named "Emmanuel" who was a panhandler.

The police called up Brian David Mitchell's name on their computer, and there he was. He had a shoplifting bust last September, and there was a bench warrant out because he never showed up for his court date. The police told the Smarts they now had a name to go with their face, although the warrant Mitchell was wanted on was for a petty crime, and he had no serious priors, nothing to indicate that he might be a predator. The police asked the relative if the family knew where Mitchell was, but the answer was no. None of the Mitchells had had any contact with him in months. He had his hangouts around town, though, and the relative, whose name has not been released, provided some of the likeliest places where he would be. It was around five in the morning on February 12 when a noise from across the street awakened a housewife on Channel Road. She looked out the window and saw a man in long johns trying to pry open the window of one of the preschool classrooms at the Lakeside Presbyterian Church. He forced it open, put something in the frame that looked like cardboard, and crawled inside. The housewife quickly called the police.

Mitchell was sleeping on the floor of the classroom when police came into the church. His long johns were grimy and he smelled terrible. The police roused him awake, handcuffed him, and booked him. He said his name was Michael Jenson, and his birthday was October 17, 1954, an adjustment of the date and the year when Mitchell was actually born. He was in jail for six days. Police checked his fingerprints, and they showed up as belonging to Brian David Mitchell. But the computer didn't reveal the warrant out for Mitchell on his skipped court date for the shoplifting incident back in September because it was only a misdemeanor. Either way, police knew he was using an alias; what they didn't know was why.

The face and name of Brian David Mitchell were broadcast into millions of homes on February 15 when "America's Most Wanted" aired that night. This was the man wanted for questioning in the Elizabeth Smart case, the show said. A relative had called police after the sketch was released and told investigators that she didn't know where he was. But she provided information about him and said he may look different than he does in the sketch. He may have left Utah for a warmer climate.

"Police now know Emmanuel's real name is

Brian David Mitchell. He calls himself Emmanuel for religious reasons. He's believed to be traveling with his wife, named Barzee," the show said. "Police stress he's not a suspect. They want to question him about Elizabeth's disappearance."

When the show aired, Mitchell was in a lock-up in San Diego where none of the deputies who'd become familiar with him over the past months had seen the "America's Most Wanted" broadcast. They knew they had a man who was going by an alias, but there were no nationwide alerts in the system for him, and that was all they had.

Derrick Thompson was sitting at home when "America's Most Wanted" aired, and for some reason he decided to watch it, even though he hadn't seen the show in about a year. He almost choked at what he saw. He picked up his phone and called his brother, Mark. "Turn on the TV," he later recalled saying.

Their stepfather was being featured on the crime show as someone wanted for questioning in the Elizabeth Smart case. The Thompson brothers gathered their thoughts and then went out into Salt Lake, looking for their mom and Mitchell.

Barzee was at the campsite with Elizabeth when Mitchell was arrested. She had no idea what had happened to him, and she was becoming manic with worry about where he might be. On the fourth or fifth night that he was behind bars, Barzee came undone. She was terrified that he wasn't coming back, and she believed he might have died. Late one night, Barzee left Elizabeth alone at the campsite and went to pray at "Golgotha," the altar they had built.

Barzee would later tell friend Vicki Cottrell that she had prayed and cried for hours. She was in terrible pain. She thought she was dying. She stretched out in front of the altar, waiting for some sign from God. She was eventually visited by "attending angels" who helped her through the night. There were many who came to her, she told Cottrell. Her father was there, and her grandfather, and Johann Sebastian Bach, her favorite composer.

At the campsite, Elizabeth was all alone for hours, yet she stayed where she was. She may have been too terrified to run, or unsure of whom she could trust if she tried to get help. Whatever the reason, when the sun rose over Lakeside the next morning, Barzee had made it through her torment. She made her way back to the campsite, where Elizabeth was waiting for her.

"She said Elizabeth told her that she was worried about her and was going to go out to look for her, but she knew she was supposed to stay where she was," Cottrell said.

Ed Smart stood outside Shriners Hospital with his brothers on February 18. With a brilliant sun shining above him, he said he was grateful that someone had identified Brian David Mitchell, and that now he hoped he would be found. It was hard to put a value on whether the roofer who'd once helped him at the house was "the one." But the key was that Mary Katherine had said he looked like the person in her room. She remembered his hair being slicked back.

The Smarts didn't call Brian David Mitchell a suspect, but they were clearly interested in him. At that point, they believed his alias was "David Emmanuel Isaiah." But it was significant that Mary Katherine had come forward with the information about him, Ed said. "I couldn't imagine how Mary Katherine could have remembered this person," he said. He added that "she doesn't know that it was him."

The information from his daughter "was a possible, it wasn't a definite."

Dwayne Baird, the Salt Lake PD spokesman, said in press reports that cops had been looking for "Emmanuel" since October. They'd checked homeless shelters and other places, but "he's one of dozens of people who worked on the house," Baird said. The cops hadn't confirmed that "Emmanuel" and Brian David Mitchell were one and the same.

But the family, at that point, was near certain they were. And hundreds of miles away, at the other end of the country, the man the family was looking for was in court for his sentencing hearing for breaking into Lakeside Presbyterian. The hearing had been delayed by the President's Day holiday that had shut courts around the country a day earlier. The hearing was a videotape conference, where Mitchell appeared via closed-circuit camera. He looked almost frail during the appearance, his blue prison shirt hanging off his shoulders. His wild hair hung in his face, a scruffy contrast to the court-appointed lawyer, David Lamb, by his side. Mitchell's voice was throaty as he pleaded guilty to breaking into the church. Superior Court Judge Charles Ervin asked Mr. "Jenson" where he would be living in the future. Mitchell said he didn't know.

"Um, my wife and my daughter are staying with some friends presently in, uh, Lakeside and, uh, I'll be, I'll be there, too," Mitchell said. He sounded nervous. "We're staying with some friends in the Lord Jesus Christ. Uh, I'm a minister for the Lord and, uh—"

"Where are you living? Do you have a place to stay?" the judge interrupted.

"With, with these friends," Mitchell replied.

Judge Ervin said that he would release "Mr. Jenson" from custody and put him on probation.

"Now, you just told me that you're a minister for Jesus Christ, and I appreciate that," the judge said. "But if you're going into the Presbyterian church or any of those churches out there in Lakeside for the purpose of ministering and they don't want you on the property—if you don't have permission on the property, that's gonna be a violation of the charge of burglary that I'm sure Mr. Lamb's gonna discuss with you momentarily.

"Also," Ervin continued, "if you're going into

those churches and you're breaking the window and you're going in there because you don't have a place to live, that likewise could be a violation of the law. You understand that?"

"I do, your honor," Mitchell said, leaning toward the microphone in front of him. "And that, that was the worst night and the worst week of my whole life."

Mitchell stammered slightly. "I, I had, I had for the first time in 22 years—I got drunk that night and, uh, and the whole night was just a nightmare and, and it's, and, and I, this week in jail has, uh, been like, uh, Jonah getting swallowed by the whale," he said.

"It's, it's turned me right around and, and I know I need to do what the Lord wants me to do with my life and," he paused for a second, then pressed on. "And I am deeply sorry and, and, uh, nothing like that's gonna happen again."

Mitchell had pleaded guilty to a misdemeanor charge of vandalism, and he was given three years of probation. He was told to pay a $250 fine, $100 of which was payment to the church for damaging their property. He vowed to abide by his probation, and he was released. Before he was out of custody, sheriff's deputies warned him that they knew he was hiding something.

"We know you're not Michael Jenson," Revell recalled officials saying. "We can't figure out why you won't tell us who you are, but we're trying to figure it out."

By that time, the name "Emmanuel" had been broadcast into millions of homes by John Walsh, but no one working at the Lakeside sheriff's office had been watching it, and there was no national bulletin out for Brian David Mitchell yet. There was nothing in the national crime database saying he should be kept in custody, so they let him go. But they had warned him that they were trying to figure out who he was, and Revell thought that might have frightened him.

Barzee gave Vicki Cottrell a different story later on. She told Cottrell that she and Mitchell had had a "revelation," God's voice telling them that they were to go home, back to Utah. There would be no fulfillment of "Immanuel's" prophecy, and they would "be arrested by the evil-doers," she told Cottrell.

In the days immediately after the Smarts' press conference at Shriners Hospital, national TV networks aired blurbs about the new name in the case. The Associated Press put a story over the wire about the search, and a smattering of newspapers around the country used it. One was the *San Diego Union-Tribune*. It was a small piece about the hunt for the drifter whom the Smarts were asking people to keep an eye out for.

Tom Smart heard that Brian David Mitchell sometimes went into the Wild Oats market, and he added it to his list of places to check. A friend told Tom that he'd seen Mitchell camping out in the hills, and the friend gave a detailed map of exactly where he'd seen the drifter. Tom later said he gave that map to police to check out sometime in February. At the stores Tom checked, several people reported seeing him. He heard a rumor from his daughter that Brian David Mitchell had been seen around the University of Utah. The people who'd seen him around said he'd had two women with him.

While Tom was trying to gather every scrap he could about Brian David Mitchell, Barzee's sons were also trying to find them. They went to the Greyhound bus terminal, to the malls, to street corners where they knew their stepfather often went to preach or to beg for money. They showed people pictures of their mom and stepdad, hoping anyone could help. Time was elastic, and some people thought they'd seen the robed man around town within recent weeks, reports that would later prove wrong, and there was suspicion that Brian David Mitchell might have fled the area once he learned people were looking for him. But the Smarts hoped they were getting closer, and they would turn out to be right.

After the "America's Most Wanted" episode aired, Debbie Mitchell made contact with the Smarts. She said she immediately thought her ex-husband could be the man with Elizabeth, and she wanted police to be aware of everything she remembered from their marriage. She said she told them what she knew, including the stories her daughter Rebecca had told her after Debbie and Mitchell separated. By then, the Smarts were starting to put together a map of Brian David Mitchell's life. Debbie offered the Smart family an insight that later proved true: She felt that if Mitchell had Elizabeth, then Elizabeth was still alive.

The new man wanted for questioning was starting to get some attention. Police were getting tips of possible Brian David Mitchell sightings from all over, and they were trying to track them. They were looking for him, but none of the leads called in had panned out so far. In the press, the Salt Lake police department downplayed the possibility that "Emmanuel" could have committed the crime. Ricci was still at the top of the list. Whatever their efforts were, their ultimate boss wasn't happy with the way the case had gone.

Mayor Anderson sent Chief Dinse a memo on February 28 saying he was "concerned" about the investment that had been placed in Richard Ricci as a suspect. With everything that was coming out about "Emmanuel," it seemed like it had been the wrong track to follow.

"Although I have tried to stay out of the Elizabeth Smart investigation as much as possible, leaving it for the Police Department to do its job, I have felt it appropriate to intervene on occasion to follow up on matters that have, in my view, negatively impacted members of the Smart family or the investigation.

"I have been especially concerned with the public commitment of the investigators to the Richard Ricci theory," Anderson went on. He gave nine points that troubled him:

"1. The only eyewitness, Mary Katherine Smart, has maintained from the beginning that she did not think Richard Ricci was the abductor.

"2. There is no physical evidence tying Richard Ricci to the abduction.

"3. Richard Ricci has no past history of sexual abuse or abductions.

"4. Mary Katherine independently suggested the abductor may have been 'Emmanuel.'

"5. Emmanuel was somewhat familiar with the Smart home.

"6. Emmanuel has a history of child sexual abuse.

"7. Emmanuel was seen nearby, at a Kinko's on 1st South, near the University of Utah, on the afternoon Elizabeth was abducted.

"8. Emmanuel was known to camp out near the Shoreline Trail, above the Smart home.

"9. Perhaps most telling, Emmanuel apparently has left the area since information about his possible involvement was disclosed."

"I am at a loss as to why the Police Department did not aggressively pursue the Emmanuel angle and why it (and you) discouraged Ed Smart from disclosing the possibility of Emmanuel being involved," Anderson fumed.

"Why is the Police Department, through its investigators and public information officer, downplaying the possibility that Emmanuel was involved?"

The memo, released publicly a month after it was sent, again mentioned the murder cases that Anderson worked on when he was in private practice. In those cases, he said, police had committed to a theory, and he was afraid that was happening all over again. The long-standing mistrust between Anderson and his police force was about to boil over.

On March 1, "America's Most Wanted" aired a fresh segment on the hunt for Brian David Mitchell. There were new photos of him, some with a beard and some without, provided by Barzee's sons. Around that time, authorities put out the first nationwide bulletin to be on the lookout for Brian David Mitchell, who used the alias "Emmanuel." More tips poured in from the latest "Most Wanted" episode. One was from someone in the Lakeside, California, area, who said they'd seen a man who matched the description of "Emmanuel." He had been seen around town with two women in veils.

On Sunday, *Deseret News* columnist Lee Benson ran a piece about the search for the roofer and the

family's efforts to track him down. He quoted
Irene Mitchell as saying she was "absolutely positive my son did not do this." He wrote another col-
umn the following week, saying police needed to
keep up their own search for "Emmanuel."

Members of the Mitchell and Thompson families had provided the Smarts with as much information as they could about Mitchell and Barzee,
but the thought that the couple could have had
anything to do with what happened was surreal
and disturbing. The Smarts were still saying publicly that they wanted Mitchell only for questioning, but it was becoming clear that they thought he
was definitely involved. That week, an investigator
from Salt Lake was sent to the Lakeside area after
the tip that the trio had been seen there, officials
said. Exactly when the cop arrived wasn't made
clear, but he was trying to locate the trio.

Dusty Harrington watched as three filthy people
stood by the counter. Harrington, the manager at
the Lakeside branch of the San Diego County library system, had seen them come in before, back
in the late fall. But that time they were dressed in
off-white robes. That time the man had read one
of the newspapers, either the *San Diego Union-
Tribune* or *USA Today*. Other times, she saw them
panhandling near the library. The man passed out
little religious pamphlets telling people to "believe
in the Lord" or that "Jesus is your friend." She often gave them money just to make them go away.
But on that day during the first week of March,

the three were dressed in mud-spattered street clothes. They all wore jeans. The man wore a red-and-blue-plaid shirt, and the young girl wore cat-eyed sunglasses that hugged her face. Her hair was pulled back in a sloppy ponytail. The man asked for an atlas of the western United States. He was particularly interested in looking at Arizona, he said.

Dusty looked them over, wondering why the girl wasn't in school. But as she took in their smudged clothes, she realized they were homeless. The man, especially, was a mess, his hair a gnarled halo around his head.

The young girl looked at the man and started to say something to him. But the older woman reached over quickly and circled her fingers around the girl's wrist, Dusty recalled later, and the teenager stayed silent. They went to a table, where the man studied the atlas for about an hour. If he had something to say to the older woman he would tap her, and she'd lean over the table to hear him. The girl sat at the table, saying nothing.

On March 4, a skateboarder who'd been in the mountains in the morning, rock climbing with friends about 35 miles north of San Diego, saw the robed travelers standing on the street, *Time* magazine reported later. It was pouring, and they were out in the middle of nowhere, so the young man offered them a ride, he recalled later. The man in the robes called himself Peter and said he was with his wife and daughter. The girl was named Augustine, and she was fresh out of high school. They were heading to Las Vegas, he said, where he would spread the word of God. They got about 40 miles into the drive when the man asked to be let out. The driver could pull over at a nearby store, he said. They got out and went on their way.

People who encountered Mitchell, Barzee, and Elizabeth remember him providing different names for the girl he called his daughter. Investigators haven't said exactly when he began calling her Augustine, or why he chose the name. Saint Augustine, considered by many Christians to be the founder of theology, considered adultery to be the ultimate transgression for men and women. In his book *The Confessions,* St. Augustine wrote about trying to reconcile his spiritual life with the one he lived on earth, filled with material needs. Mitchell wasn't lying when he said they were headed for Las Vegas. It was one of the final stops of the horrible, circular nine-month trip. By March 12, the world would know what Ed Smart had always believed— that Elizabeth was still alive, but there was a long road left to travel before it happened.

SIXTEEN

The workers in the Burger King in North Las Vegas watched the three people stand in front of the restaurant for awhile, panhandling. It was around lunchtime on March 11 when one of the workers called North Las Vegas police about a group of people hanging out in front of the fast-food place. But when the cops showed up, the trio was gone.

The police drove up the street until they caught up to the three, who were simply walking down the street. The police asked to see identification from the group, who looked like transients. They had no identification, they said. But the man gave his name, Peter Marshall. The older woman was Juliette Marshall, and the younger one was Augustine. They gave their birth dates, but they didn't seem to want to answer questions.

The cops talked to them for almost a half hour, until around 1:30 p.m., standing on the street in a city that abuts the Las Vegas most people call Sin City. The Strip, with its casinos, can be seen from the distance. While the trio waited, the police ran a check on their names, and their identities "checked out," officials said later. The cops sent the three on their way.

Police would later say they suspected the three were actually Brian David Mitchell, Wanda Barzee, and Elizabeth Smart, although they hadn't known it at the time, and they had no reason to hold them. The encounter was on a street about a block from Interstate 15, the main route running from California, through Las Vegas and straight to Utah. The Beehive State border was less than 100 miles from the Burger King. Fourteen hours later, Brian, Wanda, and Elizabeth had crossed it. By that time the next day, Elizabeth Smart would be discovered.

Ryan Johnson was getting breakfast when a stranger started a conversation with him at a McDonald's in Springville. Johnson was on a break from his job, and the man mentioned he was heading to Salt Lake City. Johnson offered to give him a lift to a bus stop. The man was traveling with two women, one wearing a gray wig, although her uncovered face was clearly young.

The man told Johnson that he'd had a vision from God to go to Salt Lake City and preach a new religion. The three had been staying in San Diego until they came to Utah, he said. The girl looked frightened, as if she wanted to speak up but couldn't, Johnson thought.

Something about the girl's face stayed with him, and he tried calling police, but he couldn't get through. He later learned that he had dialed the wrong number. He also later learned who he had ferried from Springville to Provo.

SEVENTEEN

When Salt Lake residents opened their copies of the *Tribune* the morning of March 12, they found a story in which Tom Smart, for the first time, came out swinging against the police. He accused them of being too slow in trying to find Brian David Mitchell, the man he called "the biggest lead right now."

"They should have caught this guy by now," Tom told the paper. But he accused the cops of placing too much stock in the theory that Ricci was the top suspect.

"It's a way to cover your ass," he said.

It was completely uncharacteristic of how the family had publicly handled their relationship with the police in the months after Elizabeth's abduction. Before then, the family gave measured statements about the authorities. Ed Smart occasionally mentioned having "words" with the cops, but that was the extent of it, until that morning.

Tom said that when his niece, Mary Katherine, made the connection between the man in her room the morning of the kidnapping and "Emmanuel," it was "the mother of all epiphanies."

In the story, Ed's criticism was more muted than Tom's. But he did say he was frustrated that police were, in their comments to the press, suggesting that Brian David Mitchell wasn't a major lead. He wasn't displeased with the work of the detectives on the case, he said. But he didn't agree with a decision to keep Mitchell from the press.

"I hope police comments aren't downsizing the chance to find Elizabeth," Ed said. "When the only eyewitness says it could be him, that is important."

Police at that point said the FBI was tracking a sighting of Mitchell in Miami, and that many people were trying to flush him out.

"Look, if we wanted to blame Ricci for this, we would have closed the case by now and told the Smarts we were no longer investigating it," Lieutenant Jim Jensen, who had taken over the role of task force leader after Cory Lyman left, told the paper.

But Tom Smart said days later that he thought police had "completely discounted" Mary Katherine. "By October, they were completely focused on Ricci. But Mary Katherine always said he didn't do it. She said, 'They don't think it's Richard, do they, Dad?' She was the only eyewitness, and they didn't take her seriously."

The article was the talk of people who had followed the case that morning. But by the afternoon, it would be replaced by a much bigger story.

A few hours after the *Tribune* hit the newsstands, the investigator tasked with finding Elizabeth after the sighting in San Diego was in California, working out a plan to extradite Brian David Mitchell from that state to Utah for his missed court appearance on his shoplifting charge, law enforcement would later say. They hadn't found the man, but they thought the person they'd been tipped off to might be him, and he might have Elizabeth. He'd been seen around town with two women, one of them a young girl.

That morning, the Santee sheriff's office got a call from Salt Lake investigators about "Emmanuel" possibly being in their area. When they downloaded the picture from the "America's Most Wanted" website, they had no doubt that he was the drifter they'd spoken to about a dozen times during the last four months. They were taking the picture around and asking if anyone had seen him, when they got another call. "They said, 'Never mind. We've got him,'" Revell recalled later.

"911."

"Is this where I call if I think I see that Emmanuel they're looking for?" Nancy Montoya asked the 911 operator from her cell phone.

On March 12, at 12:52 p.m., Nancy and her husband Rudy sat in their car, watching a man in a green T-shirt and a brown hat with flowers on it, followed closely by two women in robes. Nancy was nervous as she spoke to the operator. She kept her gaze fixed on the three as they walked by the Southtowne Mall. She was an avid "America's

Most Wanted" viewer, and she was pretty sure
she'd just seen someone John Walsh had talked
about on the show.

The three carried filthy bedrolls and a Wal-Mart
shopping bag as they slowly made their way north
on State Street.

"Is he wearing robes?" the 911 operator asked.
Nancy could hear him typing furiously in the
background.

"He's wearing, like, quite a bit of something,"
she replied. "They're carrying sleeping bags, and
he's got a big, bushy beard.

"He's with two ladies," she added. "One of
them has gray hair, and the other one has her head
covered."

Seven minutes earlier, the Montoyas had
walked out of the Kinko's in downtown Sandy,
climbed into the car, and caught sight of the peculiar travelers.

"Those look like homeless people," Nancy told
Rudy, who thought the man looked familiar.

"That looks like that 'Emmanuel' on 'America's
Most Wanted,'" Rudy said. They swung their car
around to get a better look.

"That's him," they told each other, and Nancy
reached for her phone.

Nancy Montoya's call was technically the second one to come into 911 related to the transients.

Seconds earlier, Anita and Alvin Dickerson were
heading north in their car when they spotted the
bearded man and his two companions.

"Pull in there!" Anita told her husband as he circled back and eased the car onto the blacktop outside the Kinko's.

She got out of the car and waited for the man to get close enough to make eye contact. She could swear she'd seen his face on the local news. One look was more than she needed.

Anita dialed 911 and told the operator she was calling about the man wanted in the Elizabeth Smart case. But the operator accidentally switched Anita to the Salt Lake police. The Salt Lake switchboard transferred her back to Sandy, just as Nancy was finishing her call.

Nancy's heart was racing, as was Anita's. They might have seen the man connected to Elizabeth Smart's disappearance. But they were so focused on Mitchell, they didn't even wonder about the faces of the two women behind the veils.

The transients' slow walk up the boulevard came after a trip to a Wal-Mart a few blocks from the Sandy police station. At the Wal-Mart, Mitchell, Barzee and Elizabeth roamed the aisles for about an hour. Elizabeth drew odd looks from store clerks, her gray wig framing her face and her oversized sunglasses shielding her eyes.

No one said a word to them.

They lingered over three sleeping bags and blue tarps, "the kind kids make pup tents out of," a store clerk recalled. As always, they took advantage of a public bathroom, spending 15 minutes getting themselves together before they left. They were headed toward the bus stop near 104th South and State Street when a patrol car arrived.

Sandy Police Officer Karen Jones had been on patrol nearby and was the first to answer the call over her radio about sightings of a group of transients.

Jones, a short redhead with an open face and a quiet manner, didn't know what to expect while she was en route. As she pulled up to the curb, she spotted the trio and immediately thought the man looked like the face of the "Emmanuel" everyone was looking for.

The robed group, smelling of funk and covered in grime, was similar to the frequent drifters that police in the Salt Lake City area are accustomed to, the type the police often pass by if there's no complaint called in.

But the man's face burned in Jones's brain. She stopped them and told them she needed to detain them for a few minutes. She asked them their names and for some identification. The two women didn't speak. They stood off to the side and nervously watched Jones as she spoke to Mitchell.

"What's your name, sir?" Jones would later recall asking.

"Peter Marshall" was the answer. He said he was with his wife, Juliette, and their daughter, Augustine.

Jones pressed him for ID, but the man insisted they didn't need it. The older woman with him barely spoke.

"We are messengers of God," Mitchell insisted,

according to police accounts. "We are free of all worldly things."

Just a few feet away, Elizabeth was under her makeshift veil—a T-shirt wrapped from its neck around her head—and the gray wig. Their clothes were soiled. Jones didn't realize that she might be just feet away from Elizabeth, focusing, just as the Montoyas and the Dickersons had, on Mitchell. As she pressed him, another officer, Troy Rasmussen, arrived at the scene. Rasmussen, a soft-voiced, barrel-chested cop, honed in on the wigged young girl. "She looks like Elizabeth Smart," he said to Jones.

Jones asked the girl whom she was traveling with. She said they were her parents. Jones and Rasmussen glanced at each other. Jones went to her squad car to alert Salt Lake City police to what was happening, and Sergeant Victor Quezada and Officer Bill O'Neal arrived.

The officers took turns talking to the adults and to the young girl whom they were growing convinced was Elizabeth. She said she was 18 years old, and when they told her she didn't look that old, she said, "Well, I am," the officers recalled. Elizabeth was defiant, even petulant with the Sandy police, the authorities said. For most of the next 45 minutes, she acted as if they were prying into her privacy. They peppered her with questions, and her story gradually changed each time.

Quezada pulled her aside and tried to talk with her about topics other than her identity. She told

him about all the things she had done with her
"parents." They were ministers of God, and the
girl said she couldn't imagine doing anything else.
Her name was Augustine Ann Marshall, from Miami, Florida, she said. When she couldn't answer
basic questions about the couple she called her
parents, she said they were her "stepparents."

Quezada told her he didn't believe she was 18
years old, and he would like it if she'd admit to
who she was. "I know who you think I am," she
said. When he asked who, she said, "That Elizabeth girl."

When Rasmussen questioned her, he asked
where her mother was born, and Elizabeth faltered. "Well, this is my stepmother, and that's my
father," he recalled her saying. The cops were
growing convinced with each stumbling answer
from Elizabeth that she was the girl authorities
were searching for. But they were dumbfounded
that she was denying her identity.

The scene was surreal for the officers, who expected the girl to simply step forward and say who
she was, and that she needed help. Instead, she did
everything she could to steer them in the wrong direction. The hold that "Emmanuel" had on her
was so strong that she maintained the charade
even as the story began to crumble.

Rasmussen asked Elizabeth why she was wearing her big sunglasses.

She claimed to have just had eye surgery in San
Diego and said she was sensitive to light. "Why are

you wearing a wig?" Rasmussen recalled asking, looking at the mop of salt-and-pepper curls.

He said the girl insisted, "This isn't a wig, it's my real hair." Incredulous, Rasmussen asked about the wig again, and why the girl would need it. She told him it was "personal," none of his business.

At one point, O'Neal, who had been briefed by Rasmussen about the situation, took Mitchell aside while some of the other officers talked to Elizabeth, and he asked where the three were from.

"We're from Miami," Mitchell replied to O'Neal, a Florida native. "Miami, Florida?" O'Neal asked.

"Miami, Miami," Mitchell answered. When O'Neal asked him which part of Florida, Mitchell said it was the "Dade County area." O'Neal pointed out that Miami is in Dade County, and Mitchell said, "All I know is that we're ministers of God and we're traveling to spread his word." Investigators later recognized the name Peter Marshall as the longtime host of the show "Hollywood Squares."

One of the officers went to get one of the "missing" fliers bearing Elizabeth's picture. By then, Salt Lake detectives had arrived. The girl in the photo looked a little different from the one standing on the street—her face was fuller, and her cheeks were ruddy—but they knew it was her.

When Jones questioned Elizabeth on her own, the girl who was calling herself Augustine made some reference to Elizabeth Smart, and Jones started talking about how much all of Salt Lake missed her, and how no one had ever stopped looking for her. The girl seemed to falter for a minute, as if she was going to cry, and Jones even called her Elizabeth to her face. The girl didn't object to the name, but her eyes were blank.

O'Neal eventually started questioning the girl, and Elizabeth also told him she was from Florida. When he asked her what her zip code was, Elizabeth told him that the three had moved around so much "that I never learned all those numbers." Then, she gave him six digits-110223. The cop told her she'd given one digit too many.

He asked her date of birth, and she paused just a second too long. It was November 4, 1984, she said—one day later than her real birthday, and four years earlier. "I know who you think I am," she told the officers, her eyes darting, O'Neal recalled.

"Okay, who do we think you are?" O'Neal asked.

"You think I'm that Elizabeth Smart girl that ran away, but I'm not," she said. She would at some point add: "Everyone in this city thinks I'm that Elizabeth Smart girl who ran away."

O'Neal and Rasmussen took her aside and told her that if she needed help, they would get it for her. Rasmussen told her how much everyone loved her and missed her. They knew she was lying. It's over, they told her. She was safe.

The officers held the "missing" poster of Elizabeth right up to her face. Her eyes grew damp as her own face peered out of the poster, the officers said. The cops gave each other a thumbs-up sign. A positive identification had been made.

Rasmussen said he could see Elizabeth's heart pounding, and hear her breathing grow heavy. She didn't respond, but by this time, the officers were sure.

"Tell us you're Elizabeth Smart," Quezada said. "I need you to tell us you're Elizabeth." The answer finally came: "Thou sayeth," the girl said, a scrap of scripture carried over from the last nine months as Augustine. Quezada asked again, and her reply was the same. But this time, she began to weep.

O'Neal and Quezada looked at each other. "We'll take that as a yes," Quezada said.

Some believe that Elizabeth's biblically phrased answer to police reflected how completely Brian and Wanda had superimposed the teen's new identity over her old one. "Once the police separated her from Mitchell and Barzee, that new identity began to crumble," said cult deprogrammer Rick Ross. "It was fragile, in a sense. It was very dependent on Elizabeth's environment being controlled and enforced by Mitchell."

Quezada, O'Neal and Rasmussen took Mitchell and Barzee off to the side and handcuffed them. Elizabeth, standing next to Jones's patrol car, looked up.

"What's going to happen to them? Are they in trouble?" was Jones's memory of what Elizabeth said, the first of three expressions of concern for her captors, and one that surprised the officers.

They told Elizabeth that the couple was going to be taken away.

Tears still in her eyes, Elizabeth climbed into the back of Jones's car and crossed her arms, the cop said.

"Are you all right?" Jones asked the girl as they turned onto 100 South and headed toward the stationhouse. "What's going to happen to them?" she asked again, Jones said. "Are they in trouble?"

Jones responded carefully, saying she didn't know what would happen to Mitchell and Barzee, but yes, they would likely be in some type of trouble.

"She started to cry," Jones said later. "She just sobbed. She sobbed the whole way to the station."

It was the beginning of the end of the horrible ordeal. The trauma Elizabeth had endured was too deep for anyone to think about in the early, joyous hours of her miraculous homecoming.

Ed Smart was at his office at home when he got a call from one of the Salt Lake detectives on his case, telling him to rush to the Sandy police station. "Come quick," Ed recalled the detective saying.

The detective had given no clue about what waited for him in Sandy. There had been so many false starts, so many promising leads that had fallen through.

"So many times, we'd get a phone call that they'd found a body, and we'd go to look," Ed's brother, David Smart, said. "At least three times, we did that. I can't tell you what kind of emotional roller coaster that is.

"He had no idea what to expect when he got there," David said, and it was better that way. "If they had told him, he would never have been able to make that drive."

Ed had thought he might have been called there to identify Brian David Mitchell, he recalled. At the stationhouse, Ed barreled through the doors and was led to a back holding room. There, on the couch, sat Officer Jones and Elizabeth. Elizabeth's arms were crossed over her chest. A stunned Ed stood in the doorway.

"Sir, is this your daughter?" one of the cops asked.

"Yes," Ed said, and he burst into tears. He went over to his daughter and held her tightly. He later recalled holding her away from him and searching her face.

"Is it really you?" he asked.

"Yes," she replied.

When Elizabeth was pulled away from her captors, and then saw her father in front of her, it was the jolt she needed, Rick Ross suspected. "Her true identity began to take precedence. All the things that reinforced her old sense of self were available to her again: her home, her family, her sister. That helped make it a rapid transition."

Elizabeth soon left with her dad and investigators to go to the Salt Lake police station. She got a change of clothes and had her hair braided into two pigtails. She would later be reunited with her family, an emotional meeting where the Smarts wept and held each other. "She couldn't let go of her little brother," said Mayor Anderson, who met with the family.

The joyous reunion was tinged with the tension between the Smart family and certain police officers that had begun over the summer. Ed Smart "went berserk" when he found that an officer who he thought had leaked information during the nine-month investigation was in the stationhouse, Anderson revealed in a memo to Chief Dinse five weeks later. The officer's name was blacked out from the memo when Anderson's office released it, but the mayor later admitted that he had ordered that Sergeant Don Bell be kept away from the family that evening at the stationhouse. Anderson told Salt Lake reporters that he had done so at Ed Smart's request. Anderson also had issues with Bell, and he supported the Smarts.

"Ed Smart was outraged at the thought that Elizabeth was being interviewed at the Police Department following her recovery," Anderson wrote. "Ed Smart demanded that Elizabeth be allowed to go home, yet she was not allowed to leave until after the interview."

Mitchell and Barzee were initially held at the Sandy police station. They were placed in separate cells until they were taken to the Salt Lake County Adult Detention Center. Mitchell quoted scripture when police spoke to him. He gave his address as "Heaven on earth." His emergency contact was God.

It took all of three hours for a flurry of phone

calls among the Smart clan to turn into worldwide bulletins. Neighbors at Kristianna Circle honked their horns and raced door to door, spreading the unbelievable news. The blue ribbons that originally went up to signal prayers for Elizabeth's return were tied around trees and lampposts again, along with the bright balloons that once signified the hope that she would come home.

"Welcome home, Elizabeth!" signs were everywhere from front doors to a Wendy's restaurant on State Street. People whooped and hugged in the streets, wiping away tears. The euphoria spilled all over town. Some motorists with bumper stickers featuring Elizabeth's name as a missing child case plastered the word "FOUND" over the information.

Ed Smart called his brother Tom to tell him the news. Ironically, many members of the Smart extended family were out of the state when the moment they had been waiting for happened. Charles and Dorotha Smart had been vacationing in Palm Springs. Angela Dumke was in Maui with her husband and some of her children when Tom called. Chris Smart, the third of Ed's brothers, was in Phoenix on business. They all quickly headed home.

Charles and Dorotha drove back as fast as they could from Palm Springs. Charles later recalled calling his son on his cell phone. "Edward, is it true?" he asked.

"Dad," his son replied, "I have her in my arms."

The national media that had left Salt Lake City

months earlier when it seemed like the case would end up as another horrible statistic started booking flights to Utah. Elizabeth's safe return was the rarest of things: a happy news story. She had defied the statistics that said 98 percent of abducted children don't return after thirty days missing. Somehow Elizabeth Smart had managed to survive.

At some point that day, while investigators interviewed Wanda, she relayed that Brian had gone to the Wrights' house in July, trying to take one of Elizabeth's cousins to bring back to the mountains. It confirmed what the Smarts said they'd believed all along.

Chief Dinse stepped in front of the cameras at about 5 p.m., with the FBI, representatives from the Sandy PD, and Anderson standing by. The press conference was beamed live around the country by national TV networks, and it began in celebratory fashion. Anderson and Dinse praised the press for keeping Elizabeth's disappearance publicized.

"Welcome home, Elizabeth!" Dinse said.

Chip Burrus, the FBI special agent in charge of the Salt Lake field office, said it was "a great day for the state of Utah." The investigators were all smiling, he said. "I can't tell you how many times in the FBI we've conducted investigations with our state and local partners where this has not been the outcome."

But the questions about exactly what had gone wrong in the search for Elizabeth's abductor began that afternoon.

Dinse gave an update on Elizabeth's condition. He said she seemed alert and overjoyed to be in the arms of her family. Everyone was overwhelmed, and even shocked, at how well the case had turned out. Then, the questions turned to the police search for Brian Mitchell. Dinse was asked when cops had started looking for him.

"When we got the name—when we found out about Mr. Mitchell," the chief replied. "I believe these investigators worked very hard at trying to locate Mr. Mitchell."

Police said they were certain she was kidnapped and hadn't gone willingly, and that she always had two people by her side, Dinse said amid questions about whether the teen had ever tried to run.

The chief was asked if he regretted the focus on Ricci as his wife, Angela, sat miles away, her husband's name still linked to the kidnapping in the mind of the general public.

"If you remember, I've always said that until I can charge somebody with this crime, everybody is a suspect and we are going to continue to look through those people, and we did," Dinse replied.

"Emmanuel" was one of the people they'd wanted to find, he said. But they had only his name and a description. "Up to the point of actually finding Elizabeth with him, that was the basic information, other than the fact that Mary Katherine had thought maybe it was Emmanuel that was in that room," he said.

He fielded several questions about exactly how the police search had gone.

"I can tell you everything that we did was based on calculated information around the investigation," the chief said. "It was done to not hurt that investigation. If we held anything back it was because we thought it might have an impact on our ability to solve the case."

Dinse kept most information about what Elizabeth had endured close to the vest. Things would come out later, when there were charges. He tried to cut the news conference off. When the reporters balked, the chief said he wanted to wrap it up because "we'll be here all night. I can't answer any more." The reporters protested again, and Dinse changed his mind and stayed at the podium. The topic turned to Richard Ricci.

"As I said before, we go where the evidence takes us," Dinse said. "Emmanuel was somebody we had not talked to. The information particularly from the family was significant and we followed up on that. We were aggressively seeking him, as we were seeking everybody that we had not been able to identify or contact within or around that house. And at that point in time, Ricci—yes, he was still the guy that had all of the evidence pointing towards him."

Even as the questions began, the amazing end to Elizabeth Smart's ordeal mesmerized the country. The world fell in love with her story. Parents of other children who had been kidnapped saw new hope in what had happened. This was the miracle that they had all been praying for, and if it happened in Salt Lake, then maybe it would happen in their cases, too.

The media frenzy that surrounded her initial disappearance returned tenfold. A photographer, camped outside the Salt Lake police station, waited for an image of Elizabeth, her hair in tight braids and her mother at her side. Networks set up makeshift tents in front of the Federal Heights Ward meeting house. Ed, Tom and David would later make statements. They looked thrilled and shocked by their incredible good fortune.

On her first night home, her dad said, Elizabeth was settling back into her home. She and Mary Katherine hugged and sobbed. She slept in her own bed, from which she'd been taken nine months earlier. Mary Katherine crawled in and joined her sister, just as they used to do, and the two held hands.

"It's real!" Ed told reporters the next day. "I can't begin to tell you how happy I am. What an absolute miracle and answer to prayers this has been. God lives. He is there. He answers prayers. And the prayers of the world have brought Elizabeth home."

He said he couldn't stop embracing his daughter. "Elizabeth is happy. She's well. And we are so happy to have her back in our arms. I hate even leaving her," he said. But the father who had just been blessed with an incredible gift said his mind was on abducted children who never made it home. He raised the issue of the AMBER Alert bill, stalled in Congress, saying the blood of children would be on the heads of people who didn't help put the tracking system in place. "I hate to go into that, but it's so important and critical," he said.

Ed said he believed "some mistakes have been

made" by the police along the way. But he knew they had tried, he said. And what mattered was that his daughter was home. He'd gotten a call from Cory Lyman soon after Elizabeth had been found.

"I love that man. He was a great friend, and he said, 'Ed, I have never been so glad to be wrong in my life,' and I think that says it all," Ed recounted. "We don't have, so to speak, professional kidnapping policemen. We don't, and so we do our best, and I believe that they tried to do their best."

But there has to be "open communication," Ed said, and if that breaks down, the local police can't dictate the way the investigation runs. At that point, the FBI has to play a major role, he said.

As for his Elizabeth, she was different in some ways.

"She really is a young woman," said Ed. She had watched her favorite movie, "The Trouble With Angels," and, at her family's request, she sat down and struggled through a few songs on the harp. She was rusty as she struggled through a few pieces.

"She said, 'Well, it's been nine months!'" Ed said. "But it was absolutely wonderful to hear her play."

Tom Smart later said her musical training might have helped his niece through her ordeal. "Strangely enough, maybe her musical ability and training—her focus and discipline—helped her get through this," he said.

Ed said he wasn't pushing Elizabeth for information. He didn't have it in him to make the unbelievable experience she'd had any harder. But he was stunned when she told her family that she had been in the mountains behind the home through the summer. She had no idea how many people were looking for her, although she had seen some posters with her name on them, and she somehow knew about one of the harp recitals in her honor.

Next, Ed noted that police had clarified that Elizabeth was taken not by a gun, but by a knife. And the screen, the source of much of the debate over the summer about how the kidnapper got in the house, was the entry point Brian David Mitchell had used.

"He did come through the screen. The screen was cut from the outside! The screen was cut from the outside," Ed said, his voice growing louder, as if to make sure any reporter who was still in doubt had heard him. "And apparently, he had been watching her for quite some time."

Amid all the questions about his recovered daughter, Ed took a moment to focus on his other little girl. She was the "hero" in the story, he said. "I cannot get over that she was inspired to come forward on Emmanuel. And I hope if there is one lesson to be learned, that when there is an eyewitness there, and thinks that it is someone, that it's not just one of 250, that person goes to the top of the list," he added.

Across town, Angela Ricci struggled with dueling emotions. She was thrilled for the Smarts. She couldn't believe how well the case had ended. But she was mourning a husband who had been the prime suspect for much of the case, and whom

Dinse would acknowledge later that day apparently had no connection to the crime.

Ed was asked if he had anything to say to Ricci's family.

"No. I feel sorry for Angela. I'm sorry that she lost Richard," said Ed. "We still have all these questions that were unanswered. Obviously, it was not Richard. So this is one thing that he was not responsible for. And Angela, I know you went through a lot, and I am very sorry, and I hope that—I hope this at least gives you peace to know that he wasn't the one."

At press conferences and in interviews, the Smarts tempered their statements about the nine-month police investigation. But privately, some vented their anger.

Later that day, Elizabeth's siblings and friends showered her with the gifts they'd stockpiled over the holidays and the birthday that she'd missed. She had an impromptu birthday party, where the kids ate pizza and then ran into the cul-de-sac in front of the Smarts' house clutching balloons and then releasing them into the air.

The Smarts made clear they had no plans to bring Elizabeth outside to address the media throng, but the press was clamoring for a glimpse of the miracle girl. To satisfy the press, and to protect Elizabeth, her photographer uncle Tom took a series of photos of Elizabeth with her brothers, sister, parents, and grandparents. The photos were sent around the world, with the condition that all media had a 48-hour window for free use. The goal of the shots was to let people know that she was doing well, Tom said, and to head off a media chase. After that window of time expired and outlets were asked to pay for the pictures, questions were raised about the propriety of the pictures and potential profits from them. Tom said his only purpose was to show the world how well his niece was doing. "If there's anything that ever comes of those photos, it goes to the National Center for Missing and Exploited Children," Tom told Larry King.

Ed Smart went live on John Walsh's daytime show, broadcast from Utah that day, and stepped up his pressure on the House to bring the AMBER Alert bill to the floor. He singled out House Judiciary Committee chairman James Sensenbrenner, a Republican from Wisconsin, who wanted a bill with several other items attached to it, instead of the one that had already cleared the Senate.

"The AMBER Alert needs to come to the floor right now," said Ed. "Children out there do not have time and he needs to know that. Jim, you will be held responsible."

Ed stirred a minor dust-up in Washington, D.C., with his comments, but it was short-lived. The focus was on the good news out of Salt Lake City that day.

Elizabeth sightings suddenly became a quick claim to fame, a neo-urban legend. According to reports in the first 48 hours after she was found, she'd been as far south as Florida and Georgia, yet within days she was suddenly seen back in California.

Police in Atlanta later said they had no reason to believe she was ever there. As for Florida, that rumor may have been launched by reports of sightings of Mitchell in that area, or possibly because that's where he told the Sandy officers he was from.

Still, the videotapes and pictures seemed to crop up from every direction. Several revelers from the party at 10 East and 2nd South produced images of a veiled Elizabeth standing inside the house, her eyes drifting from the camera and her abductor no farther than two feet away.

In San Diego, there were pictures of Mitchell, Barzee and Elizabeth walking through a park, captured by people who thought they looked strange. A steady trail of missed opportunities was developing: the trips to the Souper Salad, the party in October, the various sightings around Salt Lake City and the homeless camp in San Diego, even the stop by police outside the Burger King in Nevada.

The day after Elizabeth's return, word of Brian's prophetic writings and the passages dealing with polygamy began to circulate. The local press had long known about Mitchell's writings, but now it was hitting the TV networks. Alternate theories about why he had kidnapped her were developing, as the details of the ordeal remained clouded. One theory was that Brian was a polygamist, and Dinse later acknowledged that the alleged kidnapper considered himself such. Another was that he had taken Elizabeth as a surrogate daughter for Wanda. That night, the Associated Press got hold of a copy of Mitchell's prophecy, which had been dubbed his "manifesto" by the press. The text showed that Mitchell spelled the name he'd given himself with an "I." It was "Immanuel," not "Emmanuel."

The Smarts were deluged with media requests, and spokesman Chris Thomas warned reporters that contacting family members directly would hurt their chances of landing an interview. But the Smarts weren't alone in the media glare; the families of Mitchell and Barzee were also in the midst of a media frenzy. The case was painful for many of them to talk about.

The Smarts made clear that they did not extend their feelings about the people who took their daughter to their families. Ed made a point of thanking the relatives of Mitchell who had come forward. Angela Dumke said she didn't want to see the Mitchells get hurt as the story unfolded. Without them, she noted, the Smarts wouldn't have Elizabeth.

There were a number of people heralded as heroes immediately after Elizabeth was found, starting with her sister. There were also the Montoyas, the Dickersons, and the Sandy police. There were thanks to the federal officials, as well. But the praise for the Salt Lake police was noticeably muted. The sentiment that the investigation into who took Elizabeth had been flawed was growing. It was coupled with questions about why Elizabeth apparently hadn't tried to flee her captors.

Late that afternoon, Tom Smart joined Dinse and Burrus at a press conference. Dinse tossed a few barbs at reporters before he started reading from his notes, giving a lengthy timeline first of the kidnapping, and then of the search for "Immanuel." He had just come from a meeting with the Smarts, he said, and they had talked about what he was going to say at the press briefing.

Before Dinse got to the section that dealt with "Immanuel," Tom Smart stepped up to speak. It was only a day earlier that the *Tribune* quoted him criticizing the investigation, but Tom said the Smarts didn't bear a grudge.

"On behalf of the family, we want to stress that hindsight is 20/20, and we in no way want to impugn anybody," Tom said. "I mean, I think I probably made a mistake or two in the last nine months, you know?"

Tom said the family was grateful to all the officials who worked on the case. "We don't go, 'What if we would have done that? We go, 'God bless that she's here today.'"

He stepped back, and Dinse resumed. The chief gave an outline of how long the police had been looking for "Emmanuel," taking several minutes to go through exactly what the police had done to find the man they came to know as Brian David Mitchell.

Dinse was peppered with questions about why he didn't go forward with the sketch earlier.

"Let me tell you that hindsight is 20/20 vision," Dinse said. "If we had to go back over it again, that decision by the investigators, I think each and every one of them would say I wish we had gone public with that photograph sooner. The result is a happy result. We're glad she is free. We're glad she is home. We believe that we were close to maybe being able to make that occur before her discovery on the 12th, but we are ecstatic that she is home, and there isn't an investigator in this investigation that isn't happy and pleased that she's home and feels tremendous about that."

Police had searched for the campsite that the family had talked about, the one Tom's friend had told him about in the mountains, weeks back, but couldn't find it, the chief said. But now, they knew where to look.

Then came questions about Mitchell and the manifesto. Burrus said the FBI had a warrant in Montana. He wouldn't specifically say for what, but it turned out to be that officials were searching one of Brian's kid's homes, looking for more religious writings.

People wanted to know if there was any explanation for why Elizabeth hadn't tried to escape her captors. "There is clearly a psychological impact that occurred during this abduction at some point" was all the chief would say.

As for Brian David Mitchell's background, Dinse said, he had no history of being charged for sex abuse, although he said police had some information that there was some abuse in his family, possibly a reference to what Debbie Mitchell had said. But there was never any suggestion that the kidnapper might be a zealot.

Burrus said that the FBI profiler's opinions of

who Elizabeth's abductor was were helpful, but that almost nothing could have suggested what they ended up finding. Did the profiler "say he was going to be wearing robes with a weird hat and have a long beard? No, that's not specific to that."

And how did they get the money to travel?

"From God," Dinse replied. At one point, Burrus took pains to talk about the cooperation between the different law-enforcement agencies. He also tipped his hat to the Smarts for their patience, and for their ideas about where to take the investigation over the last few months.

Rocky Anderson had already begun making noises about an independent review of how his police force handled the case. The message that day was unity, but many had already started dropping the Salt Lake City police force from the list of those who deserved praise for Elizabeth's return.

It seemed like the entire city was planning to descend on Liberty Park on Friday evening for the celebration in honor of Elizabeth Smart. She stayed at home with her grandparents, while Ed and Lois joined John Walsh, Rocky Anderson, and some of the FBI agents who'd worked on the case.

Anderson had been preparing the event all day. While Tom Smart was between a string of interviews with the press earlier that day, his cell phone never stopped ringing. Some of the calls were from Anderson, who kept him posted about the plans for the city-sponsored event. Entertainment and food stands were being brought in. The crowds would be enormous. Press tents ringed the park.

Tom had been working with printers to enlarge a note Elizabeth had written in shaky handwriting so that it could be displayed to the crowd. "I'm the luckiest girl in the world! Thank you for your love and prayers. It's a wish come true!! I'm HOME! I love you all, Elizabeth Smart," the note read. It was posted on a large board over a photo of Elizabeth holding her little brother, William.

Ed and Lois arrived at the ceremony by police escort. It was Lois's first appearance since her daughter had come home, and she beamed as she and Ed strode onto the stage to "When the Saints Go Marching In." Anderson told the crowd how thrilled he was by the good fortune, which had seemed so unlikely months earlier.

"Nine months ago, we came to this same park for a candlelight vigil," Anderson said. "Now, we gather in joy." The crowd roared.

Lois spoke after the mayor, shouting out, "I am the luckiest mother in the world!"

Elizabeth was doing well, Lois said. "She's happy to be home, and she can hardly wait for a bubble bath. We've been doing her hair, painting toenails, giving manicures."

When Ed took the stage, he retold the story of seeing Elizabeth for the first time in Sandy two days earlier. But he saved most of his praise for Walsh, the man who had become one of his closest friends.

"He's a man I called numerous times, day and

night. And his heart is in the right place," said Ed. "This man has a love and a passion that cannot be described. He's not just here for the press."

Walsh, for his part, thanked the Montoyas and the Dickersons, singling them out for praise. "They thought they saw this low-life scumbag, and they called. Nancy and Anita, they saw this pollutant, and they had the courage to make that call, and *they* are the reason Elizabeth Smart is home tonight!" he said. But Mary Katherine was another hero, he said, the one who had gotten everything started months ago.

The night ended with a fireworks show, the colors streaking across the sky over Salt Lake. In the days ahead, the Smarts said their focus was protecting Elizabeth from any more damage. But that night, the young girl's third back at her home, seemed perfect.

EIGHTEEN

The Federal Heights Ward meeting house that had served as the epicenter of the early search was a media campground through the weekend. Ed hadn't held a news conference since Thursday, and Lois hadn't sat for any interviews. Except for an interview Ed did with John Walsh on his daytime show, the couple spent the weekend away from the public eye. Instead, their siblings tried to accommodate the number of interview requests pouring in, organizing the schedules in a conference room at the back of the meeting house. On a chalkboard, a graph detailed the schedule: Larry King, Ashleigh Banfield, "Good Morning America," *People* magazine.

That weekend, with the media focused mostly on talking to Mitchell's and Barzee's families, investigators took Elizabeth and Lois in a helicopter over the Wasatch Mountains to scour for spots where she had been taken during her stolen summer. Prosecutors were trying to hammer out charges against the kidnappers, and those were expected to come on Monday. Elizabeth was interviewed to help piece together a timeline, but district attorney David Yocom wanted as much physical evidence as he could get to back up a case against the abductors. Investigators had already cordoned off the woods high above the Smarts' home.

As the helicopter flew above the canyons, Elizabeth tried to point out where she'd been—campsites where she'd slept, trails she had walked. Investigators praised the Smarts and Elizabeth for their cooperation during the difficult questioning.

Tom Smart said he was impressed with his niece's composure after her ordeal. She was able to sit down and give details and draw maps to locations she'd been, he said. "Elizabeth is a very bright, articulate girl. And the details she remembered, despite everything she'd gone through, are incredible."

By Sunday, the media crush at the ward house had somewhat died down. Chris Thomas stood in the ward house parking lot, talking to a small group of reporters standing idly in the warm spring sunshine. Appearing more relaxed than he had in days, Thomas told stories about how Elizabeth was doing. "She's in good health, but the last month she has lived on a diet of junk food," he said. On Friday night, Thomas added, she'd had a home-cooked meal with her grandparents, and Dorotha made a pot roast. "She said, 'This is the best meal I've had since June 4.'"

The teen had missed her freshman year of high school and was worried about schoolwork. She had already started asking about it in the elevator at the police station, Thomas recalled. At Kristianna Circle, the family had been deluged with letters, flowers and gifts. "Their home smells incredible—I would love to be a florist in Salt Lake this week," he joked. More seriously, he talked about how important it was for Elizabeth to take her re-acclimation slowly. "It's baby steps," Thomas said. The family "has very good professional help advising them."

Elizabeth was in good shape, although she seemed a little distracted, the family said. Everyone close to the teenager said no one was pressuring her for information about what she'd been through. One family friend said Elizabeth would occasionally offer small details, and the family "was all ears." But they were leaving it up to her.

That morning, Elizabeth's brothers, cousins, aunts and uncles joined the community for a thanks-giving service at the ward house that had become like a second home. For more than an hour, Tom, Charles and Dorotha addressed the more than 350 people who'd turned out, thanking them for their prayers and support. Ed had also been scheduled to speak, but at the last minute he and Lois decided they didn't want to leave Elizabeth, Thomas said.

Tom Smart stood first. He joked about how the day marked the first time he'd been in church in a decade, and he couldn't think of a better reason to have been drawn back. "What a happy, happy day it is," said Elizabeth's elated uncle. "In the hard days of the last years—the uncertainty since September 11—it is a beautiful thing to be granted this miracle."

The discord and frustration over the police investigation seemed to evaporate as he spoke. "You can't look back or second-guess—how can our hearts be anything less than full of joy?"

Elizabeth's improbable return, and the response it had prompted around the globe, was astonishing, Tom said. At some point, he said, he realized "this is bigger than the Olympics."

When Dorotha spoke she was stoic, though her voice quivered with emotion as she spoke of the dark hours that had tested her faith. To see her children attacked in the media, she said, had added to her despair.

To her husband, Charles, Elizabeth's homecoming was the greatest blessing of his life. He and Dorotha had driven through the night from California, hardly daring to believe it was true she'd been found. But the phone call to Ed confirmed it. When they got to Salt Lake and saw Elizabeth, he threw his arms around her and said, "Welcome home."

The retired surgeon told of his granddaughter's nine-month "camping trip," her days of living in the hills and under railroad trestles. Then, he addressed the question that had peppered conversations across the country since Elizabeth's return. Why didn't she run? Charles, too, believed his granddaughter had been brainwashed. Church members listened intently as Charles recounted the depth of Mitchell's control. "In all that time, she didn't try to run away, even during the one day she was left by herself," he said, apparently referring to the days in San Diego when Mitchell was in jail and Barzee was praying at "Golgotha." "She had no ability to control her life. She was completely controlled by Emmanuel."

Whatever might have happened during her time away, Charles said, "Elizabeth is pure before the Lord."

Mental health and behavioral experts were also appalled at the suggestion that Elizabeth could have walked away from her captors at any time. They became frequent commentators on talk shows, trying to explain what might have been going on in the teen's mind.

"The questions about why she didn't run are insulting," said David Smart. "People should remember that she did what she had to do to survive. If she hadn't, she wouldn't be back here today."

David said his family had been speaking with Patty Hearst, the newspaper heiress who assumed a new identity after an extremist group abducted her three decades earlier.

The Smarts would have to field other difficult questions that weekend. Elizabeth had gained weight while she was gone, and her face was fuller. Reporters began to ask if she was pregnant. She wasn't, David said, nor had she ever been. More unsettling was a story that began circulating the day after Elizabeth came home: Mitchell, it was said, had performed a bizarre marriage ritual, sealing the teen to him as a plural wife.

Distasteful as the scenario was, David Smart addressed it calmly. "He could have done something like that, but whatever kind of radical, bizarre, evil thing he could think up, it doesn't matter. Elizabeth was forced. Whatever this beautiful and innocent girl went through, to us she's just as beautiful and innocent as she ever was."

Sunday night brought a bizarre announcement from a man who claimed to be Brian David Mitchell's lawyer. Larry Long, a personal injury lawyer who primarily handled DUI cases, met with Mitchell at the jail that day. As Long walked down the ramp outside the prison, a reporter from Salt Lake's KUTV approached, and the lawyer stopped to talk. He said Mitchell considered Elizabeth his wife. In fact, Mitchell didn't consider what he'd done a crime. It was "a call from God."

"He wanted me to tell the world she is his wife, and he still loves her and knows that she still loves him," Long said. "No harm came to her during their relationship and the adventure that went on." The defense lawyer used the term "perpetrator" when he talked about Mitchell—not a word most lawyers use to describe their own clients.

Long said Mitchell's name for Elizabeth was Shear Jashub Isaiah, or "Remnant who will return." The lawyer described Mitchell as "very intelligent, very knowledgeable, very coherent and very articulate." Mitchell should be given consideration for bringing Elizabeth back alive, Long argued, a point that Shirl Mitchell also made that weekend. "She came back in good health," said Shirl.

Long met with Mitchell again the next day, and said the prisoner seemed "upbeat." He said he'd been referred by a relative of Mitchell. But almost as quickly as he'd burst onto the scene with his startling comments, Long was gone. By the time Mitchell was charged a few days later, Long was out of the picture, replaced by a court-ordered attorney.

Five days after her return, Elizabeth was receiving a steady stream of friends and relatives at the sprawling house on Kristianna Circle. Lois stood outside the house, greeting visitors as they walked up the stone steps.

Six miles away, her uncle David sat at the head of a conference room table in Chris Thomas's office. He was visibly upset.

"We're not going to put up with fumbling," David said. "We are not going to tolerate it."

It was the sharpest public comment from any of the Smarts since Elizabeth was returned, and it was aimed, in part, at Yocom, whose office had made noises that morning about filing formal charges against Mitchell and Barzee. That afternoon, after a meeting with Ed and Lois, Yocom abruptly backed off, leaving a horde of media standing in front of the courthouse, looking for answers to the sudden turnaround.

Mitchell and Barzee had been held on aggravated kidnapping charges until then, and by law, they were supposed to have a first court appearance. But the DA's office got a two-day extension.

The major issue over the charges became clear within hours. The sticking point, several law-enforcement sources said, was sexual abuse charges. The Smarts were concerned about forcing Elizabeth to relive everything she'd been through, and one of the issues was testifying about what had happened. But the concern of prosecutors was that a kidnapping sentence didn't carry the seriousness of the alleged crime against Elizabeth. Mitchell's goal in the crime, they argued, wasn't just kidnapping, it was assault.

The Smarts were also disgusted by what Long said outside the jail after visiting Mitchell. "The definition of love is not kidnapping, coercion, assault, degradation or ripping one's life of identity or self-respect," David said. It was the most that any of the Smarts had said about what Elizabeth had been through.

The controversy was delayed only by a day. On March 18, Yocom called a press conference to announce the formal charges against Mitchell and Barzee. The charges were aggravated kidnapping, aggravated burglary, attempted aggravated kidnapping, and aggravated sexual assault. The probable cause statement, which cited information culled from Lois, Elizabeth, detectives, and FBI agents, said that Mitchell had held the girl against her will. It also said he had "committed a rape, attempted rape, forcible sexual abuse or attempted forcible sexual abuse."

Yocom, the jowled, longtime district attorney in Salt Lake, was prepared for the questions about why the sexual abuse charges were included. "We are not dealing with just a religious zealot," he said. "We are dealing with a predatory sex offender. If he ever hits the streets, he should carry that label for the rest of his life."

Yocom knew that the charges meant Elizabeth might have to take the stand, but there were options for dealing with it, he said. She could testify by video, or in a closed courtroom. "We will do what we can do to look out for Elizabeth's interests."

Even as he announced the charges, Yocom made an unusual request. He cautioned reporters that Elizabeth's parents had asked the media not to press for details about the sexual abuse charges, "for reasons that should be very obvious to everyone." Her sister, Mary Katherine, wouldn't be called to testify because the kidnapper's identity was known, he said. There was a mountain of evidence that investigators were sifting through. They had combed campsites from Utah to San Diego, and they had turned up several things, including the knife they believed Mitchell used to break into Elizabeth's house and pieces of burnt clothing.

Federal prosecutors were still looking at their own set of charges, but they would wait and do it only if it was "necessary."

Yocom also debunked Larry Long's claim that

he was representing Mitchell as "bull-something." He said Long never was Mitchell's lawyer and shouldn't have been making comments on his behalf. Ed and Lois had hired a lawyer to represent Elizabeth's interests, and he was already speaking with prosecutors.

Chris Thomas said the sexual abuse charges were "hurtful" to Elizabeth and that Yocom would be "held accountable" for anything that revictimized the teenager. But he also said the family had been assured that Yocom would do everything he could to protect her privacy.

Yocom held his press conference a day before the first B-52 bombers started flying over Baghdad, signaling the beginning of the war against Iraq. Most of the national media had already packed up and left, on to the next major story. The miracle girl who had captivated the nation's attention disappeared from the headlines. The national cameras were gone, leaving a city coming to grips with a plague that could strike any family, and a young woman who needed to heal.

EPILOGUE

At the end of April, Mitchell and Barzee were behind bars on $10 million bail. They were undergoing mental competency evaluations that would determine whether they were fit to stand trial.

It is hard to find a criminal case in which there are no recriminations, and the Elizabeth Smart case was no exception. There were many people given credit, and many others assigned blame.

The day after Elizabeth Smart was found, Mayor Rocky Anderson talked about a possible internal investigation into the way police handled the case. The day before Yocom announced charges against Mitchell and Barzee, Anderson made the panel official. His police chief, Rick Dinse, was safe in his job, Anderson said. But the mayor was aware of the enormous public outcry immediately after Elizabeth returned over how the girl had been virtually in her own backyard for months and yet wasn't found.

The panel was to focus on leaks to the media, the attention paid to Ricci as a suspect, and, most importantly, exactly how hard police tried to track the man known as "Emmanuel." The panel wouldn't be tasked with those duties until after any trial in the Smart case. In the meantime, it would examine the four 1980s homicides that the mayor himself had investigated when he was a private lawyer. They were the same cases he referenced in his memos to Dinse during the Smart investigation, in which he had claimed that cops had hurt the cases by focusing on the wrong suspect. There was one investigator in common in all four—Sergeant Don Bell, the man who had led the Elizabeth Smart task force for a short time and who was in charge when Ricci appeared on investigators' radar screens.

The panel was controversial. The Smarts praised it, saying they were grateful to the work law-enforcement officials had done but that people needed to be held accountable for mistakes so that changes could be made. The panel prompted a swift rebuke from Cory Lyman, who had taken over for Bell on the Smart case over that summer. Lyman, who had already taken responsibility for not releasing the Brian David Mitchell sketch, called the panel an "insult" to officers who'd worked day and night on the case. Anyone who pointed fingers at police, he said, didn't know what had really happened. As for Bell, he said the probe was nothing more than a settling of personal scores, serving under the guise of a truth mission. The mayor hated him, Bell said, and it was all because of Anderson's involvement with the four murder cases years earlier. Anderson denied that, although he acknowledged that Bell was involved in all four murder investigations.

There were accusations that the panel was an election-year ploy. Some investigators felt the entire department was being painted with a broad brush over the Smart case. Others insisted they had worked hard, citing the hundreds of hours they spent on the investigation. Most were people with children of their own, who empathized with the Smarts' situation and said that investigators always acted in good faith. They conceded mistakes might have been made, but in the end, several said, they were simply happy that Elizabeth was found.

The Mitchells and the Barzees, whose lives were upended by what Brian and Wanda had done, tried to make sense of what had happened. In preparation for a possible trial, Shirl Mitchell and Dora Corbett were asked to trace as many memories as they could of their children's lives, painful roadmaps that always led back to the same question: How?

Like the Smarts, their lives were changed. The two families struggled to comprehend the horrible crimes of which their loved ones were accused. Dora Corbett, unable to get a jailhouse visit with her daughter, went to one of her April court hearings. "I just wanted to tell her I love her," Dora said. Shirl Mitchell visited his son, reading to him and putting money in his commissary account.

"What he did was beyond the pale, but he needs to know that somebody is there for him," Shirl said. "Maybe I didn't get it right the first time, and

I can't go back and fix it, but the least I can do is be there now."

There were other reverberations from the kidnapping, on a more local level. When Elizabeth's abductor turned out to be one of Salt Lake's most well-known transients, the city's homeless community braced for a backlash. Advocates quickly stepped forward to make sure people knew that Mitchell was atypical in the community. When Elizabeth disappeared, many Salt Lake homeless searched for her. The homeless population at large in Salt Lake is protective of children, outreach workers said, and they were horrified by the crime. They also feared that temporary jobs on which they depended would dry up, as prospective employers became wary of hiring them.

The rewards in the case had eventually grown to about $300,000. Anderson was charged with distributing the money and asked for nominees. Among the roughly 30 names suggested were the Montoyas and the Dickersons—the two couples who spotted Elizabeth with Mitchell and Barzee on the street in March—and Mary Katherine Smart. By May, Anderson said he'd decided how to divide the pot of money.

To prevent leaks in the case, gag orders were placed on law enforcement, prosecutors, and defense lawyers.

Even after the charges were filed against Mitchell and Barzee, there were lingering questions by the public about the crime. Many people still couldn't understand how she could have remained captive for so long, when chances to escape presented themselves. Others were fascinated by the fact that she had denied her own identity when she first was stopped by the Sandy police officers, and they wondered if she had resisted going home.

The Smarts never held another press conference after that first week Elizabeth was home. While they said they recognized the role the media played in her return, they also insisted they wanted privacy. Elizabeth's miraculous return was the kind of story that captured the attention of producers and filmmakers. The Smarts said they were deluged with offers and hired an entertainment lawyer to help sift through proposals.

The Smarts also hired another lawyer, Randy Dryer, to monitor leaks from law enforcement as the specter of a trial loomed, and to root out the sources on some of the coverage from the summer Elizabeth went missing. The first action came against the *National Enquirer* and reverberated to the *Salt Lake Tribune*. Two *Tribune* reporters who had covered the case were fired after they moonlighted for the tabloid, without their editor's permission, on the story that had infuriated the Smarts. The tabloid later retracted the information in the article. The reporters had also lied to their bosses about the degree of their involvement in the story, which had prompted Anderson's July 4 memo to Dinse. Their editor, who believed their original claims of limited involvement, resigned himself, saying he had lost the backing of his other newsroom reporters.

Rocky Anderson fired off a fresh memo, 18 pages long, to Dinse on April 30, once again demanding answers about who the police "leaks" were. This time, Anderson imposed a deadline of May 19. He reprinted entire sections of the July 2, 2002, *Enquirer* article as he ordered his police chief to find out who was behind the information. He strongly defended the Smarts' right to be upset by the "leaks." The memo only heightened the ill will between Anderson and his police force, whose members accused their mayor of conducting a "witch hunt" that was diminishing morale. The missive, which was released to the press, came just days before the *Enquirer* issue exploded as a national news story.

The two *Tribune* reporters, faced with the threat of a lawsuit by the Smarts, agreed to name their confidential investigative sources—a move that is virtually unheard of in the journalism profession. The anonymity of sources is sacrosanct and the fact that two reporters unmasked theirs so quickly dealt a serious blow to the relationship between investigators and the Salt Lake media. Dryer, the Smarts' lawyer, held a press conference to describe what he'd learned from reporters Kevin Cantera and Michael Vigh. Cantera, he said, had admitted to embellishing when he spoke to the *Enquirer* and even acknowledged making up out of whole cloth a key detail in the tabloid story: a journal outlining the sexual preferences of the Smart brothers. Cantera neither confirmed nor denied Dryer's account. Dryer passed along his list of names of the sources, which he said were from four law-enforcement agencies, to District Attorney David Yocom to investigate for possible criminal charges. He also sent the list to the agencies in question—the police, the FBI, the U.S. Secret Service, and the Utah Department of Public Safety.

Within five days, Yocom publicly cleared Salt Lake police officers of any connection to the *Enquirer* piece. None of the Salt Lake cops had provided information for the story, Yocom said. And even if they had, he hadn't been able to find any statute in Utah law that would make leaks a criminal offense. The Utah State Attorney General also cleared Department of Public Safety workers on Dryer's list of any criminal wrongdoing. The other two agencies involved said they were reviewing the lists of names.

The day Yocom cleared the Salt Lake police, Sergeant Don Bell said he had been told by Dinse that he wasn't one of the names on the Cantera–Vigh list. He had never been one of the leaks, Bell said, and he expected that to be acknowledged by Anderson.

"If this man has any principles at all, I expect an apology," Bell said on KSL radio. "I'm not going to roll over and play dead," he said. "If this continues, I have the right to seek redress like the Smarts."

Bell said Vigh had called him once the *Enquirer* imbroglio began. The reporter asked whether the sergeant had been a source for the controversial tabloid story. "They were the ones that told me that they had heard the mayor had been saying I was the responsible person for the leaks to the *National Enquirer*," Bell told KSL-TV.

But Anderson made clear an apology wouldn't be forthcoming. He noted that he never used Bell's name publicly in connection with the hunt for leaks.

"I didn't use his name," Anderson told the TV station. "It really is Don Bell that has made himself the center of attention here. And I don't understand, if someone doesn't want public attention, [why] he keeps going out publicly."

Several legal observers and law-enforcement officials were perplexed that such a public inquiry came before a trial had even taken place. It could potentially discredit, in the eyes of prospective jurors, the same investigators who might be called to testify to bolster the case against Mitchell and Barzee.

The day of Dryer's press conference on May 2 the Smarts gave a statement about the whole affair, saying they held "no personal animosity toward those who have acted in less than honorable ways" and appreciated the hard work of others.

"Our desire is to return to our private lives," the statement read. "We have asked not to know the names of the law-enforcement sources who may have acted inappropriately and are confident that the relevant authorities will take the proper action."

At Kristianna Circle, Elizabeth Smart began settling back into her life. With the press gone, she began venturing out of the house. She spent time with friends, went to meetings in her ward, and studied at home so she could be ready when school started in the fall.

On April 30, 2003, Elizabeth Smart joined her parents, and the families of other children who had been abducted, in Washington, D.C., for an event that was broadcast live on national television. They stood in the Rose Garden at the White House, looking on as President George W. Bush signed nationwide AMBER Alert legislation into law. Thousands of children disappear from schools, from playgrounds, street corners, and homes each year, and the AMBER Alert was designed to bring them home. Many are abducted by family members, others by strangers, and many run away. No matter what the cause, the effect of a missing child on a parent is devastating. To many of those parents, Elizabeth Smart became a symbol that the statistics can be beaten.

Later that day, all three of the Smarts sat for a taping of John Walsh's daytime talk show, set on a rooftop somewhere in Washington. Parents of children saved by AMBER Alerts sat in a makeshift audience during the nearly 20-minute segment with Ed and Lois Smart. The show had been heavily promoted with still photos and TV teasers the day before because it featured Elizabeth. When the show aired, promotions ran at each commercial break, reminding viewers that Elizabeth would soon be on, playing her harp. Elizabeth didn't speak during her performance, which was saved for the very end of the show. The camera panned in on the young girl's face and her hands as she played.

In the last two decades, the awareness of the epidemic of missing children has risen sharply. Once the domain of the occasional made-for-TV movie based on a particularly disturbing case, abductions now regularly make headlines in newspapers across the country. People pay more attention to such crimes than they once did. But in most instances, the story of a missing child fades quickly.

The Elizabeth Smart case never completely faded from the public eye, even during lulls in the coverage over the nine long months she was gone. The way in which she was kidnapped was haunting. It stirred fears that no one is safe, even in their homes. But it was her amazing return that captured the most attention. She was not unchanged, but she was alive. Her family, like those of many other kidnapped children, never stopped searching and never gave up hope. The Smarts were the all-too-rare exception whose efforts were rewarded.